LaTeX Cookbook

Over 100 practical, ready-to-use LaTeX recipes
for instant solutions

Stefan Kottwitz

LaTeX Cookbook

Group Product Manager: Aaron Tanna

Publishing Product Manager: Uzma Sheerin

Senior Editor: Kinnari Chohan

Technical Editor: Rajdeep Chakraborthy

Copy Editor: Safis Editing

Project Coordinator: Prajakta Naik

Proofreader: Safis Editing

Indexer: Manju Arasan

Production Designer: Prashant Ghare

DevRel Marketing Coordinator: Mayank Singh

First published: October 2015

Second edition: March 2024

Production reference: 1230224

Published by Packt Publishing Ltd.

Grosvenor House

11 St Paul's Square

Birmingham

B3 1RB

ISBN 978-1-83508-032-0

www.packtpub.com

A big thank you to the technical reviewers Izaak Neutelings and Stephan Lukasczyk for their valuable contributions during the book development process. Additional appreciation goes to Prajakta Naik and Kinnari Chohan from Packt Publishing, with whom I have collaborated on a book for the second time.

I would also like to thank the DANTE e.V. TeX users group for their enduring support over the years of the website projects I maintain.

– Stefan Kottwitz

Contributors

About the author

Stefan Kottwitz studied mathematics in Jena and Hamburg. He works as a network and IT security engineer at Lufthansa Industry Solutions.

For numerous years, Stefan has been providing LaTeX support on internet forums. He manages the web forums `LaTeX.org` and `goLaTeX.de`, along with the question-and-answer platforms `TeXwelt.de` and `TeXnique.fr`. He maintains the TeX graphics gallery sites `TeXample.net`, `TikZ.net`, and `PGFplots.net`, the `TeXlive.net` online compiler, the `TeXdoc.org` documentation service, and the `CTAN.net` software mirror.

A moderator of the TeX Stack Exchange site and matheplanet.com, he publishes ideas and news from the TeX world on his blogs `LaTeX.net` and `TeX.co`.

He also authored the *LaTeX Beginner's Guide* in 2011, with the second edition in 2021, and *LaTeX Graphics with TikZ* in 2023, all published by Packt.

About the reviewers

Izaak Neutelings earned his master's and Ph.D. degrees from the University of Zurich (UZH). He is currently engaged in fundamental research in experimental particle physics at the CMS experiment in CERN, searching for new particles in proton collisions.

He previously served as a technical reviewer for the book *LaTeX Graphics with TikZ*. His extensive use of LaTeX includes writing lecture notes for introductory physics courses at UZH, fully illustrated with TikZ figures. He is a primary contributor to the example collection websites `TikZ.net` and `FeynM.net`.

Stephan Lukasczyk holds a B.Sc. and M.Sc. degree in Computer Science and is currently a research assistant and PhD student at the University of Passau, Germany. His research focuses on automated test generation for dynamically typed programming languages, along with static and dynamic analysis techniques for such languages.

He has been an avid LaTeX user since approximately 2006. Since 2021, he has held a position on the German-speaking TeX User Group (DANTE) board.

Table of Contents

2

Tuning the Text   55

3

Adjusting Fonts   91

4

Creating Tables   119

5

Working with Images 145

6

Creating Graphics 163

7

Creating Beautiful Designs   199

8

Producing Contents, Indexes, and Bibliographies   223

11

Using LaTeX in Science and Technology — 319

12

Getting Support on the Internet   365

13

Using Artificial Intelligence with LaTeX   375

Index   389

Other Books You May Enjoy   400

Preface

LaTeX is a high-quality typesetting software and is very popular, especially among scientists. Its programming language gives you precise control over every aspect of your documents, regardless of complexity. LaTeX's many customizable templates and supporting packages cover most writing aspects with embedded typographic expertise.

This book will enable you to leverage the latest document classes' capabilities and explore the newest packages' functionalities.

This book starts with examples of common document types. It provides samples for refining text design, using fonts, embedding images, and creating legible tables. Supplementary parts of the document, such as the bibliography, glossary, and index, are addressed with LaTeX's modern approach.

You will learn to create excellent graphics directly within LaTeX; this includes creating diagrams and plots with ease. The book shows the application of LaTeX in various scientific fields, focusing on creating figures with new graphics packages.

The example-driven approach of this book will quickly increase your productivity.

The second edition incorporates enhancements, featuring code adjustments to align with LaTeX and package upgrades. It includes supplementary examples and a new chapter exploring the application of Artificial Intelligence through ChatGPT, aiding in generating LaTeX code and supporting various writing tasks.

Who this book is for

If you possess a foundational understanding of LaTeX and seek quick and practical solutions to your challenges, this book is tailored for you. Advanced readers can leverage the example-driven format to elevate their expertise. Familiarity with LaTeX's basic syntax and proficiency in using your preferred editor for compilation are prerequisites for optimal engagement.

What this book covers

Chapter 1, *Exploring Various Document Classes*, gives insight into diverse document types, and you'll discover how LaTeX is versatile for creating theses, books, CVs, presentations, flyers, and large posters with tailored examples.

Chapter 2, Tuning the Text, focuses on customizing text details within documents. Beginning with essential fundamentals, we'll cover practical tips and conclude the chapter with demonstrations of LaTeX's capabilities beyond standard paragraph formatting.

Chapter 3, Adjusting Fonts, shows how to make global font choices and explore techniques for adjusting fonts within your document.

Chapter 4, Creating Tables, explains how to craft visually appealing tables. This includes guidance on creating legible tables, aligning numeric data, and incorporating colors. It introduces the concept of floating tables and figures, enabling automated positioning. Additionally, the chapter discusses advanced topics such as merging and splitting cells and importing table data from external files.

Chapter 5, Working with Images, begins by exploring considerations related to image quality. You'll find practical instructions on incorporating, positioning, shaping, and aligning images in LaTeX.

Chapter 6, Creating Graphics, provides step-by-step instructions for crafting compelling graphics. The chapter leverages modern graphics packages, enabling the creation of comprehensive graphics, including various types of diagrams and charts.

Chapter 7, Creating Beautiful Designs, guides you on incorporating background images, crafting attractive ornaments, integrating appealing headings, generating calendars and word clouds, incorporating symbols for computer keys and menu items, and simulating terminal output.

Chapter 8, Producing Contents, Indexes, and Bibliographies, provides practical solutions for quickly customizing the table of contents, lists of figures and tables, bibliographies, glossaries, and indexes.

Chapter 9, Optimizing PDF Files, explores the functionalities of PDFs, including metadata, PDF comments, and fillable forms. You'll learn techniques for merging PDF files, adjusting margins, optimizing output for e-books, and creating animations in a PDF.

Chapter 10, Writing Advanced Mathematics, works with LaTeX's enduring strengths—its exceptional typesetting capabilities for mathematical formulas. After a quick tutorial, you'll learn advanced techniques for refining formulas and creating theorems, diagrams, geometric figures, and plots in 2D and 3D.

Chapter 11, Using LaTeX in Science and Technology, deals with additional scientific fields, including chemistry, physics, computer science, and various technologies such as electronics. This chapter provides a comprehensive overview, showcasing how LaTeX can be effectively applied across diverse fields through specific examples.

Chapter 12, Getting Support on the Internet, starts with a guide to the most valuable Internet resources for LaTeX. Then, it demonstrates how to efficiently seek support from the TeX online communities.

Chapter 13, Using Artificial Intelligence with LaTeX, provides guidance and examples on harnessing the capabilities of ChatGPT to streamline code work and enhance your content efficiently.

To get the most out of this book

The required software for this purpose is TeX Live, version 2023 or later, or MiKTeX, a version of 2023 or later. It is advisable to install a LaTeX editor as well. Chapter 1's introduction will provide details on obtaining TeX software and editors, while Chapter 12 will direct you to additional online resources.

An essential tool is `texdoc`, which opens manuals and additional documentation. To use `texdoc`, enter "`texdoc keyword`" in the Command Prompt. For packages and bundles, the keyword typically corresponds to the name. If you don't have the documentation installed or use an online compiler such as Overleaf, you can access the documentation online at `https://texdoc.org/pkg/keyword`.

All the code examples in this book are available for download, as explained later in the Customer Support section. This eliminates the need for manually typing the code or copy-pasting, allowing us to present the code in the book in snippets and explain it step by step.

If you are using the digital version of this book, we advise you to type the code yourself or access the code from the book's GitHub repository (a link is available in the next section). Doing so will help you avoid any potential errors related to the copying and pasting of code.

Download the example code files

You can download the example code files for this book from GitHub at `https://github.com/PacktPublishing/LaTeX-Cookbook`. If there's an update to the code, it will be updated in the GitHub repository.

We also have other code bundles from our rich catalog of books and videos available at `https://github.com/PacktPublishing/`. Check them out!

Conventions used

There are a number of text conventions used throughout this book.

`Code in text`: Indicates code words in text, database table names, folder names, filenames, file extensions, pathnames, dummy URLs, user input, and Twitter handles. Here's an example: "You can access each package's documentation by calling `texdoc` at the command line."

A block of code is set as follows:

```
\documentclass{article}
\begin{document}
\end{document}
```

When we wish to draw your attention to a particular part of a code block, the relevant lines or items are set in bold:

```
\begin{figure}[htbp!]
  \centering
  \includegraphics{filename}
  \caption{Some text}
  \label{fig:name}
\end{figure}
```

Any command-line input or output is written as follows:

```
$ bibtex document
```

Bold: Indicates a new term, an important word, or words that you see onscreen. For instance, words in menus or dialog boxes appear in **bold**. Here are some examples:

"**Artificial Intelligence (AI)** refers to machine or software-simulated intelligence."

"Click the **editGPT** button to enable the editing mode."

> **Tips or important notes**
> Appear like this.

Get in touch

Feedback from our readers is always welcome.

LaTeX questions: If you have any questions about LaTeX, you can post them at the author's forum at `https://latex.org`.

General feedback: If you have questions about any aspect of this book, email us at `customercare@packtpub.com` and mention the book title in the subject of your message.

Errata: Although we have taken every care to ensure the accuracy of our content, mistakes do happen. If you have found a mistake in this book, we would be grateful if you would report this to us. Please visit `www.packtpub.com/support/errata` and fill in the form.

Piracy: If you come across any illegal copies of our works in any form on the internet, we would be grateful if you would provide us with the location address or website name. Please contact us at `copyright@packt.com` with a link to the material.

If you are interested in becoming an author: If there is a topic that you have expertise in and you are interested in either writing or contributing to a book, please visit `authors.packtpub.com`.

Share Your Thoughts

Once you've read *LaTeX Cookbook*, we'd love to hear your thoughts! Scan the QR code below to go straight to the Amazon review page for this book and share your feedback.

https://packt.link/r/1835080324

Your review is important to us and the tech community and will help us make sure we're delivering excellent quality content.

Download a free PDF copy of this book

Thanks for purchasing this book!

Do you like to read on the go but are unable to carry your print books everywhere?

Is your eBook purchase not compatible with the device of your choice?

Don't worry, now with every Packt book you get a DRM-free PDF version of that book at no cost.

Read anywhere, any place, on any device. Search, copy, and paste code from your favorite technical books directly into your application.

The perks don't stop there, you can get exclusive access to discounts, newsletters, and great free content in your inbox daily

Follow these simple steps to get the benefits:

1. Scan the QR code or visit the link below

https://packt.link/free-ebook/978-1-83508-032-0

2. Submit your proof of purchase
3. That's it! We'll send your free PDF and other benefits to your email directly

1

Exploring Various Document Classes

Documents vary in shape and size, with distinct formats, sections, and designs. You can use LaTeX for any kind of document type. This chapter is packed with recipes suitable for an assortment of document types.

Specifically, we will cover the following:

- Preparing your LaTeX tools
- Writing a short text
- Developing a thesis
- Designing a book
- Creating a presentation
- Designing a **curriculum vitae (CV)**
- Writing a letter
- Producing a leaflet
- Building a large poster

Throughout this chapter, you will get step-by-step instructions, tips, and tricks to help you create each document type easily. By the end of this chapter, you'll have a solid foundation in creating a wide range of documents using LaTeX.

All example code is available on GitHub for download. You can find all examples of this chapter at `https://latex-cookbook.net/chapter-01`, where you can also compile them online.

Preparing your LaTeX tools

LaTeX has been around for many years. Over time, developers and authors contributed numerous extensions to its code base.

Such an extension could be one of the following:

- **Document class**: A base file that is the frame of your document. It provides various formatting styles and usually comes with meaningful default settings, which can be changed via options when loading it. It often provides commands for authors to modify settings.

- **Package**: A style file with a specific purpose that you can load in addition to the document class. Packages can be combined. Most of the time, we load many of them by executing the \usepackage command.

- **Bundle**: A set of closely related packages or classes. In our next recipe, *Writing a short text*, we will get to know some bundles.

- **Template**: A document with dummy text that you can take as a starting point and fill in your headings, texts, formulas, and images. We will look at templates in another recipe, *Developing a thesis*.

Those add-ons are incredibly valuable. They are one reason for the enduring success of LaTeX. We all agree that learning LaTeX can be challenging with its steep learning curve. However, if you don't reinvent the wheel and start with a good template or class and a quality set of packages, you can quickly achieve great results.

The purpose of this book is to assist you in this regard.

Getting ready

To be able to work with LaTeX, you need to have the following installed on your computer:

- TeX and LaTeX software, called a **TeX distribution**

- A LaTeX editor, though you could use any text editor

- A PDF viewer for seeing the final output

If you already have those installed, great! In that case, you can skip the following paragraphs and immediately proceed to the first recipe.

A PDF reader is probably already installed on your computer, such as Adobe Reader or the Preview app on the Mac. Furthermore, most editors come with an integrated PDF previewer. So, let's have a look at TeX software and editors.

TeX and LaTeX distributions

There are TeX and LaTeX software collections ready to use and easy to install. Their websites provide install and update information. You may choose the download site for your system:

- **TeX Live**: On `https://tug.org/texlive`, you can find download information and installation instructions for the cross-platform TeX distribution, which runs on Windows, Linux, Mac OS X, and other Unixes. It is supported by the **TeX Users Group** (**TUG**).

- **MacTeX**: This is based on TeX Live and has been significantly customized for Mac OS X. Essential information is available at `https://tug.org/mactex`.

- **MiKTeX**: A download and documentation for the Windows-specific distribution can be found at `https://miktex.org`.

If you own a Mac, I suggest selecting MacTeX. Otherwise, I recommend using TeX Live because the TUG provides excellent development and support.

Describing the setup is outside the scope of this book. For TeX Live, you can find a step-by-step explanation with screenshots in the *LaTeX Beginner's Guide* by Packt Publishing. Generally, you can find detailed setup instructions when you visit the aforementioned internet addresses.

Finally, on Linux systems, such as Ubuntu, Debian, Red Hat, Fedora, and SUSE versions, a TeX Live-based software package is usually available via the operating system repositories. While it's usually not as up to date as an installation via the TeX Live website or a TeX Live DVD, it's straightforward to install using the Linux package manager you deploy to install any software there.

I strongly recommend choosing a complete LaTeX installation containing all available software, packages, and fonts. At the time of writing, it typically requires around 8 GB of disk space, but it guarantees you won't encounter any missing packages or dependencies later.

LaTeX editors

There are many LaTeX editors, from small and quick to feature-rich editors. The TeX distributions already provide the fine editor **TeXworks**, which I use myself. You set it up with TeX or a package manager on Linux, and it can be downloaded from `https://tug.org/texworks`.

You can find a collection of LaTeX editors and additional software at `https://latex.net/software`. You may look for alternative editors running on your operating system there.

Using LaTeX online

A complete online cloud solution for LaTeX saves you from installing LaTeX software yourself. The most advanced one is called **Overleaf** and comes with an online LaTeX editor that runs in a web browser, so you can use it even on tablets and smartphones for storing, editing, and compiling even large LaTeX projects. You can find it at `https://www.overleaf.com`. While registration is necessary, basic access to the platform is free. Some advanced features require purchasing a subscription, but it's worth noting that many universities and institutions partner with Overleaf and provide enhanced licenses for their students and employees.

The *LaTeX Beginner's Guide* explores Overleaf in more detail; you can find this section online at `https://latexguide.org/overleaf`.

If you need help setting up and using LaTeX or an editor, you can visit a LaTeX web forum such as `https://latex.org`. In *Chapter 12*, *Getting Support on the Internet*, you can find their addresses and how to use them. You can also meet me there and ask me and our fellow forum users any LaTeX-related questions.

Once you have done the installation or online setup, you can start with a LaTeX recipe from the following sections.

See also

Many LaTeX tutorials available on the internet can help you with the first steps. I recommend looking at the following:

- `https://learnlatex.org` covers the most essential LaTeX basics in short lessons in 10 languages. It is very modern and comes with an online compiler for its examples.

- `https://texdoc.org/pkg/lshort` is the web link for *The not so short introduction to LaTeX2e*, a famous introductory text. It has been translated into more than 20 languages, available at `https://ctan.org/pkg/lshort`.

- `https://www.overleaf.com/learn` takes you to the *Overleaf knowledge base* with various guides and many articles about LaTeX.

- `https://en.wikibooks.org/wiki/LaTeX` takes you to the *LaTeX Wikibook*, a collaboratively created extensive guide.

- `https://www.dickimaw-books.com/latex/novices` contains the free introductory book *LaTeX for Complete Novices* by Nicola L. C. Talbot. It is somewhat dated but OK for the first steps.

- `https://latex2e.org` hosts the *Unofficial reference manual for LaTeX*, an excellent resource whenever you need to know how to use specific LaTeX commands, environments, arguments, and syntax in general.

- `https://latexguide.org` is the website for the *LaTeX Beginner's Guide*, with a sample chapter, all code examples by chapter, reviews, and additional information in case you're considering buying a modern book on paper or in electronic format.

If you still need to learn LaTeX, read one of the guides, and you will then be well prepared to get the best out of this book.

Writing a short text

While LaTeX is excellent for large documents, it's as useful for smaller ones, and you get all the features to work with. Writing down homework or producing a seminar handout, for example, doesn't need book-like chapters, and the layout would not be very spacy. So, we will choose a document class that suits it best.

Class bundles cover commonly used document types. Every LaTeX installation contains a base bundle with standard classes. There is a class file for articles, one for books, one for reports, one for letters, and more. It is stable stuff; it has stayed the same for many years. It can be sufficient if you don't care about the latest style. It would run even on a 10-year-old LaTeX installation.

In this recipe, we will use a class of the **KOMA-Script** bundle. This is a set of document classes and packages designed initially to replace the standard classes and provide more features. In contrast to the stable base bundle, KOMA-Script has been extensively developed in recent years. It has become feature-rich and has an excellent user interface. Parts of its functionality are provided in packages that can be used together with other classes as well. You can identify KOMA-Script classes and packages by the `scr` prefix. This prefix stands for **Script**, which was the initial name of this bundle.

How to do it...

We will start with a complete small document, already using various features. This can be your template, where you can fill in your own text later.

While we go through the document step by step, you may open the complete code directly with your editor, so you don't need to type it. It is contained in the code bundle available on the book's page at `https://www.packtpub.com` and `https://latex-cookbook.net`:

1. Create a `.tex` document in the editor of your choice. Start with a document class. We will use the `scrartcl` KOMA-Script class with A4 paper size, a base font size of 12 pt, and inter-paragraph space instead of default paragraph indentation:

   ```
   \documentclass[paper=a4,oneside,fontsize=11pt,
       parskip=full]{scrartcl}
   ```

2. Begin the document:

   ```
   \begin{document}
   ```

3. By running this command, you let LaTeX print a table of contents:

```
\tableofcontents
```

4. Start a section without numbering:

```
\addsec{Introduction}
```

5. Add some text:

```
This document will be our starting point for simple
documents. It is suitable for a single page or up to
a couple of dozen pages.

The text will be divided into sections.
```

6. Start an automatically numbered section with some text:

```
\section{The first section}
This first text will contain
```

7. Add a bulleted list using an `itemize` environment. Each list item starts with an `\item` command. Using the `\ref{label}` command, we will already refer to labels we will create later:

```
\begin{itemize}
  \item a table of contents,
  \item a bulleted list,
  \item headings and some text and math in section,
  \item referencing such as to section
    \ref{sec:maths} and equation (\ref{eq:integral}).
\end{itemize}
```

8. Continue with the text, and start another numbered section:

```
We can use this document as a template for filling
in our own content.
\section{Some maths}
```

9. Set a label so that we can refer to this point when we would like to refer to this section:

```
\label{sec:maths}
```

10. Continue with the text. We start using some math expressions in the text. We mark them by enclosing them in parentheses with a prefixing backslash as follows:

```
When we write a scientific or technical document, we
usually include math formulas. To get a brief glimpse
of the look of maths, we will look at an integral
```

```
approximation of a function \( f(x) \) as a sum with
weights \( w_i \):
```

11. Write a math equation using the `equation` environment. Again, place a label:

```
\begin{equation}
\label{eq:integral}
  \int_a^b f(x)\,\mathrm{d}x \approx (b-a)
  \sum_{i=0}^n w_i f(x_i)
\end{equation}
```

12. End the document:

```
\end{document}
```

13. Compile the document. Do it twice so that the references work. The first page of the output will be as follows:

Contents

Introduction   1

1 The first section   1

2 Some maths   1

Introduction

This document will be our starting point for simple documents. It is suitable for a single page or up to a couple of dozen pages.

The text will be divided into sections.

1 The first section

This first text will contain

- a table of contents,

- a bulleted list,

- headings and some text and math in section,

- referencing such as to section 2 and equation (1).

We can use this document as a template for filling in our own content.

2 Some maths

When we write a scientific or technical document, we usually include math formulas. To get a brief glimpse of the look of maths, we will look at an integral approximation of a function $f(x)$ as a sum with weights w_i:

$$\int_a^b f(x)\,\mathrm{d}x \approx (b-a)\sum_{i=0}^n w_i f(x_i) \tag{1}$$

1

Figure 1.1 – A document with sections, math, and referencing

How it works...

In the first line, we loaded the `scrartcl` document class. In square brackets, we set options for specifying an A4 paper size with the `oneside` option for one-sided printing and a font size of 11 pt. Finally, we chose to have a full line between paragraphs in the output to distinguish paragraphs easily by adding the `parskip=full` option.

The default setting is no space between paragraphs but a small indentation at the beginning of a paragraph. Remove the `parskip` option to see it. We chose a paragraph skip because many people are used to it when working with emails, while indentation costs line space, a precious resource on small electronic devices.

Without further ado, we began the text with a table of contents.

While the `\section` command starts numbered sections, we can have an unnumbered section by the starred `\section*` version. However, we used the `\addsec` KOMA-Script command for the first unnumbered section. That's because contrary to `\section*`, the `\addsec` command generates an entry in the table of contents.

The empty line in *step 5* tells LaTeX to make a paragraph break. Note that a simple line break in the LaTeX code doesn't cause a line break or paragraph break in the output.

As bulleted lists are an excellent way to present points clearly, we used an `itemize` environment in *step 7*. Environments start with a `\begin` command and are finished by an `\end` command.

> **Note**
> If you want a numbered list, use the `enumerate` environment.

An `equation` environment has been used to display an automatically numbered formula. We used a `\label` command to set an invisible anchor mark so that we could refer to it using its label name by the `\ref` command and get the equation number in the output.

> **Choosing label identifiers**
> It is a good practice to use prefixes to identify kinds of labels, such as `eq:name` for equations, `fig:name` for figures, `tab:name` for tables, and so on. Avoid special characters in names, such as accented characters.

In *step 10*, small formulas within text lines have been enclosed in \ (. . . \) , which provides inline math mode. Dollar symbols, such as $ . . . $, can be used instead, making typing easier. However, the parentheses clarify where the math mode starts and ends, which may be beneficial when many math expressions are scattered in the text, and the "dollar syntax" is old TeX syntax.

Why did we have to compile it twice? When you use the \label command, LaTeX writes that position to the .aux file. In the next compiler run, the \ref command can read this and put the correct reference into the text.

For further information on math typesetting, refer to *Chapter 10, Writing Advanced Mathematics*, specifically to the *Fine-tuning a formula* recipe.

See also

The part of the document before \begin{document} is called the **preamble**. It contains global settings. Adding a few lines to our document preamble can improve and modify our document's general appearance. *Chapter 2, Tuning the Text*, starts with beneficial additions to the preamble that are also useful with small documents.

In *Chapter 3, Adjusting Fonts*, you can find recipes for changing an entire document's fonts or specific elements.

For further customization tasks, such as modifying page layout, adding headers and footers, and changing sectioning title font, refer to the *Designing a book* recipe in the current chapter. We will look at such settings on the occasion of a book example.

Developing a thesis

When you write a large document such as a thesis, you have two main choices: choose a ready-made template or set up your own document environment. If you have little time and need to start your thesis fast, a template can come to the rescue.

Beware of outdated and questionable templates found somewhere on the internet. Look first at the date and at user opinions, such as in web forums. The age of a template is not a problem in itself, as LaTeX can run it the same way when it's been written. However, LaTeX developed, and better solutions came up over time. Legacy code may not benefit from it.

Some universities provide their own template. That may be OK because requirements would be met for sure; just check if it can be improved – for example, by replacing obsolete packages with recommended successors.

An excellent source for checking the quality of a template is the guide to obsolete commands and packages in LaTeX2e; people call it **l2tabu**. You can open the English version by typing `texdoc l2tabuen` at Command Prompt or at `https://texdoc.org/pkg/l2tabuen`.

To be clear, the LaTeX base is stable and solid, but there are changes in community-contributed packages.

In the previous recipe, *Writing a short text*, we took a bottom-up approach and built a document from scratch, adding what we desired. Now, we will go top-down: let's use and understand a complete template, removing what we don't need.

As we need to choose a template now, let's take a real gem. The `ClassicThesis` package by Prof. André Miede is a thesis template of excellent quality. The design follows the book classic *The Elements of Typographic Style* by Robert Bringhurst; we will see some particular points later in this recipe. Its implementation is thoughtful and modern. Initially written in 2006, it's also maintained today and shipped with TeX distributions.

Getting ready

Though the `ClassicThesis` package may already be installed on your TeX system, named `classicthesis.sty`, the whole template is an archive of files that should go into your working directory.

Download the `ClassicThesis` archive from the following **Comprehensive TeX Archive Network (CTAN)** address: `https://ctan.org/pkg/classicthesis`.

Instead of fetching single files, choose to download them as a `.zip` file. Unzip it to where you keep your personal documents in its own directory. This directory will be your thesis directory.

This package provides a ready-made structured filesystem of the main document, style file, settings file, and document parts such as abstract, foreword, and chapters in dedicated files. You can edit all files and fill in your own text.

The `ClassicThesis.tex` file is the main document. Its filler text is the template's manual; this allows us to compile it immediately to look at the output design. Also, you can verify that your TeX installation can handle it if you need to install additional packages.

How to do it...

After unzipping, your directory will have this structure:

Figure 1.2 – The directory structure of the ClassicThesis template

Now, follow these steps:

1. Rename or copy the `ClassicThesis.tex` file and choose your own name, such as `MyThesis.tex`, but keep it in the same directory.

2. Open the main document, `MyThesis.tex`, and look around to get a feeling of the structure. Compile it for testing at least twice to get correct referencing so that you know that this starting point works.

3. You can review and edit the settings in the main file, `MyThesis.tex`, and in the `classicthesis-config.tex` configuration file. On the following pages, we will examine that content.

4. Open the existing `.tex` files, such as `Abstract.tex` and `Chapter01.tex`, with your editor. Remove the filler text and type in your own text. Add extra chapter files as needed, and include them in the main file, `MyThesis.tex`, as well. The structure is given; the technical part of the editing is like cloning files and copying lines; all you need to focus on is the actual thesis content now.

Don't worry if the font or margins don't please you yet. You can change the layout at any time. Let's take a closer look now, and then you will know how.

How it works...

We will now look at the functional lines of the main file, `MyThesis.tex`.

The document preamble starts as follows:

```
\documentclass[ twoside,openright,titlepage,
                numbers=noenddot,headinclude,
                footinclude,cleardoublepage=empty,
                abstract=on,BCOR=5mm,paper=a4,
                fontsize=11pt
                ]{scrreprt}
\input{classicthesis-config}
```

The template is built on the `scrreprt` KOMA-Script class. KOMA-Script as a LaTeX bundle is described in the first recipe of the current chapter, *Writing a short text*.

You can change the pre-set options to those you need, such as font size or BCOR binding correction. There are many class options for adjusting the layout. You can read about them in the KOMA-Script manual, such as by running `texdoc koma-script` at the command line or at `https://texdoc.org/pkg/koma-script`. In our next recipe, *Designing a book*, we will discuss some of them in more depth.

Loading of packages and all the remaining settings is done in a single file, `classicthesis-config.tex`. We will look at it later in this recipe.

The document body starts with the following text:

```
\begin{document}
\frenchspacing
\raggedbottom
\selectlanguage{american}
\pagenumbering{roman}
\pagestyle{plain}
```

The `\frenchspacing` command means that there's only a single space following the punctuation after a sentence. LaTeX puts extra space between sentences by default, or if you enter the `\nonfrenchspacing` command.

The language is set to American English, which is essential for American hyphenation. Actually, you would need the `\selectlanguage` command only if you need to switch between languages.

We start with Roman page numbers. The `plain` page style means we have no page headers for now, while page numbers are centered in the page footer.

Then, we see the **front matter**, which is the part of the document where the formal parts before the actual content go:

```
\include{FrontBackmatter/DirtyTitlepage}
\include{FrontBackmatter/Titlepage}
\include{FrontBackmatter/Titleback}
\cleardoublepage\include{FrontBackmatter/Dedication}
%\cleardoublepage\include{FrontBackmatter/Foreword}
\cleardoublepage\include{FrontBackmatter/Abstract}
\cleardoublepage\include{FrontBackmatter/Publication}
\cleardoublepage\include{FrontBackmatter/Acknowledgments}
\cleardoublepage\include{FrontBackmatter/Contents}
```

Each commonly required part of the front matter has its own file. Just edit the file as needed, comment out using a % sign at the beginning of a line, or remove what you don't need. The `\cleardoublepage` command ends a page but also ensures that the next page starts on the right-hand side. This can mean inserting an empty page if necessary – that is, a double-page break. It would not happen if you changed the `twoside` option to `oneside`, so you could keep that `\cleardoublepage` command, which would act like a `\clearpage` command when the `oneside` option was set.

Finally, we get the **main matter**:

```
\cleardoublepage
\pagestyle{scrheadings}
\pagenumbering{arabic}
\cleardoublepage
\part{Some Kind of Manual}\label{pt:manual}
\include{Chapters/Chapter01}
\cleardoublepage
\ctparttext{You can put some informational part
  preamble text here...}
\part{The Showcase}\label{pt:showcase}
\include{Chapters/Chapter02}
\include{Chapters/Chapter03}
```

In the main matter, the page style is set to `scrheadings`, and we use Arabic page numbers. The `\pagenumbering` command resets the page number to 0.

The thesis is divided into parts. Each one is split into chapters. You can omit the `\part` lines if your highest sectioning level should be the chapter level.

Each chapter gets its own `.tex` file in the `Chapters` subdirectory, so you can easily handle a massive text. Furthermore, you could use the `\includeonly` command to typeset just selected chapters to speed up writing.

Finally, the main document ends with the **back matter**:

```
\appendix
\cleardoublepage
\part{Appendix}
\include{Chapters/Chapter0A}
\cleardoublepage\include{FrontBackmatter/Bibliography}
\cleardoublepage\include{FrontBackmatter/Declaration}
\cleardoublepage\include{FrontBackmatter/Colophon}
\end{document}
```

The `\appendix` command resets the sectioning counters and changes to alphabetic numbering; the following chapters will be numbered by A, B, and so on. As with the front matter, the appendix parts are divided into several files.

Let's take a look at the configuration file. Open `classicthesis-config.tex`. It would take too much space in the book, so let's just see some sample lines:

```
\newcommand{\myTitle}{A Classic Thesis Style\xspace}
\newcommand{\myName}{Andr\'e Miede\xspace}
\newcommand{\myUni}{Put data here\xspace}
```

```
\newcommand{\myLocation}{Darmstadt\xspace}
\newcommand{\myTime}{January 2024\xspace}
```

Here, you can fill in your own data. Besides being printed on the title page, this data will be used as metadata for the generated PDF document. There are more supported macros at this place, such as `\mySubtitle`, `\myProf`, and many more. The `\xspace` command takes care of proper spacing after such a macro, inserting a space when there's no punctuation mark following it.

There's more...

As mentioned, this template contains design decisions inspired by the book *The Elements of Typographical Style* by Robert Bringhurst. The most notable are as follows:

- It doesn't use bold fonts – small caps or italics elegantly emphasize what's important.

- The text body is not very wide, allowing reading comfortably without the eyes jumping too wide from the right back to the left. So, we have wide margins, which can be used for notes.

- The table of contents is not stretched to get right-aligned page numbers. To quote the author: "Is your reader interested in the page number, or does she want to sum the numbers up?" That's why the page number follows the title.

Explore the `classicthesis-config.tex` file further to make modifications. As in the previous recipe, we apply document-wide changes within the preamble; this file is the place for doing it.

We will take a look at the selected lines of that configuration file.

Getting a right-justified table of contents

The design is not set in stone; you may adjust a lot. Look at the very beginning of `classicthesis-config.tex`:

```
\PassOptionsToPackage{
    drafting=true,
    tocaligned=false,
    dottedtoc=false,
    eulerchapternumbers=true,
    linedheaders=false,
    floatperchapter=true,
    eulermath=false,
    beramono=true,
    palatino=true,
    style=classicthesis
}{classicthesis}
```

Here, you can find the options for the actual `classicthesis` package. For example, if you would like to see the page numbers in the table of contents right aligned, set the `dottedtoc` option to `true`. These and further options are documented in the template's manual available by executing the `texdoc classicthesis` command or at `https://texdoc.org/pkg/classicthesis`.

Changing the margins

To fulfill requirements on page margins or implement your layout ideas, you can specify exact page dimensions by loading the geometry package. Here's an example:

```
\usepackage[inner=1.5cm,outer=3cm,top=2cm,bottom=2cm,
   bindingoffset=5mm]{geometry}
```

Here, you can also provide a value for the space you may lose by the binding and all margins you would like. It's a good practice to have a visible inner margin set to half the value of the outer one because margins would be added in the middle. For single-sided printing, with `oneside` options, call the margins `left` and `right`.

Place such a line at the end of `classicthesis-config.tex` so that it will override previously made original settings.

Modifying the layout of captions

In the `classicthesis-config.tex` file, you can also change the appearance of captions of figures and tables. This is the default setup in that file:

```
\RequirePackage{caption}
\captionsetup{font=small}
```

Here, the template loads the `caption` package. The `\RequirePackage` command is similar to the `\usepackage` command except that it can be used before the `\documentclass` command. The `caption` package provides many features for fine-tuning captions. With this setting, captions have a smaller font than regular text. By adding simple options, you can further adjust the appearance; for example, by adding the option `labelfont=it`, you would get italic caption labels. Refer to the `caption` package manual at `https://texdoc.org/pkg/caption` to learn more.

> **Note**
> While the `caption` package is a general solution working with most classes, including KOMA-Script, the latter now offers extended integrated caption features.

Centering displayed equations

Another option is responsible for the alignment of displayed equations:

```
\PassOptionsToPackage{fleqn}{amsmath}
\usepackage{amsmath}
```

With `ClassicThesis`, displayed equations will be left aligned. The `fleqn` option is switching to this alignment. If you want to restore the default behavior centering the equations, remove that first line that passes the option or comment it out. But keep the second line, which loads the `amsmath` package, as this is the de facto standard package for typesetting mathematics in LaTeX.

See also

You can find many recipes for content elements in the following chapters for your thesis. Especially for a beautiful thesis, elegant tables are of great value, so you may look at the *Designing a legible table* recipe in *Chapter 4, Creating Tables*.

At `https://latextemplates.com`, you can find a collection of excellent templates, including thesis templates.

Overleaf provides hundreds of thesis templates at `https://www.overleaf.com/latex/templates/tagged/thesis`, including templates of universities, so check out descriptions and tags for your university's name.

Designing a book

A book can be a large document, so we can take a similar approach to the previous recipe. Refer to that recipe to see how to split your document into handy files and how to organize the directory structure.

Commonly, books are printed two-sided. In contrast to articles, they are divided into chapters, which start on right-hand pages, have pretty spacy headings, and often a page header showing the current chapter title. Readability and good typography are essential, so you would hardly find books with an A4 paper size, double line space, and similar specs, which some institutes expect of a thesis. That's why we got dedicated book classes with meaningful default settings and features.

How to do it...

As the *Writing a short text* recipe explains, our choice will be a KOMA-Script class; this time, it has the name `scrbook`.

Follow these steps:

1. Start with the `scrbook` class and suitable options for paper and font size:

   ```
   \documentclass[fontsize=11pt,paper=a5,
     pagesize=auto]{scrbook}
   ```

2. Choose a **font encoding** with the following command; use T1, which is good for European, English, or American texts:

   ```
   \usepackage[T1]{fontenc}
   ```

3. If you want a non-default font, load it; here, we chose Latin Modern:

   ```
   \usepackage{lmodern}
   ```

4. We will load the `blindtext` package for getting English dummy texts; it also requires loading the `babel` package with English settings:

   ```
   \usepackage[english]{babel}
   \usepackage{blindtext}
   ```

5. Load the `microtype` package for better text justification:

   ```
   \usepackage{microtype}
   ```

6. By running the following command, you can switch off additional space after sentence punctuation:

   ```
   \frenchspacing
   ```

7. Begin the document:

   ```
   \begin{document}
   ```

8. Provide a title, a subtitle, an author name, and a date. You can also set an empty value if you don't want to have something in that titling field:

   ```
   \title{The Book}
   \subtitle{Some more to know}
   \author{The Author}
   \date{}
   ```

9. Let LaTeX print the title page:

   ```
   \maketitle
   ```

10. Print out the table of contents:

    ```
    \tableofcontents
    ```

11. In addition to chapters, we will divide this book into parts, so start one:

    ```
    \part{First portion}
    ```

12. Start a chapter with a heading. Having text before another heading comes is nice, so let's have some:

    ```
    \chapter{The beginning}
    Some introductory text comes here.
    ```

13. As in our first recipe, add a section and text and another part with a chapter and sections. Using the \Blindtext command, you can generate long dummy text; use the \blindtext command to get shorter dummy text. The \appendix command switches to alphabetic numbering:

    ```
    \section{A first section}
    Dummy text will follow.
    \blindtext
    \section{Another section}
    \Blindtext
    \appendix
    \part{Appendix}
    \chapter{An addendum}
    \section{Section within the appendix}
    \blindtext
    ```

14. End the document:

    ```
    \end{document}
    ```

15. Let your editor compile the text to PDF. You will get a 13-page book document with A5 paper size, a title page, part pages, chapter, section headings, and filler text.

Take a look at a sample page:

1. The beginning

Some introductory text comes here.

1.1. A first section

Dummy text will follow. Hello, here is some text without a meaning. This text should show what a printed text will look like at this place. If you read this text, you will get no information. Really? Is there no information? Is there a difference between this text and some nonsense like "Huardest gefburn"? Kjift – not at all! A blind text like this gives you information about the selected font, how the letters are written and an impression of the look. This text should contain all letters of the alphabet and it should be written in of the original language. There is no need for special content, but the length of words should match the language.

1.2. Another section

Hello, here is some text without a meaning. This text should show what a printed text will look like at this place. If you read this text, you will get no information. Really? Is there no information? Is there a difference between this text and some nonsense like "Huardest gefburn"? Kjift – not at all! A blind text like this gives you information about the selected font, how the letters are written and an impression of the look. This text should contain all letters of the alphabet and it should be written in of the original language. There is no need for special content, but the length of words should match the language.

7

Figure 1.3 – Page 7 of the sample book with chapter and section headings

Note the headings in a sans-serif font. This is an intentional default setting in KOMA-Script classes, which makes the headings lighter than the standard LaTeX big, bold, and serif headings. You know – the traditional look.

Now, you can fill in your own text, add chapters and sections, and add features described later in this recipe.

How it works...

At first, we loaded the scrbook class, made explicitly for writing books. So, it is ready for two-sided printing with meaningful margins and pleasing proportions of headings and text.

Besides the class's default settings, we chose a font size of 11 pt and A5 paper size, which is handy for a book. The `pagesize=auto` option is essential here: it ensures that the A5 printing area will be taken over to the PDF page size.

Then, we did the following things, which will be explained in more detail at the beginning of *Chapter 2, Tuning the Text*:

- Chose the **T1** font encoding when loading the `fontenc` package
- Selected the high-quality **Latin Modern T1** supporting font set by loading the `lmodern` package
- Loaded the `babel` package with support for English
- Used the `microtype` package for getting finer typography

The last package we loaded was `blindtext`. You don't need it in your final document; here, it will serve us to provide filler text. Using such dummy text, we can get a better idea of the final result already before writing the actual content.

Finally, we switched to the so-called **French spacing**, which we already saw in the thesis recipe. Remember – this means that after ending a sentence, we will get a standard interword space, not a wider space.

There's more...

You can change the layout of the book in many ways. Choose your settings at the beginning, or even better: don't hesitate and start writing your content – once you get a decent amount of text, you can better see the effect of layout changes. You can do that at any time. Let's take a look at some design ideas.

Changing the page layout

When a book is bound after printing, this binding can cost space; less of the inner margin may be visible. You can specify a **binding correction** to compensate for and preserve layout proportions. So, if you see 5 mm less of the inner margin after binding, add `BCOR=5mm` as a class option at the beginning. A similarly produced book may give you an idea about a good value.

The actual text area has the same ratios as the page itself. This is automatically done by a dividing construction, described in the KOMA-Script manual. That's really worth reading. You can open it by typing `texdoc scrguien` at Command Prompt or online at `https://texdoc.org/pkg/scrguien`. This abbreviation comes from `scr` for the original package name (Script), `gui` for guide, and `en` for English, and obviously from the ancient limit of 8 characters per filename in older filesystems.

Besides those page and text area ratios, the result shows a bottom margin twice as high as the top margin, and an outer margin with the double width of the inner margin. Imagine an opened book: the inner margins together appear with the same space as an outer margin. Sometimes, people make the mistake of thinking that the inner margin should be much bigger because of the binding, but that's done by raising BCOR as previously. In *Chapter 2, Tuning the Text*, you can use the *Visualizing the layout* recipe to inspect and understand the margins.

If you want a more extensive text area, which means narrower margins, you can keep the ratios as described. Just raise the division factor of the mentioned internal construction and take a look to see if it would suit you. For example, set the DIV=10 class option. Higher values are possible. That's a safe and easy way to preserve sane layout proportions.

To sum up, our example with 5 mm binding loss and pretty narrow margins could start like this:

```
\documentclass[fontsize=11pt,paper=a5,pagesize=auto,
    BCOR=5mm,DIV=12]{scrbook}
```

Alternatively, you could freely choose text and margin dimensions when requirements by the publisher or institute need to be met. This can be done by loading the classic geometry package with the desired measurements, as we saw in the *Writing a thesis* recipe:

```
\usepackage[inner=1.5cm,outer=3cm,top=2cm,bottom=4cm,
    bindingoffset=5mm]{geometry}
```

Designing a title page

You can create your own title page to present more information in a style you desire. Let's look at an example that shows some handy commands for it.

Remove the \maketitle command. You can do the same with the \title, \subtitle, \author, and \date commands. Instead, put this titlepage environment right after \begin{document}:

```
\begin{titlepage}
    \vspace*{1cm}
    {\huge\raggedright The Book\par}
    \noindent\hrulefill\par
    {\LARGE\raggedleft The Author\par}
    \vfill
    {\Large\raggedleft Institute\par}
\end{titlepage}
```

The `titlepage` environment creates a page without a page number on it. We started with some vertical space using the `\vspace*` command. The `\vspace` command adds vertical space, which can be of a positive or a negative value. Here, note the star at the end: this way of calling `\vspace` also works at the beginning of a page, where a simple `\vspace` instance would be ignored. That default behavior prevents undesired vertical space at the top of a page, which initially may have been intended as space between texts.

We enclosed each line in curly braces. This is also called **grouping**, and it is used to keep the effect of changes, such as the font size, local within the braces. In each line, we did the following:

- Switched to a specific font size
- Chose left or right alignment
- Wrote out the text
- Ended with a paragraph break

The `\par` command is equivalent to an empty line in the input. Sometimes, people use it to keep the code compact, such as here. We must end the paragraph before the font size changes because that size defines the space between lines. Hence, we ended the paragraph before we closed the brace group. It's good to keep this in mind for when texts are longer.

Our only non-text design element is a modest horizontal line with the `\hrulefill` command. The preceding `\noindent` command just prevents an undesired paragraph indentation, so the line really starts at the very left.

`\vfill` inserts stretching vertical space, so we got the last line pushed down to the title page bottom. If you used several `\vfill` commands on the same page, the available vertical space would be divided and distributed equally between them.

We took this scenario to show some commands for positioning text on a page. You can experiment with the `\vspace` and `\vfill` commands and their horizontal companions, `\hspace` and `\hfill`. Just avoid using such commands to "fix" local placement issues in the document when it would be better to adjust a class or package setting document-wide. If at all, don't make such tweaks until the final stage.

> **Note**
> The `titlepages` package provides 40 example title pages in various designs with complete LaTeX source code. You could choose one, use it, and customize it.

Adding a cover page

The title page, which we produced previously, is an inner page. That's why it follows the standard page layout with the same inner and outer margins as the body text.

The cover is different; for example, it should have symmetric margins and can be designed individually. To get that deviating layout, it's recommended to use a separate document for it. Another reason is that it will usually be printed on different paper or cardboard.

So, you can start with an article-like class as in our first recipe, *Writing a short text*, then use options such as twoside=false or the equivalent oneside option to get symmetric margins. Then, you can position your text as we did with the title page.

Changing the document class

A very well-designed book class is memoir. It is pretty complete in itself, so you don't need to load many packages: it already integrates many features of other packages, providing similar interfaces. memoir has a monolithic, easy-to-use approach, but it needs to take care of package conflicts. It is not as flexible as choosing the package set by yourself. KOMA-Script, in contrast, provides its features mostly in packages that can also be used with other classes.

1. Start with memoir by changing the first line to the following:

   ```
   \documentclass[11pt,a5paper]{memoir}
   ```

2. Remove the \subtitle command, which is not supported.

3. To have the title on its own page, surround \maketitle with a titlingpage environment:

   ```
   \begin{titlingpage}
   \maketitle
   \end{titlingpage}
   ```

4. Typeset and compare.

The memoir class provides an extensive manual that can help you to customize your document. It's split into two parts. Type texdoc memman at Command Prompt to read the actual manual and texdoc memdesign to read the part on book design, which is an excellent resource independent of the class. Alternatively, you can find these manuals at https://texdoc.org/pkg/memman and https://texdoc.org/pkg/memdesign, respectively.

Another great start with a unique beauty is the tufte-latex class. It comes with a sample-book.tex file, which you can also download from https://ctan.org/tex-archive/macros/latex/contrib/tufte-latex. You could open this book file containing some dummy content and fill in your text. One of its outstanding features is a wide margin for extensive use of side notes and small figures in the margin.

See also

A book may contain additional elements such as an index, a glossary, and a bibliography. Refer to *Chapter 8, Producing Contents, Indexes, and Bibliographies*, which includes such recipes.

The Overleaf book templates collection at `https://www.overleaf.com/latex/templates/tagged/book` can also give you a head start.

Creating a presentation

At a conference or a seminar, speakers often use a projector or screen to present written information in addition to the talk. Such a presentation document requires a specific kind of layout and features.

In our recipe, we will use the `beamer` class, which has been designed specifically for this purpose and provides the following features:

- A typical landscape slide format, here 128 mm x 96 mm
- Structured frames with dynamic information, such as sectioning
- Support for overlays and transition effects
- Pre-designed themes for easily changing the look
- An intelligent interface for customizing

How to do it...

We will start with a sample presentation document, which we can extend. Follow the next steps:

1. Start with the `beamer` document class:

    ```
    \documentclass{beamer}
    ```

2. Choose a theme. Here, we take the theme called `Warsaw`:

    ```
    \usetheme{Warsaw}
    ```

3. Begin the document:

    ```
    \begin{document}
    ```

4. Provide a title, a subtitle, the author's name, the institute, and a date:

```
\title{Talk on the Subject}
\subtitle{What this is about}
\author{Author Name}
\institute{University of X}
\date{June 24, 2015}
```

5. Make a slide using the `frame` environment. The first one will contain the title page:

```
\begin{frame}
   \titlepage
\end{frame}
```

6. Make a frame for the table of contents titled `Outline`. Add the `pausesections` option so that the table of contents will be shown stepwise, section by section:

```
\begin{frame}{Outline}
   \tableofcontents[pausesections]
\end{frame}
```

7. Start a section and a subsection within:

```
\section{Introduction}
\subsection{A subsection}
```

8. All visible content goes into a `frame` environment. So also do lists, which are visually better than normal text in a presentation:

```
\begin{frame}{Very Informative Title}
   \begin{itemize}
    \item First thing to say.
    \item There is more.
    \item Another short point.
   \end{itemize}
\end{frame}
```

9. This frame will show an emphasized block with a title:

```
\begin{frame}{Another Title With Uppercased Words}
  Text
  \begin{alertblock}{A highlighted block}
    Some important information put into a block.
  \end{alertblock}
\end{frame}
```

10. We add another subsection, with a frame with another titled block, and another section with a slide containing a list. We highlight some words using the \alert command. Finally, end the document:

```
\subsection{Another subsection}
\begin{frame}{Informative Title}
  \begin{exampleblock}{An example}
    An example within a block.
  \end{exampleblock}
  Explanation follows.
\end{frame}
\section{Summary}
\begin{frame}{Summary}
  \begin{itemize}
    \item Our \alert{main point}
    \item The \alert{second main point}
  \end{itemize}
  \vfill
  \begin{block}{Outlook}
    Further ideas here.
  \end{block}
\end{frame}
\end{document}
```

11. Compile and have a look at the produced slides:

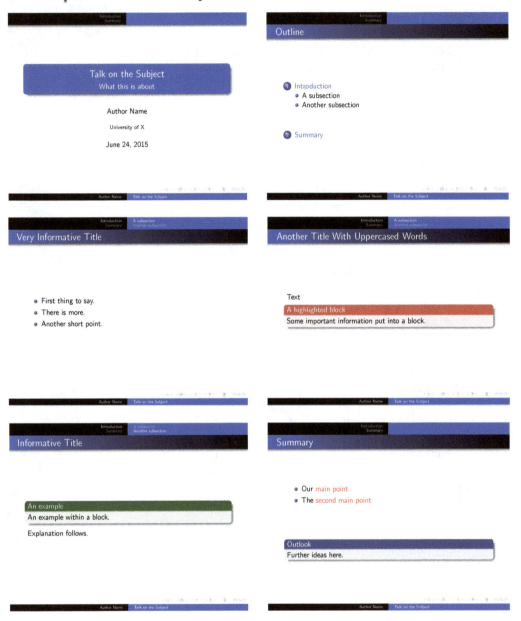

Figure 1.4 – Presentation slides

Now, you can adjust the title, author, and date and edit the text in the frames. Then, you can add your own frames with titles and text.

How it works...

We loaded the `beamer` class and chose the theme with the name `Warsaw`. You could easily replace it with another theme's name, compile, and cycle through the themes until you find the best for your occasion. Pre-installed themes are as follows:

- AnnArbor
- Antibes
- Bergen
- Berkeley
- Berlin
- Boadilla
- boxes
- CambridgeUS
- Copenhagen
- Darmstadt
- default
- Dresden
- EastLansing
- Frankfurt
- Goettingen
- Hannover
- Ilmenau
- JuanLesPins
- Luebeck
- Madrid
- Malmoe
- Marburg
- Montpellier
- PaloAlto
- Pittsburgh

- `Rochester`
- `Singapore`
- `Szeged`
- `Warsaw`

We specified the title, subtitle, author, and talk date, which is then printed by `\titlepage`. We used a `frame` environment, which we will do for each slide.

The next frame contains the table of contents. We provided an `Outline` frame title as an argument to the frame in curly braces. For the `\tableofcontents` command, we added the `pausesections` option. By doing this, section titles are printed individually with a pause in between. This allows us to explain what the auditory will hear before they read further.

As in a standard LaTeX document, we used the `\section` and `\subsection` commands. The heading is not directly printed. The sections and subsections are printed in the frame margin with the current position highlighted.

We used an `itemize` environment as in a standard LaTeX document to get a bulleted list. The `enumerate` environment for numbered lists and `description` environment for descriptive lists also work in `beamer` frames.

To highlight information, we used so-called `block` environments. Besides the standard `block` environment, we can use `exampleblock` and `alertblock` to get a different style or color. The chosen theme determines the appearance of those blocks.

A more subtle kind of emphasizing is achieved using the `\alert` command, as seen in the last frame.

Now, you have a template and tools to build up your presentation.

Here are some more quick tips:

- Keep time constraints in mind; a frame per minute is a good rule of thumb
- Use a few sections, logically split into subsections; it's better to avoid sub-subsections
- Use self-explaining titles for sectioning and frames
- Bulleted lists help to keep things simple
- Consider avoiding numbering things; one rarely cares about a reference to theorem 2.6 during a talk
- Don't disrupt the reading flow by footnotes
- Graphics, such as diagrams, help the auditory in visualizing

> **Note**
>
> Slides should support your talk, not the other way around. Did you already bear up with a presentation where the speaker just read out aloud text from the slides and used fancy transition effects? You can do it better by focusing on well-crafted content.

There's more...

The `beamer` class has unique capabilities and extraordinary design. We will explore it further.

Using short titles and names

Besides the title page, the title of the presentation and the author's name are additionally printed at the bottom of each frame. The exact position depends upon the chosen theme.

However, the space might need to be increased for long titles or names. You can give short versions used at such places, such as by specifying the following text:

```
\title[Short title]{Long Informative Title}
\author[Shortened name]{Author's Complete Name}
\date[2024/01/24]{Conference on X at Y, January 24, 2024}
```

The same is possible for the `\institute` and `\subtitle` commands if used.

In the same way, you can provide short names for sections and subsections so that they better fit into their field within the frame margin. Just use the `optional` argument in square brackets. The `\part` and `\subsubsection` commands work similarly if needed.

Uncovering information piecewise

Showing a complete slide at once may be distracting. People may read ahead instead of listening to you. You can take them by the hand by showing the content step by step.

The simplest way is by inserting a `\pause` command. It can go between anything, such as text, graphics, and blocks. It also works between two `\item` commands in a bulleted list, though consider not to pause between items but between whole lists. Use it as in the following line of code:

```
Text\pause more text\pause\includegraphics{filename}
```

Such a frame is then layered – that is, divided into overlays. They are internally numbered. If you would like to show something at a certain overlay, you can tell the `beamer` class when to uncover it:

```
\uncover<3->{Surprise!}
```

This shows your text on *slide 3* of the current frame, and it will stay on the following slides on that frame. Omit the dash for restricting it only to *slide 3*. You could also list slides (for example, <3 , 5>), give ranges such as <3 - 5>, and mix slides (<3 , 5 - >).

That syntax works with overlay specification-aware commands. Among them, there are \item, \includegraphics, and even \renewcommand, so you can use them with an overlay specification such as the following:

```
\includegraphics<3->{filename}
```

It should not be too fancy. A presentation still needs a linear structure. Complicated overlays may be handy for showing and hiding annotation to an object while you explain that.

Refer to the beamer manual for further information about using overlays.

Splitting frames into columns

You can arrange text and images in multiple columns on a frame. It's convenient for images with explaining text. Let's take a look at a sample:

```
\begin{frame}
  Some text which can use whole frame width
  \begin{columns}[t]
    \begin{column}{0.45\textwidth}
      Sample text in\\
      two lines
    \end{column}
    \begin{column}[T]{0.45\textwidth}
      \includegraphics[width=3cm]{filename}
    \end{column}
  \end{columns}
\end{frame}
```

We started the multi-column area using the columns environment. You can specify t, b, or c alignment options for the column's top, bottom, or centered alignment. Centered is the default. While t aligns at the baseline of the first line, as usual in LaTeX, there's a handy additional option, T, which aligns at the very top.

Each column has been made with the column environment. The column width has been given as an argument. It understands the same positioning options, so you can override what you set in the surrounding columns environment. We added [T] here because an image has its baseline at its bottom, and we wanted to change it to the very top.

Showing an outline for each section

You can tell the `beamer` class to give an outline at the beginning of each section by specifying the following code:

```
\AtBeginSection{
  \begin{frame}{Outline}
    \tableofcontents[currentsection]
  \end{frame}}
```

You can also use the `\AtBeginSection` command for inserting different code. If something should happen for a starred `\section*` command too, you can insert the corresponding code within an `optional` argument in square brackets.

Removing navigation symbols

By default, every slide shows small navigation symbols; here, at the bottom of a frame. If you don't need them, you can save that space and reduce distraction by specifying the following line of code:

```
\setbeamertemplate{navigation symbols}{}
```

Changing the font

The default font set with the `beamer` class is Computer Modern. You can change it to other fonts, as explained in the *Writing a short text* recipe.

The default shape is sans-serif. Even the math formulas are sans-serif. It can be more readable with a low projector resolution or at some distance than with a serif font.

However, if you would like to change to a serif font, you can load the corresponding font theme in the preamble:

```
\usefonttheme{serif}
```

Another available font theme is `professionalfonts`, which doesn't change fonts but simply uses the set you bought. Furthermore, there are `structurebold`, `structureitalicserif`, and `structuresmallcapsserif`, which change the font in the structure – that is, in headlines, footlines, and sidebars – to such a shape combination.

Changing the color

The quickest way to change colors is by loading a theme with a thoughtful selection of colors for the various structural elements. Use a single command, such as the following:

```
\usecolortheme{dolphin}
```

Outer color themes provide a color set for the headline, footline, and sidebar. The author then gave sea-animal names: `dolphin`, `whale`, and `seahorse`. Then, there are **inner color themes** for elements such as color blocks with names of flowers: `lily`, `orchid`, and `rose`. Combine inner and outer color themes as you like.

Finally, there are complete themes covering all structure aspects: `albatross`, `beaver`, `beetle`, `crane`, `dove`, `fly`, `monarca`, `seagull`, `spruce`, and `wolverine`. They are named after flying animals, except `beaver` and `spruce` as external additions.

That's a lot of names; just cycle through them using the `\usecolortheme` command to find the color set you like most.

Loading a theme from the internet

With some labor, you can create your very own theme. The extensive `beamer` manual will guide you. However, you may save much time: `beamer` is very popular among academic users who already use LaTeX for their papers. So, you can find many themes prepared for universities and institutes but also designed by various `beamer` users.

You can find an overview at `https://latex-beamer.net`.

Explore the gallery there, download a theme you like, add your logo, and tweak it. Instructions are on that website.

Providing a handout

You can give your auditory a printed version of slides. Just create a version of your document with the handout option so that no overlays will be used:

```
\documentclass[handout]{beamer}
```

Slides are commonly small, so it's good to print several slides on a single page:

```
\usepackage{pgfpages}
\pgfpagesuselayout{4 on 1}[a4paper,
  border shrink=5mm, landscape]
```

This prints four slides on one A4 page in landscape. You can get bigger prints, two slides on each page, in portrait mode by specifying the following line of code:

```
\pgfpagesuselayout{2 on 1}[a4paper,border shrink=5mm]
```

We used the `pgfpages` package, a utility package coming with the `pgf` package.

See also

For best quality with included graphics, refer to *Chapter 5, Working with Images*. In *Chapter 6, Creating Graphics*, you can find recipes for quickly creating diagrams and charts, which are excellent tools for visualizing data in a presentation.

Beyond common academic documents such as a thesis, papers, books, and slides, you may need to present yourself in the working world. The following recipe will prepare you for applying for a job with style.

Designing a CV

Tabular layouts are prevalent today for a CV. When applying for a job, inform yourself about typical requirements for the content of a CV. You can then create a simple document with tables that are consistent and readable.

You can use a template if it needs to be quick or you would like to base it upon a proven modern layout. We will use the `moderncv` class and its template in this recipe to quickly produce a CV.

Getting ready

If it's not already installed on your computer, download and install the `moderncv` class from CTAN at `https://ctan.org/pkg/moderncv`. The easiest is to download it as a `.zip` file from `https://mirrors.ctan.org/macros/latex/contrib/moderncv.zip`.

If your TeX installation provides a package manager, use it for the installation.

There's a directory of examples containing templates that you can use. Either locate it in the documentation branch of your TeX directory tree or visit the preceding CTAN link: `https://ctan.org/tex-archive/macros/latex/contrib/moderncv`.

How to do it...

We will start using a sample file provided by the `moderncv` bundle. Follow these steps:

1. Copy the `template.tex` file into your document directory, rename it, and choose your own name, such as `MyCV.tex`.

2. Open that document, `MyCV.tex`, and look around to understand the template. Luckily, it is full of comments on how to use it. Compile it to ensure that this document works.

3. Review and edit the class and package options in `MyThesis.tex`.

4. Remove the filler text and type in your own data. At the beginning, your document may look like this:

```
\documentclass[11pt,a4paper,sans]{moderncv}
\moderncvstyle{classic}
\moderncvcolor{blue}
\usepackage[scale=0.75]{geometry}
\name{John}{Doe}
\title{CV title}
\address{street and number}{postcode city}{country}
\phone[mobile]{+1~(234)~567~890}
\phone[fixed]{+2~(345)~678~901}
\email{john@doe.org}
\homepage{www.johndoe.com}
\photo[64pt][0.4pt]{picture.jpg}
\begin{document}
\makecvtitle
\section{Education}
\cventry{year--year}{Degree}{Institution}{City}%
  {\textit{Grade}}{Description}
\cventry{year--year}{Degree}{Institution}{City}%
  {\textit{Grade}}{Description}
\section{Experience}
\subsection{Vocational}
\cventry{year--year}{Job title}{Employer}{City}{}%
  {General description\newline{}%
  Detailed achievements:%
\begin{itemize}%
  \item Achievement 1;
  \item Achievement 2, with sub-achievements:
    \begin{itemize}%
    \item Sub-achievement (a)
    \item Sub-achievement (b)
  \end{itemize}
\item Achievement 3.
\end{itemize}}
\cventry{year--year}{Job title}{Employer}{City}{}
  {Description line 1\newline{}Description line 2}
\subsection{Miscellaneous}
\cventry{year--year}{Job title}%
  {Employer}{City}{}{Description}
\section{Languages}
\cvitemwithcomment{Language 1}{Skill level}{Comment}
```

```
\cvitemwithcomment{Language 2}{Skill level}{Comment}
\end{document}
```

5. Compile and have a look at the following result:

street and number
postcode city
country
📱 *+1 (234) 567 890*
📞 *+2 (345) 678 901*
✉ *john@doe.org*
🌐 *www.johndoe.com*

John Doe

CV title

Education

year–year **Degree**, *Institution*, City, *Grade*
Description

year–year **Degree**, *Institution*, City, *Grade*
Description

Experience

Vocational

year–year **Job title**, *Employer*, City
General description
Detailed achievements:
○ Achievement 1;
○ Achievement 2, with sub-achievements:
  - Sub-achievement (a)
  - Sub-achievement (b)
○ Achievement 3.

year–year **Job title**, *Employer*, City
Description line 1
Description line 2

Miscellaneous

year–year **Job title**, *Employer*, City
Description

Languages

Language 1 Skill level   *Comment*
Language 2 Skill level   *Comment*

Figure 1.5 – A CV

How it works...

We loaded the moderncv package. We used an 11 pt base font size; 10 pt and 12 pt are also supported. We selected A4 paper; further paper size options are a5paper, b5paper, letterpaper, legalpaper, and executivepaper. You can also add landscape as an option. We chose a sans-serif font, which is fine for such a kind of list; alternatively, you could write roman for a serif font.

We selected the classic style. Other available styles are casual, oldstyle, and banking.

Our color style is blue. Other color options are orange, green, red, purple, gray, and black.

We loaded the geometry package with a scaling factor for reducing the margins.

Using commands such as \name and \address, we entered our personal data.

The \photo command includes our photo; the size options are the height to which it is scaled and the thickness of the frame around the photo. In this recipe, we used the picture.jpg dummy photo contained in the moderncv bundle.

The document body is divided into sections and subsections with a unique design.

Then, the \cventry command makes a typical resume entry for a job or education. Use it as follows:

```
\cventry[spacing]{years}{job title}
  {employer}{localization}{detail}{job description}
```

You can alternatively use this:

```
\cventry[spacing]{years}{degree}
  {institution}{localization}{grade}{comment}
```

You can leave the last four arguments empty if you don't need them.

A simpler line is done using the \cvitem command as follows:

```
\cvitem[optional spacing length{header}{text}
```

The \cvitemwithcomment command works similarly, just with another argument printed at the right.

Some more commands and options are explained in the well-documented template.tex file and the moderncv.cls class file itself if you look for deeper information beyond this quick start guide.

Writing a letter

Letters have a specific structure. Commonly, they have an addressee field at a fixed position, which should be visible in the envelope window. It also should show a back address of yourself as the sender. An opening text and a closing phrase are usual elements; you may add fold marks and enclosures.

How to do it...

We will use a KOMA-Script class specifically designed for letters named `scrlttr2`. Follow the following steps:

1. Use the `scrlttr2` class, activate the address field and fold marks via an option, and align the sender's address to the right:

   ```
   \documentclass[addrfield=true, foldmarks=true,
       fromalign=right]{scrlttr2}
   ```

2. Provide your name and your address using the `\setkomavar` command:

   ```
   \setkomavar{fromname}{Thomas Smith}
   \setkomavar{fromaddress}{123 Blvd \\ City, CC 12345}
   ```

3. Write a date, either `\today` for today or any date as text:

   ```
   \date{\today}
   ```

4. Begin the document:

   ```
   \begin{document}
   ```

5. Open a `letter` environment with the recipient's address as an argument:

   ```
   \begin{letter}{Agency \\ 5th Avenue \\
                   Capital City, CC 12345}
   ```

6. Start with an opening, and let your letter text follow:

   ```
   \opening{Dear Sir or Madam, }
   the actual content of the letter follows.
   ```

7. End with closing words:

   ```
   \closing{Yours sincerely}
   ```

8. End the `letter` environment and the document:

   ```
   \end{letter}
   \end{document}
   ```

9.   Compile the document. Here is the upper part of the output:

Thomas Smith
123 Blvd
City, CC 12345

Thomas Smith, 123 Blvd , City, CC 12345

Agency
5th Avenue
Capital City, CC 12345

October 12, 2015

Dear Sir or Madam,

the actual content of the letter follows.

Yours sincerely

Thomas Smith

Figure 1.6 – A letter template

That was pretty easy! You got fully fledged formal letter addressing information, envelope window support, today's date, phrases, signature, and even fold marks.

Now, you can enter real addresses and actual letter text.

How it works...

When loading the scrlttr2 letter class, we activated the address field, switched on fold marks, and set the options for right aligning the sender's address.

The scrlttr2 class is quite different from others, so it has a unique interface. Using the \setkomavar command, we set the content of class variables, similar to \renewcommand. Here, we put names and addresses. The KOMA-Script manual explains all available variables. As mentioned in the *Developing a thesis* recipe, you can open it by executing texdoc koma-script at Command Prompt or online at https://texdoc.org/pkg/koma-script.

We used a `letter` environment for the actual content, including the opening and closing phrases. The address is a mandatory argument for that environment. You can have several `letter` environments in a single document.

There's more...

To improve input and hyphenation and change the font, look at the first recipes in *Chapter 2, Tuning the Text*.

Let's take a look at some letter-specific options.

Separating paragraphs

Instead of indenting the beginning of paragraphs, you can visualize a paragraph break with an empty line. For this, add the `parskip=full` option to the comma-separated list of class options at the beginning.

Use `parskip=half` for less space.

Changing the signature

If you would like to use a signature different from your specified name for the address, you can modify the corresponding variable content in the preamble:

```
\setkomavar{signature}{Thomas}
```

It would be indented. You can get it left aligned by specifying the following code:

```
\renewcommand{\raggedsignature}{\raggedright}
```

The code just shown also belongs to the preamble.

Adding enclosures

If you would like to add enclosures to your letter, it's common to mention them. You can do this by inserting an `\encl` command right before `\end{letter}`:

```
\encl{Curriculum vitae, certificates}
```

You can change the default `encl:` option if you like by modifying the corresponding variable before calling the `\encl` command:

```
\setkomavar*{enclseparator}{Attached}
```

We used the `\setkomavar*` starred version, which modifies the description of a variable instead of its content, which actually is : – that is, a colon followed by a space.

Producing a leaflet

Flyers are a common way to promote an event or to inform about a product. A folded **leaflet** is particularly handy as a giveaway and to carry around, so let's see how to produce one.

How to do it...

The intended layout is very different compared to the already shown document types. Fortunately, there's a document class for it, with the name `leaflet`. We will use this one now. Let us start filling it with some content:

1. Start with the `leaflet` document class. Choose a base font size of 10 pt, and set the `notumble` option, which keeps the back side printed in the same direction:

    ```
    \documentclass[10pt, notumble]{leaflet}
    ```

2. Use an extended font encoding:

    ```
    \usepackage[T1]{fontenc}
    ```

3. If you want a non-default font, load it. This time, we chose the **Linux Libertine** font:

    ```
    \usepackage{libertine}
    ```

4. Switch to sans-serif as the default font family:

    ```
    \renewcommand{\familydefault}{\sfdefault}
    ```

5. For better text justification, load the `microtype` package:

    ```
    \usepackage{microtype}
    ```

6. Load the `graphicx` package for including a picture:

    ```
    \usepackage{graphicx}
    ```

7. Switch off the page numbering:

    ```
    \pagenumbering{gobble}
    ```

8. Begin the document:

    ```
    \begin{document}
    ```

9. Set title, author, and date. Then, print the title:

```
\title{\textbf{\TeX\ Live Install Party}}
\author{\Large\textbf{Your \TeX\ team}}
\date{\textbf{August 11, City Hall Cellar}}
\maketitle
```

10. Include a centered image. For a demonstration, we chose the CTAN lion, which you can download at https://ctan.org/lion and convert to PDF:

```
\begin{center}
    \includegraphics[width=\linewidth]{ctanlion.pdf}
\end{center}
```

11. Add some text:

```
We'd like to welcome you to our famous yearly
\TeX\ install party! Bring your laptop and have free
cold soft drinks while we assist you in installing
the latest \TeX\ version on your computer.

We will provide
```

12. A bulleted list can be a good idea for a catchy text. Use an itemize environment for it; each list item starts with an \item command:

```
\begin{itemize}
    \item a fast internet connection for downloading,
    \item media such as DVDs and USB sticks with
          the latest \TeX,
    \item \TeX\ books for buying with a discount,
    \item chat with \TeX\ experts.
\end{itemize}
```

13. End the page. Fill in more text on the next leaflet pages, which will be printed on the back side of the paper, next to each other:

```
\clearpage
Fill in text for page 2 (on the back side)
\clearpage
Fill in text for page 3 (on the back side)
\clearpage
Fill in text for page 4 (on the back side)
\clearpage
```

14. Now, *pages 5* and *6* of the leaflet come to the front side of the paper. Use \section to get a heading:

```
\section{Schedule}
```

15. You can add a timetable using a tabular environment. By inserting @{ } in the column format options, we suppress spacing at the left and right:

```
\begin{tabular}{@{}rl@{}}
  6 pm     & Welcome \\
  7:30 pm & Live install presentation \\
  8 pm     & Book authors available for talks
            and signing \\
  9:30 pm & Bar closing
\end{tabular}
```

16. End the paragraph using an empty line, continue with writing text, and finally, end the document:

```
From 6pm to 10pm: install support
and free \TeX\ copies on DVD on our welcome desk.
\section{Accomodation}
Hotel, Meals, Travel information here
\section{Sponsors}
Information about our local \TeX\ user group
and Open Source projects sponsor
\clearpage
\section{Contact}
Names, Phone numbers, email addresses
\end{document}
```

17. Compile and have a look at the first page:

Schedule

6 pm   Welcome
7:30 pm   Live install presentation
8 pm   Book authors available for talks and signing
9:30 pm   Bar closing

From 6pm to 10pm: install support and free TeX copies on DVD on our welcome desk.

Accomodation

Hotel, Meals, Travel information here

Sponsors

Information about our local TeX user group and Open Source projects sponsor

Contact

Names, Phone numbers, email addresses

TeX Live Install Party

Your TeX team

August 11, City Hall Cellar

We'd like to welcome you to our famous yearly TeX install party! Bring your laptop and have free cold soft drinks while we assist you in installing the latest TeX version on your computer.

We will provide

- a fast internet connection fow downloading,
- media such as DVDs and USB sticks with the latest TeX
- TeX books for bying with a discount,
- chat with TeX experts.

Figure 1.7 – A foldable leaflet

The back side still contains just some dummy text, helping to identify the position where the text finally lands on the page.

How it works...

In the first line, we loaded the `leaflet` class with a font size of 10 pt. The `tumble` option enables printing the back side upside down, which can be helpful for double-sided printing. This is the default. We used the `notumble` option instead, which suppresses that default behavior so that the output is better readable on the screen.

The next three lines contain our font settings. We used the Linux Libertine font. We specified T1 font encoding. You can read more about encodings in *Chapter 2, Tuning the Text*, specifically in the *Improving justification and hyphenation* recipe. Furthermore, we set the default font family to be sans-serif. I prefer the clean look of sans-serif on a flyer or a leaflet, which usually contains little text in narrow columns.

The remaining part of the preamble is as follows:

- We loaded the microtype package, which improves the justification capabilities by tiny font adjustments. This is especially useful in a situation with narrow columns, such as in this case.

- We loaded the graphicx package to include images such as a logo or a geographic map.

- We hid page numbers. The gobble option stands for \gobble, which is a TeX command that removes the following command or control sequence so that the page number will be absorbed.

Our document body shows the usual sectioning commands and text. You can see that we added an explicit space after the TeX logo with a backslash and a following space. That's because a space after a macro, such as \TeX, indicates the end of the macro. It doesn't produce a space in print because punctuation may follow.

To have an image in our template, we used the CTAN lion drawn by Duane Bibby; simply replace it with your own image – a geographic map or a logo, for example.

The remaining text is straightforward and shows some useful layout details, such as the following:

- Centering using the center environment:

```
\begin{center}
  ...
\end{center}
```

- Arranging points in a bulleted list by using an itemize environment

- Setting up a tabular environment for text, which should be aligned in columns

In the \begin{tabular}{@{}rl@{}} line, the rl characters stand for two columns, where the first one is right-aligned and the second one is left-aligned. The @{code} expression inserts a piece of code instead of a space before or after a column, so @{} replaces it with nothing, which means removing it. We've got two columns without additional whitespace on the left or the right, saving our previous line space.

There's more...

The leaflet class provides some options and commands for customization.

Adding fold marks and cut lines

By default, a small folding mark is printed on the backside. If you would like to omit it, add the nofoldmark option when loading the class:

```
\documentclass[10pt,notumble,nofoldmark]{leaflet}
```

You can draw a vertical dotted line with scissor symbols using the `\CutLine` command in the preamble with a page number as an argument. The line will go between this one and the preceding page, which is as follows:

```
\CutLine{3}
```

It would print a dotted line with two scissor symbols on the back side, between *pages 2* and *3*, where a folding mark would be placed by default. The `\CutLine*` starred command version would not print the scissors.

Adjusting the margins

Similar to standard classes, you could use page headers and footers. There are none by default here. Standard commands such as `\setlength{\headheight}{...}` and `\pagestyle` could be used. `leaflet` provides an additional command to declare the margins:

```
\setmargins{top}{bottom}{left}{right}
```

Adding a background image

You can add an image to the background of a certain page:

```
\AddToBackground{pagenumber}{\includegraphics{filename}}
```

Use the `\AddToBackground*` starred version to let it be printed onto the background of the combined page.

Instead of using the `\includegraphics` command, you could use another positioning, including or drawing code. Here, the *Absolute positioning of text* recipe in *Chapter 2, Tuning the Text*, may be helpful.

Changing the sectioning font

The font size of the section headers is already a bit smaller than with standard classes. If you want to change the headings' size, shape, or color, you can redefine the `\sectfont` macro. For example, if we also enabled using color by `\usepackage{xcolor}`, we could write the following code:

```
\renewcommand{\sectfont}{%
  \large\sffamily\bfseries\color{blue}}
```

This would give a large sans-serif font in bold and with blue color.

For further information regarding fonts, refer to *Chapter 3, Adjusting Fonts*.

Building a large poster

We know, for example, informational or scientific posters seen at conferences or on walls in universities or institutes.

They mostly have specific characteristics in common:

- They are large, such as A2, A1, or even A0

- People may look at them from far away but also very close

In consequence, we have some requirements for typesetting:

- Page layout dimensions should work with such an enormous size.

- We need a wide range of font sizes. We should be able to read while standing close, but we also need large, catchy headings.

- The poster should be partitioned into digestible blocks. Specifically, each block should be at most the usual line width we know from body texts. Too wide lines would make it hard to focus and skip back to the start of the following line. So, block lines should not be much wider than 40 or 50 characters long.

- Blocks should have distinct headings.

- Graphic elements such as colors and lines can divide the text into parts.

- Images should be vector graphics or should have a high resolution.

In this recipe, we would like to create a poster of A0 size in landscape orientation. It will show some blocks containing dummy text as a placeholder, math, and images. As sample images, we will take a flowchart from *Chapter 6, Creating Graphics*, and a plot from *Chapter 10, Writing Advanced Mathematics*. There, you can find the source code. You can later replace the dummy text and other parts with your own content.

How to do it...

We will use the `tikzposter` class. The document is structured in columns and blocks. Follow these steps:

1. Begin with the document class. A0 is the default paper size. We state landscape orientation as an option:

   ```
   \documentclass[landscape]{tikzposter}
   ```

2. Choose a theme that provides a set of colors and decorations. We chose the blue `Wave` theme:

   ```
   \usetheme{Wave}
   ```

3. Load the `lipsum` package to generate dummy text:

    ```
    \usepackage{lipsum}
    ```

4. For dividing wider blocks into text columns, we load the `multicol` package. Because of the large paper, we set the column separation and the separation line width to high values:

    ```
    \usepackage{multicol}
    \setlength{\columnsep}{4cm}
    \setlength{\columnseprule}{1mm}
    ```

5. Start the document:

    ```
    \begin{document}
    ```

6. Declare the author and title, and print it out:

    ```
    \title{\LaTeX\ in Use}
    \author{John Doe}
    \maketitle
    ```

7. Begin a set of columns:

    ```
    \begin{columns}
    ```

8. Start a column with a width of 65% of the available text width:

    ```
    \column{.65}
    ```

9. Define a block with the title `Workflow` in the first argument; the second argument contains dummy text and an image with a caption:

    ```
    \block{Workflow}{
      \lipsum[1]
      \begin{tikzfigure}[\LaTeX\ workflow]
        \includegraphics[width=\linewidth]{flowchart}
      \end{tikzfigure}
    }
    ```

    The `tikzposter` package provides the `tikzfigure` environment as a replacement for the `figure` environment. The `optional` argument will be the caption of the figure.

10. We are still in the first column and start a set of subcolumns:

    ```
    \begin{subcolumns}
    ```

11. The first subcolumn will take half of the available width – in this case, the width of the left column:

    ```
    \subcolumn{.5}
    ```

12. Create a block with a bulleted list and a mathematical equation to see how it looks on a poster. We will also use a colored box and an inner block with a title for the equation:

```
\block{Mathematics}{
  Take a coffee, then:
  \bigskip
  \coloredbox{\begin{itemize}
    \item State
    \item Proof
    \item Write in \LaTeX
  \end{itemize}}
  \bigskip
  \innerblock{Integral approximation}{
    \[
      \int_a^b f(x) dx \approx (b-a)
        \sum_{i=0}^n w_i f(x_i)
    \]
  }
}
```

13. Add a note that will have a callout shape, pointing into the formula:

```
\note[targetoffsetx = 4.5cm, targetoffsety = -5cm,
    angle = -30, connection]{Weight function}
```

14. Make another subcolumn, talking the other half of the available width. Insert a block filled with text, and then end the subcolumns environment:

```
\subcolumn{.5}
\block{Text}{\lipsum[1]}
\end{subcolumns}
```

15. Now that we are back in our primary column environment, make another column, print a block with an image and some text, and then end the columns environment:

```
\column{.35}
\block{Plotting functions}{
  \includegraphics[width=\linewidth]{plot}
  \lipsum[4]
}
\end{columns}
```

16. As we ended the columns, a block would use the whole available width. To keep text readable, we will now use the `multicol` package. We divide the text itself into columns using a `multicolumn` environment with four columns:

```
\block{Conclusion and outlook}{
  \begin{multicols}{4}
    \lipsum[10-11]
  \end{multicols}
}
```

17. End the document:

```
\end{document}
```

18. Compile, and take a look:

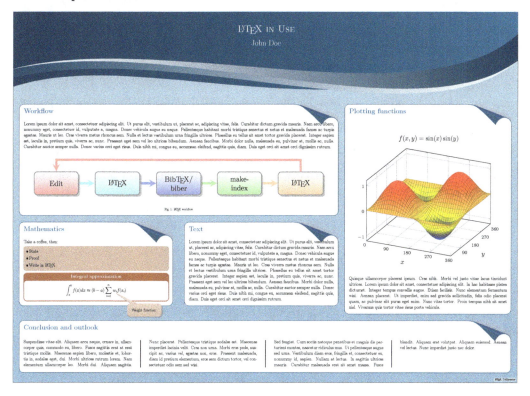

Figure 1.8 – A colorful poster with a block layout

How it works...

The `tikzposter` class supports huge paper sizes and large fonts and handles block heights and spacing between columns. We, as the users, just decided about the relative column width.

Several class options are provided. You can add them to the `\documentclass` command as we did with the preceding `landscape` option:

- The paper size can be chosen by `a0paper`, `a1paper`, or `a2paper`. `a0paper` is the default.

- Available font sizes are `12pt`, `14pt`, `17pt`, `20pt`, and `25pt`. The last one is the default.

- With either `landscape` or `portrait`, you can select the orientation. `portrait` is the default.

- The standard `fleqn` option for flush-left equations is supported.

- The standard `leqno` option for equation numbering at the left side is also supported.

You can adjust several lengths. Give them as class options in the `key=value` form with a measurement unit such as mm or cm:

- `margin`: The distance between the edge of the poster area and the edge of the paper

- `innermargin`: The distance from the outermost edge of the blocks to the edge of the poster

- `colspace`: The horizontal distance between consecutive columns

- `subcolspace`: The horizontal distance between consecutive columns in a subcolumn environment

- `blockverticalspace`: The distance between the bottom of a block and the top of the next block below

A sample call using the exact defaults would be:

```
\documentclass[a0paper, portrait, 25pt, margin=0mm,
    innermargin=15mm, colspace=15mm, subcolspace=8mm,
    blockverticalspace=15mm]{tikzposter}
```

The package makes use of the very capable graphics language, TikZ. We will see more of TikZ in *Chapter 6, Creating Graphics*. For now, the main benefit is that `tikzposter` provides a lot of predefined styles and color schemes.

You can use a main layout style with `\usetheme{name}`. At the time of writing, there were nine themes available:

- `Wave`: As seen in this recipe

- `Default` (left) and `Basic` (right):

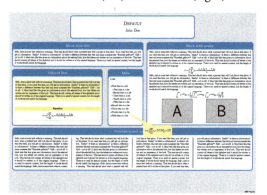 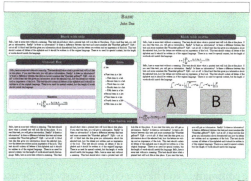

- `Rays` (left) and `Simple` (right):

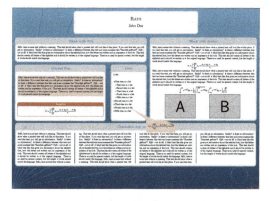 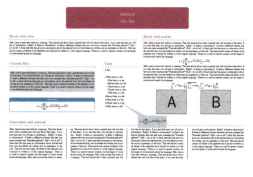

- `Envelope` (left) and `Board` (right):

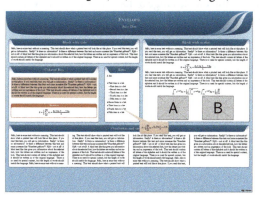 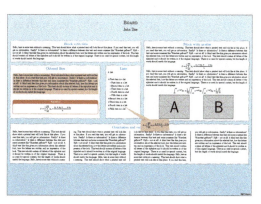

- Autumn (left) and Desert (right):

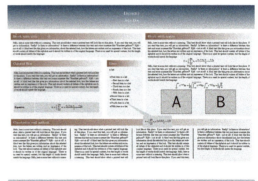

Furthermore, predefined styles for color, title, background, notes, blocks, and inner blocks can be chosen and composed. There's support for creating further styles.

The commands you have seen previously can be used immediately without further options. However, they can be customized via several options.

A complete reference is available by executing `texdoc tikzposter` at Command Prompt and online at `https://texdoc.org/pkg/tikzposter`. You can find a style guide, a feature guide, and more at `https://bitbucket.org/surmann/tikzposter/downloads`.

There's more...

One of the first poster classes is the `a0poster` class. It supports A0, A1, A2, and A3 paper sizes. It provides font sizes from 12 pt up to 107 pt. Math formulas are printed in a suitable size. There's no specific support for graphics, color, or text placement. For this, you would need additional packages such as TikZ.

In a previous recipe, you already saw `beamer` as a presentation class. The `beamerposter` package can be used together with it for producing presentations in poster size. It combines the `beamer` class with `a0poster` code. So, you can produce large posters with a wide range of font sizes together with `beamer`'s color and graphics capabilities, such as `beamer` boxes with titles.

As noted before, you can use the `texdoc` command or the `https://texdoc.org` website to access the documentation of the mentioned classes and packages.

2

Tuning the Text

The previous chapter provided recipes for creating entire documents. You may use them as starting points. Now, we will focus on fine-tuning text elements, such as shaping paragraphs and manipulating, positioning, and arranging text.

This chapter shows recipes for:

- Improving justification and hyphenation
- Adding margin notes
- Converting numbers to words
- Putting text into a colorful box
- Visualizing the layout
- Visualizing boxes of letters and symbols
- Typesetting in a grid
- Absolute positioning of text
- Adding drop caps
- Fitting text to a shape
- Creating a pull quote

We will not yet deal with fonts. This topic deserves a whole chapter and will be covered in *Chapter 3, Adjusting Fonts*.

This chapter will start with some fundamental principles, explore helpful techniques, and conclude with practical recipes that illustrate LaTeX's capabilities that extend beyond conventional paragraph formatting.

Improving justification and hyphenation

Occasionally, you may get warnings such as "overfull \hbox" or notice words hanging into the margin. This indicates that LaTeX had severe problems with justification. Now, we will look at how to improve such a situation by ensuring proper hyphenation and integrating microtypographic support.

How to do it...

We can start with any document. We will optimize it by applying particular settings in the preamble. If you don't have a document readily available, you can take one from the code package for this book, specifically for the first chapter, or download one from https://latex-cookbook.net. Take the following steps:

1. Load the `babel` package with your document languages as options. Use the preferred language as the last option:

    ```
    \usepackage[ngerman,english]{babel}
    ```

2. If you would like to use handy shortcuts of `ngerman` with English too, add the following lines:

    ```
    \useshorthands{"}
    \addto\extrasenglish{\languageshorthands{ngerman}}
    ```

3. Load the `fontenc` package with the `T1` option set:

    ```
    \usepackage[T1]{fontenc}
    ```

4. Load the `microtype` package for improved micro-typography:

    ```
    \usepackage{microtype}
    ```

How it works...

Using the `babel` package, LaTeX employs hyphenation patterns in the chosen language. Here, we specified two language options:

- `ngerman`: This option adds hyphenation patterns and features for the new German orthography. This includes commands for German umlauts and quotation marks but also additional shortcut commands supporting hyphenation, such as the following:

    - `"-`: This shortcut adds an optional hyphenation point at a specific position in a word. It keeps other hyphenation points, unlike the standard `\-` command.

    - `""`: This shortcut adds a possible hyphenation point, where, in the case of a separation, no hyphen is added.

- " ~: This shortcut inserts a hyphen, but the word will not be hyphenated here.

- " ~ This shortcut inserts a hyphen, and hyphenation is allowed before and after it.

- english: This option enables language support with hyphenation patterns for US American English. If you need British English, use one of the equivalent options british or Ukenglish.

As you've observed, babel can also load the convenient ngerman shortcuts for hyphenation commands so that you can use them with languages other than German. You can find more such shorthand commands in the babel manual. You can access it by typing texdoc babel at the command line or by visiting https://texdoc.org/pkg/babel.

Utilizing the modern font encoding **T1** enhances the situation further. In the early stages of TeX and LaTeX, fonts did not contain glyphs for accented characters. They were printed as two characters, one being the actual accent. That isn't good for copying and pasting from the final PDF output and can also disrupt hyphenation.

> **Note**
>
> The term **glyph** refers to the visual representation of a letter or symbol in writing, particularly within the context of fonts.

The default encoding is **OT1** encoding and encompasses 128 glyphs, meaning it encodes 128 characters. T1 provides 256 glyphs, so many accented characters are included. That's why T1 is recommended for Western European languages. There are further encodings tailored to other languages, such as Cyrillic and Asian languages. If you want to work with them, look at the fontenc manual by typing texdoc fontenc at the command line or read it online at https://texdoc.org/pkg/fontenc.

Lastly, we introduced the microtype package to implement microtypographic extensions. For instance, this package slightly adjusts font sizes, even for individual letters, to improve the full justification. You can hardly notice the change with the naked eye but can see the effect of less hyphenation and better overall greyness of the text. Consequently, there are usually smaller white gaps between words.

> **Note**
>
> In typography, **greyness** refers to the distribution of black and white elements on the page. A well-balanced visual density can achieve a pleasing overall visual impression.

Furthermore, the microtype package subtly adjusts punctuation at the margin for better optical alignment rather than relying solely on mechanical justification.

Regarding hyphenation, you may encounter situations where (La)TeX doesn't hyphenate the very first word in a paragraph. This occurrence is rare, typically in narrow columns starting with a very long word. A quick remedy is inserting the command \hspace{0pt} at the beginning of the paragraph so that the long word is technically not at the paragraph's start.

Adding margin notes

You can add notes to the margin to make a text more dynamic, annotate critical passages, and explain or comment on a piece of the body text. This can enhance understanding and aid in studying.

How to do it...

For our first document with margin notes, we will use the very first document from *Chapter 1, Exploring Various Document Classes*. Edit that document as follows:

1. Load the `marginnote` package in the document preamble:

    ```
    \usepackage{marginnote}
    ```

2. To highlight margin notes using color, load the `xcolor` package :

    ```
    \usepackage{xcolor}
    ```

3. Choose a font shape, color, or size for the margin notes, such as the following:

    ```
    \renewcommand*{\marginfont}{\strut\color{blue}%
        \sffamily\scriptsize}
    ```

4. Within the document text, add margin notes in the lines where you want them to be positioned. For example, like this:

    ```
    \addsec{Introduction}
    This document will be our starting point for simple
    documents.\marginnote{No chapters supported!}
    It is suitable for a single page or up to
    a couple of dozen pages.

    The text will be divided into sections.
    \marginnote{Subsections are the next level.}
    ```

5. Compile the document. In the very first run, the margin notes don't appear. Compile a second time and look at the section where we added the margin notes:

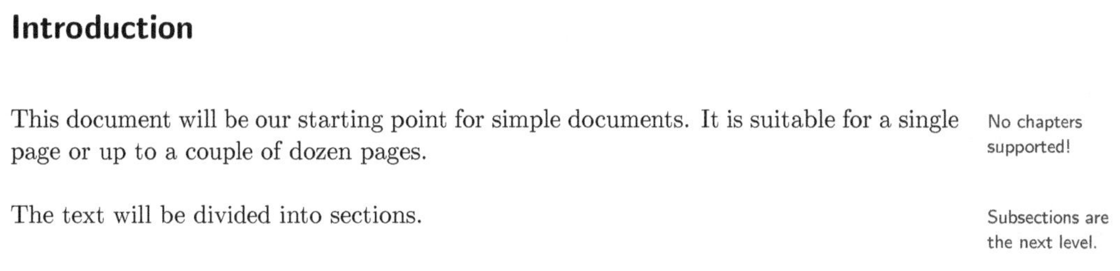

Introduction

This document will be our starting point for simple documents. It is suitable for a single page or up to a couple of dozen pages.

No chapters
supported!

The text will be divided into sections.

Subsections are
the next level.

Figure 2.1 – Margin notes

How it works...

The \marginnote command puts the text into the right margin when the document is one-sided. In a two-sided document, it places the text in the outside margin.

You can achieve the opposite placement using the \reversemarginpar command. The \normalmarginpar command restores the default placement.

The \marginnote command also supports an optional argument for text in the left margin. The complete syntax is as follows:

```
\marginnote[left margin text]{right margin text}
```

This feature is particularly useful in a two-sided layout. Depending on the position in the text, the note may be in the left margin on an even-numbered page or in the right margin on an odd-numbered page. The optional argument allows you to prepare different text versions accordingly.

The \marginfont macro can be used for choosing a specific font, size, color, or any command that you want to employ before the margin note. In particular, we inserted a \strut command here, representing a zero-width vertical line with the height of the current text. This ensures that the margin note's baseline aligns with the text line's baseline where it appears, even when using a smaller font.

A margin note should be treated as a single paragraph, so avoid inserting empty lines or using the \par command within it.

There's more...

LaTeX already provides margin notes using the following command:

```
\marginpar[left]{right}
```

It works very similar to the \marginnote command. However, it uses a float mechanism, so we cannot use \marginpar in floats or footnotes. That's one of the reasons why the marginnote package has been written.

If you want to explore this alternative approach, you can find more information at `https://latex2e.org/Marginal-notes.html`.

Another option for placing notes in the margin is the `todonotes` package.

Converting numbers to words

Numbers are sometimes written as text instead of using numerals. LaTeX is capable of automatically converting numbers to words. This feature is especially useful for values originating from LaTeX counters, such as page or section numbers.

How to do it...

We will load the `fmtcount` package and use its commands for conversion.

1. Start with any document class, such as the `article` class:

   ```
   \documentclass{article}
   ```

2. Load the `fmtcount` package:

   ```
   \usepackage{fmtcount}
   ```

3. Begin the document:

   ```
   \begin{document}
   ```

4. Write some text. Proceed the following way:

   - Whenever you like to convert a number to a word, use the command \numberstringnum.

   - For printing a counter value as a word, use \numberstring.

   - For a similar purpose, but in ordinal form, use \ordinalstringnum or \ordinalstring.

   Enter the following lines to practice the new commands:

   ```
   This document should have \numberstringnum{32}
   pages. Now, we are on page \numberstring{page}
   in the \ordinalstring{section} section.
   ```

5. End the document:

   ```
   \end{document}
   ```

6. Compile the document. All numbers and counters are displayed as text so that you will get the following text in the PDF document:

   This document should have thirty-two pages. Now, we are on page one in the first section.

How it works...

The fmtcount package provides the following set of commands that print out numbers as words:

- \ordinalstring{counter}: This prints the value of a counter as an ordinal in text.
- \numberstring{counter}: This prints the counter's value as text.
- \ordinalstringnum{number} and \numberstringnum{number}: These two commands do the same job but are based on an actual number instead of a counter.
- \Ordinalstring{counter}, \Numberstring{counter}, \Ordinalstringnum{number}, and \Numberstringnum{number}: These are the capitalized versions; they print the initial letter in uppercase.

There's more...

The fmtcount package offers even more, such as multilingual capabilities, gender support, and support for new enumeration styles. We shall take a look at these features now.

Multilingual support

The fmtcount package supports several languages, such as English, Spanish, Portuguese, French, German, and Italian. It tries to detect the language option already passed to the babel or polyglossia packages. You can explicitly load required definitions by adding \FCloadlang{language} to the preamble, with a language name understood by the babel package.

Gender

All the preceding commands support an optional gender argument at the end, taking one of the following values: m (masculine), f (feminine), or n (neuter). It is used like the following:

```
\numberstring{section}[f]
```

The masculine value is the default setting.

Enumerated lists

The moreenum package provides new enumeration styles based on the fmtcount package. Here's an example:

```
\documentclass{article}
\usepackage{moreenum}
\begin{document}
\begin{enumerate}[label=\Nthwords*]
  \item live
  \item long
```

```
    \item prosper
\end{enumerate}
\end{document}
```

The items will now be numbered **First**, **Second**, and **Third** instead of the default 1., 2., and 3. A label command \Nwords* would print **One**, **Two**, and **Three**. Lowercase versions start with a small letter n.

In addition to the fmtcount package, the moreenum package loads the enumitem package and provides a similar key=value interface.

Putting text into a colorful box

You often see important content put into a colored box, a common practice on posters and slides, although it's also used in other documents. In this recipe, we will put a little text and whole paragraphs into a colored box, including making a title for the box.

How to do it...

We will use the tcolorbox package. It is based on the pgf bundle, so you need to have also that package installed.

We will create a box with the defaults, a titled box with split content, and boxes placed inline that fit the width of the content. Proceed as follows:

1. Create a small document based on any document class. The article class is a simple choice. Load the blindtext package to generate dummy text. This time, we will use the pangram option to create short pangrams as dummy text. The blindtext package requires the babel package, so we will load it before. We also set English as the language. Furthermore, load the tcolorbox package. So, our base document looks like this:

    ```
    \documentclass{article}
    \usepackage[english]{babel}
    \usepackage[pangram]{blindtext}
    \usepackage{tcolorbox}
    \begin{document}
    \end{document}
    ```

2. Create a simple box by inserting this code right after the \begin{document} line:

    ```
    \begin{tcolorbox}
        \blindtext
    \end{tcolorbox}
    ```

This gives you the following box with the text:

> The quick brown fox jumps over the lazy dog. Jackdaws love my big Sphinx of Quartz. Pack my box with five dozen liquor jugs. The five boxing wizards jump quickly. Sympathizing would fix Quaker objectives.

Figure 2.2 – Text in a box

3. Now, use the following code snippet:

```
\begin{tcolorbox}[title=\textbf{Examples},
  colback=blue!5!white, colframe=blue!75!white]
  The text below consists of pangrams.
  \tcblower
  \blindtext[3]
\end{tcolorbox}
```

The new box has a title and is divided into two parts, as shown here:

> **Examples**
>
> The text below consists of pangrams.
>
> ------
>
> The quick brown fox jumps over the lazy dog. Jackdaws love my big Sphinx of Quartz. Pack my box with five dozen liquor jugs.

Figure 2.3 – A colored box with a title

4. Now try this setting and box command in the same document:

```
\tcbset{colframe=green!50!black,colback=white,
  colupper=green!30!black,fonttitle=\bfseries,
  center title, nobeforeafter, tcbox raise base}
  Normal text \tcbox{Boxed text}
```

It results in this:

Normal text Boxed text

Figure 2.4 – Drawing a box around inline text

5. Then, try this variation:

```
\tcbox[left=0pt, right=0pt, top=0.5ex, bottom=0pt,
  boxsep=0pt, toptitle=0.5ex, bottomtitle=0.5ex,
  title=Sample table]{
\begin{tabular}[t]{rl}
  Number & 100 \\
  Sum    & 350
\end{tabular}}
```

You can see that we can create boxes with titles, even with nontrivial content, such as this tabular material:

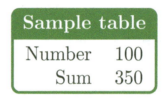

Figure 2.5 – Putting a table into a colored box

How it works...

We loaded the `blindtext` package with the `pangram` option, enabling us to generate short sample texts that served as placeholder content within our boxes.

We loaded the `tcolorbox` package. The LaTeX environment with the same name then generated the boxes for us.

The first box was done without any option with default settings. In the subsequent box, we used the `key=value` interface to specify a title and the colors for the frame and the background. The `\tcblower` command split the box for us using a dashed line.

Moving forward, we used the `\tcbset` command to define options that would apply to all subsequent boxes. Using it in the preamble is a good idea when we have multiple boxes sharing common characteristics. We set the color, applied a bold typeface, and centered the title. Furthermore, we used the `nobeforeafter` option to avoid additional space before and after the box. The `raise base` option lifted the entire box so that the content's baseline aligns with the baseline of the outer text. This is apparent in *Figure 2.4*.

The last boxes were created using the `\tcbox` command. While it understands most options of the `tcolorbox` environment, there are two differences:

- The `\tcbox` command doesn't provide a lower part, unlike the `tcolorbox` environment with the `\tcblower` command.

- The `\tcbox` command cannot be split across pages, a limitation absent in the `tcolorbox` environment.

The `\tcbox` command is a good choice for boxes within text. As in our example, it works seamlessly with tabular code and images.

There's more...

The `tcolorbox` package is highly versatile and provides many options and styles. The latter are referred to as **skins**. For in-depth information, I recommend consulting the package manual. The wealth of its features is described on more than 500 pages. You can access the manual by typing `texdoc tcolorbox` at the command line or by visiting `https://texdoc.org/pkg/tcolorbox`.

The `mdframed` package offers a similar approach. Based on the classic `framed` package, it works with the modern graphics packages **TikZ** and **PSTricks** to create colored boxes that can be split across pages.

Visualizing the layout

When designing a document, obtaining precise information about the dimensions and positioning of layout elements, such as the text body, header, footer, and the space allocated for the margin notes, is often helpful. LaTeX can print helplines for you to examine and finetune the layout.

How to do it...

We will use the `showframe` package. Take the following steps:

1. Open your document or any sample for testing. Here, we will use the very first document from *Chapter 1, Exploring Various Document Classes*.

2. Add the following line at the end of your preamble:

   ```
   \usepackage{showframe}
   ```

3. Compile the document. You can see frames around the text body, the margin note area, the header, and the footer as you can see here:

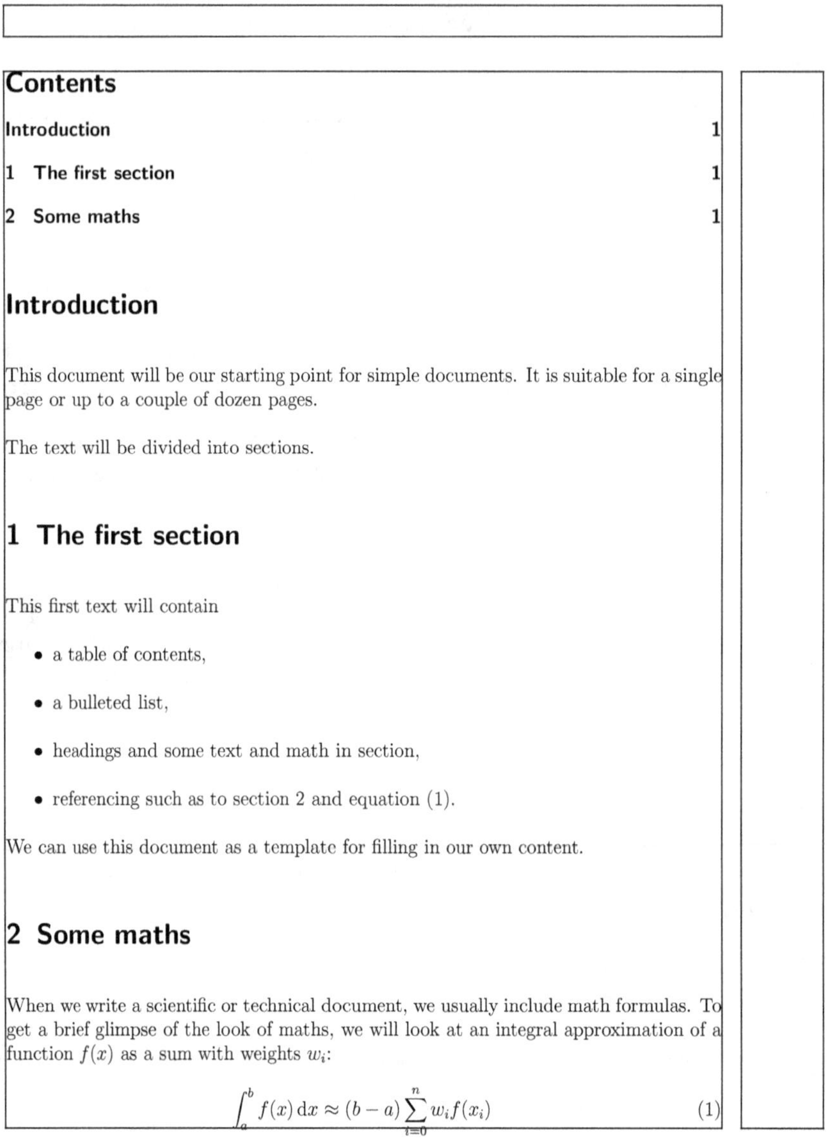

Contents

Introduction 1

1 The first section 1

2 Some maths 1

Introduction

This document will be our starting point for simple documents. It is suitable for a single page or up to a couple of dozen pages.

The text will be divided into sections.

1 The first section

This first text will contain

- a table of contents,
- a bulleted list,
- headings and some text and math in section,
- referencing such as to section 2 and equation (1).

We can use this document as a template for filling in our own content.

2 Some maths

When we write a scientific or technical document, we usually include math formulas. To get a brief glimpse of the look of maths, we will look at an integral approximation of a function $f(x)$ as a sum with weights w_i:

$$\int_a^b f(x)\,\mathrm{d}x \approx (b-a)\sum_{i=0}^{n} w_i f(x_i) \tag{1}$$

Figure 2.6 – A page layout overview

Examining the layout can inspire adjustments, such as modifying the margins or other page dimensions. When you no longer need these helplines, you can deactivate the package by either commenting out `\usepackage{showframe}` or simply removing that line.

How it works...

We loaded the showframe package that generated the desired help lines on all document pages. The package belongs to the eso-pic bundle, which will help us in the recipe *Absolute positioning of text* later in the current chapter. As the showframe package visualizes layout dimensions, it can help with positioning in relation to margins or text body.

There's more...

There are alternatives to the showframe package. Let's take a look at them.

Using geometry

If you have already loaded the geometry package to specify page dimensions such as paper size and margin, you could add the showframe option instead of loading the separate package with the same name in one of the following ways:

- You can add it while loading the package as follows:

```
\usepackage[a4paper, bindingoffset=5mm,
   showframe]{geometry}
```

- Alternatively, you can activate it by calling the \geometry command after the geometry package has already been loaded, but also in the preamble:

```
\geometry{showframe}
```

Examining the page layout details

The layout package provides a command that prints an overview of the layout and, in addition, the values of various page layout variables. Let's take a look at the following steps:

1. Load the layout package:

```
\usepackage{layout}
```

2. Insert the \layout command right after the \begin{document} line.

3. Take a look at the output, here done with our very first recipe in *Chapter 1, Exploring Various Document Classes*:

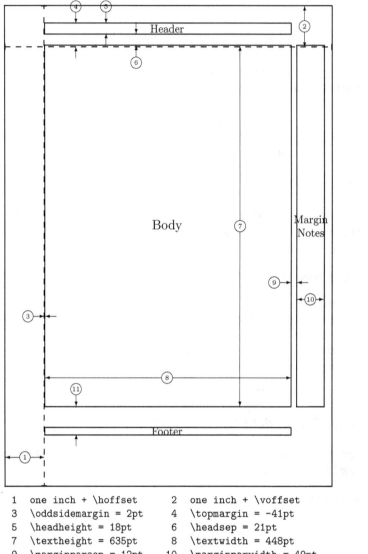

1   one inch + \hoffset   2   one inch + \voffset
3   \oddsidemargin = 2pt   4   \topmargin = -41pt
5   \headheight = 18pt   6   \headsep = 21pt
7   \textheight = 635pt   8   \textwidth = 448pt
9   \marginparsep = 12pt   10 \marginparwidth = 49pt
11 \footskip = 50pt   \marginparpush = 6pt (not shown)
    \hoffset = 0pt   \voffset = 0pt
    \paperwidth = 597pt   \paperheight = 845pt

Figure 2.7 – A detailed page layout with dimensions

This image is entirely generated by the \layout command, showing the current values of the document you are working on.

Visualizing boxes of letters and symbols

LaTeX utilizes boxes to organize and position text and symbols, whether entire paragraphs or individual letters and symbols. In this recipe, we will closely examine the dimensions of these boxes, the spacing between them, and the resulting dimensions of dynamically adjusted space. This will give us a deeper understanding of typesetting.

In this section, we will use **LuaLaTeX**. LuaLaTeX is a variant of LaTeX based on the **LuaTeX** compiler that integrates the **Lua** scripting language within TeX. It's a modern alternative to the **pdfLaTeX** compiler we usually utilize in this book if not mentioned otherwise. In *Chapter 11, Using LaTeX in Science and Technology*, we will explore Lua programming.

How to do it...

We will additionally load the `lua-visual-debug` package. Then, we will compile with LuaLaTeX as follows:

1. Open your document or any sample file. Again, we will use the document from our first recipe in *Chapter 1, Exploring Various Document Classes*.

2. Add the following line at the end of your preamble:

   ```
   \usepackage{lua-visual-debug}
   ```

3. In your editor, switch to LuaLaTeX for typesetting and compile the document. Take a look at these cut-outs of the output. The text has some annotations as follows:

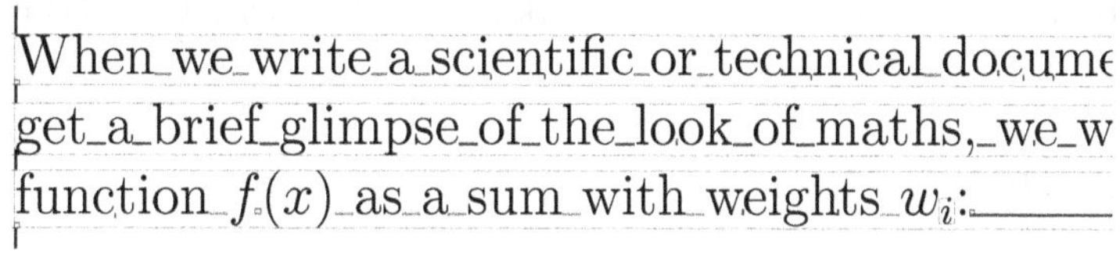

Figure 2.8 – Visualizing text layout

Formulas consist of many tiny boxes:

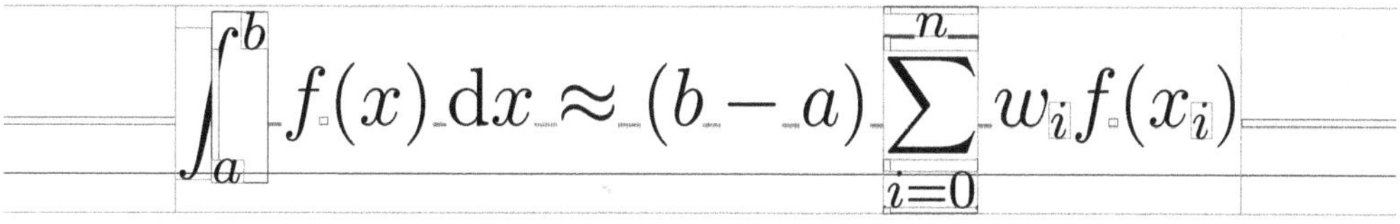

Figure 2.9 – Visualizing math layout

Examining the boxes may give us insight into tweaking formulas. In *Chapter 10, Writing Advanced Mathematics*, you can read about fine-tuning math formulas. When you no longer need the box visualization lines, you can deactivate the package by either commenting or deleting the line `\usepackage{lua-visual-debug}`.

How it works...

We simply loaded the `lua-visual-debug` package, which requires LuaLaTeX because of the package's dependency on LuaTeX. It did all the work for us; now we need to understand the output:

- LaTeX's boxes are highlighted with a thin border. A red rule denotes a zero-width box.
- A filled rectangle means a **kern**. This is a fixed vertical or horizontal spacing. A positive kern is colored yellow. A negative kern is colored red.
- Tick lines stand for **glue**. This means vertical or horizontal space. Unlike **kern**, it can be stretched or shrunken. The lines start and end with a tick. So you can recognize places where glues are touching.
- The blue rectangle below the baseline marks a point where hyphenation is allowed.
- A square means a **penalty**. This is an internal value that TeX tries to minimize in its line-breaking algorithm. A blank square means a maximum penalty. Otherwise, it's filled with gray.

This visualization can help you with debugging the document's typesetting.

Even if you use pdfLaTeX, you could briefly switch to LuaLaTeX just for this purpose, and then continue with pdfLaTeX. Alternatively, you could work with a simplified copy of that document part you need to analyze with LuaLaTeX.

Typesetting in a grid

In addition to full horizontal justification, LaTeX adjusts the page content vertically to maintain a consistent page height. Consequently, the internal spacing within a page can vary. As a result, lines on adjacent pages may look shifted.

For two-sided prints with very thin paper, matching baselines would look much better. Especially in two-column documents, it may be desirable to have baselines of adjacent lines at precisely the same height.

In this recipe, our goal is to arrange lines on a grid. Regular text lines shall be placed at a baseline grid. Displayed formulas, figures, tables, and captions are allowed to have a different baseline, but the subsequent text should return to the grid.

How to do it...

We'll use the `grid` package specifically developed for grid typesetting. Follow these steps:

1. Begin by creating a small two-column example with placeholder text to which we can apply the `grid` commands. Here is a straightforward code snippet that you can use for the start:

```
\documentclass{article}
\usepackage[english]{babel}
\usepackage{blindtext}
\usepackage{microtype}
\begin{document}
\twocolumn
\section*{Two columns}
\blindtext[3]
\begin{figure}
  \centering
  \fbox{\makebox(50,50){}}
  \caption{A dummy figure}
\end{figure}
\begin{equation}
  \sum_n f(n)
\end{equation}
Text
\end{document}
```

2. Take a first look. Compare the height of the text lines in the left- and right-hand columns. Observe that the baselines of the text are not yet aligned:

Two columns

Hello, here is some text without a meaning. This text should show what a printed text will look like at this place. If you read this text, you will get no information. Really? Is there no information? Is there a difference between this text and some nonsense like "Huardest gefburn"? Kjift – not at all! A blind text like this gives you information about the selected font, how the letters are written and an impression of the look. This text should contain all letters of the alphabet and it should be written in of the original language. There is no need for special content, but the length of words should match the language. Hello, here is some text without a meaning. This text should show

Figure 1: A dummy figure

all letters of the alphabet and it should be written in of the original language. There is no need for special content, but the length of words should match the language.

$$\sum_n f(n) \qquad (1)$$

Text

Figure 2.10 – Text without alignment on a grid

3. Now we add the `grid` package to the preamble with font size options as follows:

    ```
    \usepackage[fontsize=10pt,baseline=12pt]{grid}
    ```

4. Then, put the equation into a `gridenv` environment. It shall look like this:

    ```
    \begin{gridenv}
      \begin{equation}
        \sum_n f(n)
      \end{equation}
    \end{gridenv}
    ```

5. Compile the document and take a look at what has changed. Examine the baselines in the following screenshot closely:

Two columns

Hello, here is some text without a meaning. This text should show what a printed text will look like at this place. If you read this text, you will get no information. Really? Is there no information? Is there a difference between this text and some nonsense like "Huardest gefburn"? Kjift – not at all! A blind text like this gives you information about the selected font, how the letters are written and an impression of the look. This text should contain all letters of the alphabet and it should be written in of the original language. There is no need for special content, but the length of words should match the language. Hello, here is some text without a meaning. This text should show what a printed text will look like at this place. If you read this text, you will get no information. Really? Is there no information? Is there a difference between this text and some nonsense like

Figure 1: A dummy figure

"Huardest gefburn"? Kjift – not at all! A blind text like this gives you information about the selected font, how the letters are written and an impression of the look. This text should contain all letters of the alphabet and it should be written in of the original language. There is no need for special content, but the length of words should match the language.

$$\sum_n f(n) \tag{1}$$

Text

Figure 2.11 – Text and math with alignment on a grid

How it works...

We specified the font size and the baseline height as options for the `grid` package because the default settings don't produce the desired results.

The `grid` package makes some changes that help to stay in the grid. This is how it works:

- Elastic space, also called **glue** or **rubber space**, is either removed or replaced with fixed space.

- The heights of many frequently used items are adjusted to be multiples of the baseline height, ensuring they fit precisely within the grid. This has been made, for example, for the following elements:

  - Section headings

  - Figures and tables

  - Displayed equations

> **Note**
>
> Enclosing `equation` environments within a `gridenv` environment is advisable for proper spacing.

We have a quick solution for double-column grid typesetting. Some compromises are necessary, such as accepting a changed section heading size.

There's more...

The `gridset` package provides a command, `\vskipnextgrid`, which advances to the next grid position. It can be used as a simple fix without being a complete solution. It requires two or more typesetting runs until all is adjusted. So, you need to look at the affected place and repeat compiling if needed, mainly when repeatedly using the `\vskipnextgrid` command.

> **Note**
>
> At the time of writing, the `gridset` package was still in alpha status without official support.

The `gridset` package and the `\vskipnextgrid` command can also be used in addition to the `grid` package. If you encounter issues with `grid` package, you can rectify them by inserting a `\vskipnextgrid` command.

For instance, the `amsmath` package's multiline displayed equations could challenge the `grid` package. We will illustrate such a case and demonstrate how to fix it as follows:

1. Load the `amsmath` package in the preamble:

   ```
   \usepackage{amsmath}
   ```

2. Additionally, load the `gridset` package:

```
\usepackage{gridset}
```

3. In the document, create an `align` environment as follows:

```
\begin{align}
    y &= \sum_{n=1}^3 f(n) \\
      &= f(1) + f(2) + f(3)
\end{align}
```

4. Directly after it, add the following line. It ends the paragraph, skips to the next position in the grid, and avoids inserting paragraph indentations:

```
\par\vskipnextgrid\noindent
```

5. Add some text following it.

6. Compile the document once. The position of the previously added text may still not yet fit the grid.

7. Compile again. The `\vskipnextgrid` command will adjust the spacing to match the baseline grid.

The `\vskipnextgrid` command may have problems in the two-column mode. In such instances, we can resolve the problem by breaking the paragraph, adjusting the position, and suppressing the indentation of the following paragraph.

Absolute positioning of text

LaTeX takes care of full justification, balancing text height, and positioning floating objects such as figures and tables. It does a great job, but sometimes, we may need to tell LaTeX to put text or an image precisely at a specific position on a page.

Most positioning commands work in relation to the current position in the document. Now, we would like to output text at an absolute position.

How to do it...

We will use the `eso-pic` package for precise positioning. We will print text at the edge of the page, in the middle, and at specific positions. We will break down the code into small steps. However, you can copy the entire code from GitHub or the book's website at `https://latex-cookbook.net`.

Follow these steps:

1. Start with any document class. We chose the `article` class with A5 paper size.

```
\documentclass[a5paper]{article}
```

2. Load the `lipsum` package so that you can generate placeholder text:

    ```
    \usepackage{lipsum}
    ```

3. Load the `graphicx` package; we will later use its rotating feature:

    ```
    \usepackage{graphicx}
    ```

4. Load the `showframe` package for visualizing page dimensions, just to help us in the draft state:

    ```
    \usepackage{showframe}
    ```

5. Load the `eso-pic` package, which does the positioning for us:

    ```
    \usepackage{eso-pic}
    ```

6. Load the classic `picture` package to place pictures with coordinates:

    ```
    \usepackage{picture}
    ```

7. We will print the page number by ourselves, so disable the original page numbering:

    ```
    \pagestyle{empty}
    ```

8. Start the document:

    ```
    \begin{document}
    ```

9. Add the page number to all pages as follows:

    ```
    \AddToShipoutPictureBG{%
      \setlength{\unitlength}{1cm}%
      \put(2.5,2){Test document}%
      \put(\paperwidth-2cm,2cm){\llap{\thepage}}%
    }
    ```

10. Add some text to a single page as follows. Note the star (*) that we will discuss below.

    ```
    \AddToShipoutPictureBG*{%
      \AtPageLowerLeft{Page bottom left}%
      \AtPageUpperLeft{\raisebox{-\height}{Page
        top left}}%
      \AtTextUpperLeft{\raisebox{-\height}{%
        \color{red}Text area top left}}%
    }
    ```

11. Add a **Confidential** sign on top of the page:

```
\AddToShipoutPictureFG{%
  \AtPageCenter{\rotatebox{15}{\makebox[0pt]{%
    \Huge\bfseries\color{red}Confidential}}}%
}
```

12. Print some placeholder text. It starts at the beginning of the page, as usual. Finally, end the document.

```
\lipsum
\end{document}
```

13. Compile the document and take a look at the first page:

Figure 2.12 – A page with overprinted text

How it works...

We've loaded several packages. Here's a breakdown of what each package does:

- The `lipsum` package provides us with placeholder text, which we get by the `\lipsum` command.

- While the `graphicx` package is primarily for including images, we loaded it because we use its `\rotatebox` command to rotate text in *Step 11*.

- The `showframe` package draws lines around text and margin areas, as we saw in the recipe *Visualizing the layout*.

- The `eso-pic` package does the main job here. It provides commands for printing text or graphics independent of the current position on the page. It can do this in the background, which means behind the text, but also in the foreground, overwriting the regular text.

- The `picture` package is a classic package for drawing simple pictures. In our case, we use it for putting text at specific coordinates. The `\put` command expects `(x,y)` formatted cartesian coordinates with plain numbers, which are interpreted as factors of the `\unitlength` size. Alternatively, you can use lengths as arguments with arbitrary units, such as `10mm`.

We configured an `empty` page style to ensure that there are no default header and footer texts. In the document, we called the following `eso-pic` commands:

- The `\AddToShipoutPictureBG` command takes LaTeX's `picture` commands, which are put into a `picture` environment at the lower left corner of the page. This is printed onto the page background behind the standard text layer.

  Here, we first defined the base unit length to be 1 centimeter. In the following `\put` command, we used factors to this length for printing **Test document** near the lower left corner. Finally, we printed the current page number near the lower right corner. We calculated with paper width and centimeter values. The `picture` package brings this syntax. The `\llap` command puts its argument to the left side of a zero-width box, thus making it right-aligned.

  This background content will be repeated on subsequent pages.

- The `\AddToShipoutPictureBG*` command works like the `\AddToShipoutPictureBG` command but applies only to the current page.

- Using the `\AtPageLowerLeft` command, we positioned text in the lower-left corner of the page. The `\AtPageUpperLeft` command works similarly for the upper-left corner. We just lowered the text by its own height. The `\AtTextUpperLeft` command is the corresponding command for the text area.

- The `\AddToShipoutPictureFG` command works like the `\AddToShipoutPictureBG` command but operates on the page foreground. We positioned the word **Confidential** in huge red lettering, rotated above the text, in the middle of the page.

- The `\AddToShipoutPictureFG*` command works the same in the foreground but affects only the current page.

There's more...

There are alternative ways to achieve what we just did. There are several packages that offer a similar functionality:

- While the `eso-pic` package is based on the `atbegshi` package, the latter can be used directly.
- The `everyshi` package does a similar job. The `atbegshi` package is a modern reimplementation of it.
- The `textpos` package is based on the `everyshi` package, focuses on positioning blocks of text on a page, and provides a convenient user interface.

Comprehensive graphics packages provide their own methods in addition.

- The **TikZ** package can be used to place text in relation to the `current page` node in `overlay` mode. This is explained in *LaTeX Graphics with TikZ, Chapter 9, Using Layers, Overlays, and Transparency*. You can find the examples from this chapter at `https://tikz.org/chapter-09`.
- The **PSTricks** bundle contains the `pst-abspos` package for placing an object at an arbitrary position on the page.

If any of it aligns better with your work tools, you may look closer. As you saw in other recipes, you can access each package's documentation by calling `texdoc` at the command line, followed by the package name, and hitting the return key. For online access, just type the package name into the search field at `https://texdoc.org`.

Adding drop caps

In older texts, such as in fairy tale books, we sometimes see the first paragraph in a text starting with a huge letter while the following text flows around it. This design element is referred to as a **drop cap** or an **initial**. We will now use this design for our own text.

How to do it...

We will use the `lettrine` package, which offers a dedicated command for this purpose. Follow these steps:

1. Start a document with any document class. In this example, we've opted for the `book` class. We will use A6 paper size because the recipe is easier to show with little text.

    ```
    \documentclass{book}
    \usepackage[a6paper]{geometry}
    ```

2. Load the `lettrine` package:

    ```
    \usepackage{lettrine}
    ```

3. Begin the document:

    ```
    \begin{document}
    ```

4. Start a paragraph with the command `\lettrine{letter}{further introduction}`, as follows:

    ```
    \lettrine{O}{nce upon a time}, professional writers
    used a mechanical machine called a typewriter. It
    commonly printed fixed-width characters. Emphasizing
    was done by writing all capitals and by underlining.
    ```

5. End the document:

    ```
    \end{document}
    ```

6. Compile the document. Now, look at the shape of our paragraph:

ONCE UPON A TIME, professional writer used a mechanical machine called a typewriter. It commonly printed fixed-width characters. Emphasizing was done by writing all capitals, and by underlining.

Figure 2.13 – A paragraph starting with a drop cap

How it works...

For this simple example, we used the basic `book` class. We loaded the `geometry` package to get a handy A6 paper size. The final command in the preamble loaded the `lettrine` package, which provides precisely the design we are looking for. The command `\lettrine{O}{nce upon a time}` prints one large letter O, followed by the text in the second pair of braces, which is printed in small caps. The remaining text flows around the large letter.

There's more...

The design of the dropped capitals can be customized. Let's take a look at some available options.

Changing the drop cap size

By default, the dropped capital spans two lines. You can alter the number of lines it covers by setting the optional argument lines as follows:

```
\lettrine[lines=3]{O}{nce upon a time}
```

Now, a huge O covers three lines. Additionally, you can enlarge it by setting the `loversize` option, either independently or in conjunction with the previously mentioned option:

```
\lettrine[lines=3,loversize=0.2]{O}{nce upon a time}
```

The `loversize` option accepts values greater than -1 and smaller than or equal to 1, indicating the resizing factor. For instance, a value of 0.1 means enlarging by 10 percent.

The `lettrine` package provides a `key=value` interface. More options are available to control further aspects, such as the gap between the drop cap and the subsequent text and vertical shifting. You can also let drop caps hang into the margin. Those features are explained in the manual. You can open it using `texdoc lettrine` at the command line or by visiting `https://texdoc.org/pkg/lettrine`.

Coloring the initial

The easiest way to get colored drop caps is using the well-known commands of the `color` or `xcolor` package, such as:

```
\usepackage{xcolor}
...
\lettrine{\textcolor{red}{A}}{nother} time
```

> **Color names**
>
> A complete list of available colors and names is contained in the `xcolor` manual. You can open it by typing `texdoc xcolor` at the command prompt or at `https://texdoc.org/pkg/xcolor`. You may need to set an option to access predefined names, such as `svgnames`, `dvipsnames`, or `x11names`.

The `coloredlettrine` package provides an even fancier way. It provides bicolor initials that are based on the **EB Garamond** font. Internally, the initials are divided into two fonts. One provides the background ornaments, the other the actual letters. This separation allows individual coloring. We will use the **OpenType** version of EB Garamond. OpenType requires compilation with XeLaTeX or LuaLaTeX. Many LaTeX editors support those compilers too.

As of the time of writing this book, the `coloredlettrine` package was still in development. There was just a small set of initials available. 'That's why we will refer to the development sources.

1. Download the package files from `https://github.com/raphink/coloredlettrine`. There you find a `.ins` file and a `.dtx` file. Put them together into the same folder on your computer. Compile the file `coloredlettrine.ins` with LaTeX. This produces `coloredlettrine.sty`, which you can place in your TeX installation or your document folder.

2. Get the latest version of EB Garamond from `https://bitbucket.org/georgd/eb-garamond/downloads` and install the font. Specifically, unzip the downloaded file and install at least the `EBGaramond-InitialsF1.otf` and `EBGaramond-InitialsF2.otf` files. On a Mac, double-click the files to see the contents and then click the install button shown.

3. The `coloredlettrine` package contains an example that you can compile. Here, let's modify our example from the recipe's start:

```
\documentclass{book}
\usepackage[a6paper,hmargin=1.5cm]{geometry}
\usepackage{microtype}
\usepackage{coloredlettrine}
\renewcommand{\EBLettrineBackColor}{SlateBlue}
\setcounter{DefaultLines}{3}
\renewcommand{\DefaultLraise}{0.25}
\renewcommand{\DefaultFindent}{0.3em}
\renewcommand{\DefaultNindent}{0pt}
\begin{document}
\coloredlettrine{O}{nce upon a time}, professional
writers used a mechanical machine called a typewriter.
It commonly printed fixed-width characters.
Emphasizing was done by writing all capitals
and by underlining.

\coloredlettrine{T}{oday}, we prefer variable-width
letters. It's common to provide subtle emphasis by
using italics or to add greater emphasis by using
bold text.
\end{document}
```

4. Choose XeLaTeX or LuaLaTeX for typesetting, compile, and have a look:

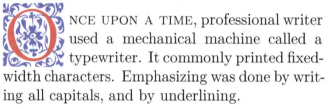

Figure 2.14 – Colorful drop caps

You can use the \coloredlettrine command exactly like the \lettrine command since it is just a wrapper for it. You can redefine the macros \EBLettrineBackColor and \EBLettrineFrontColor to choose the color.

In this example, we set default values for lettrine parameters, which we otherwise would have needed to provide as key=value options, as explained earlier in this recipe. This way can save you from defining your own macro. It is described in the manual, which you can open by texdoc lettrine or at https://texdoc.org/pkg/lettrine.

Fitting text to a shape

There are situations when text doesn't have a strict rectangular shape. For example, if you want to print on a DVD or compact disc label, the whole text should fit within a circular boundary.

How to do it...

The shapepar package can typeset paragraphs in a particular shape, such as a circle, a hexagon, or a heart. The shape size will be automatically adjusted to accommodate the provided text. We will now try it with a heart:

1. Start a small document, load the blindtext package for dummy text and the shapepar package:

```
\documentclass{article}
\usepackage{blindtext}
\usepackage{shapepar}
```

2. In the document body, use the `\shapepar` command with a shape type argument, and then your text, as follows:

```
\begin{document}
\shapepar{\heartshape}\blindtext[2]
\end{document}
```

3. Compile and have a look:

Lorem   ipsum   dolor sit amet,
consectetuer   adipiscing   elit. Etiam lobortis facilisis sem. Nullam nec mi et neque   pharetra sollicitudin. Praesent
imperdiet mi nec ante. Donec ullam-   corper, felis non sodales commodo,
lectus velit ultrices augue, a dignissim nibh lectus placerat pede. Vivamus nunc
nunc, molestie ut, ultricies vel, semper in, velit. Ut porttitor. Praesent in sapien.
Lorem ipsum dolor sit amet, consectetuer adipiscing elit. Duis fringilla tristique
neque. Sed interdum libero ut metus. Pellentesque placerat. Nam rutrum augue
a leo. Morbi sed elit sit amet ante lobortis sollicitudin. Praesent blandit blandit
mauris. Praesent lectus tellus, aliquet aliquam, luctus a, egestas a, turpis. Mauris
lacinia lorem sit amet ipsum. Nunc quis urna dictum turpis accumsan semper.
Lorem ipsum dolor sit amet, consectetuer adipiscing elit. Etiam lobortis facilisis
sem. Nullam nec mi et neque pharetra sollicitudin. Praesent imperdiet
mi nec ante. Donec ullamcorper, felis non sodales commodo, lectus velit
ultrices augue, a dignissim nibh lectus placerat pede. Vivamus nunc nunc,
molestie ut, ultricies vel, semper in, velit. Ut porttitor. Praesent in
sapien. Lorem ipsum dolor sit amet, consectetuer adipiscing elit.
Duis fringilla tristique neque. Sed interdum libero ut metus.
Pellentesque placerat. Nam rutrum augue a leo. Morbi
sed elit sit amet ante lobortis sollicitudin. Praesent
blandit blandit mauris. Praesent lectus tellus,
aliquet aliquam, luctus a, egestas a, turpis.
Mauris lacinia lorem sit amet
ipsum. Nunc quis urna dictum turpis accum-
san   sem-
per.

Figure 2.15 – Text in the shape of a heart

How it works...

We loaded the `blindtext` package, which provides filler text via the `\blindtext` command, which is excellent for testing. Then we loaded the `shapepar` package.

That package provides the `\shapepar` command, which is used as follows:

```
\shapepar[scale length]{shape command}
   text of the paragraph
```

Here, we used \heartshape as the shape command, which typesets the following paragraph of text with the shape of a heart. The shape applies only to the next paragraph's text. The text is not an argument; it just follows like plain text.

The scale length value is optional. It's a LaTeX length, which will be used as a base unit within the shape definition. If not given, it's automatically calculated for optimal shape filling.

There's a short command version as follows:

```
\heartpar{text}
```

This command is equivalent to this code:

```
\shapepar{\heartshape} text\ \ $\heartsuit$\par
```

It prints the text in a heart shape and ends it with a heart symbol.

There's more...

We can shape text in various ways. Furthermore, we can let the text flow around a shape. In other words, we can cut out shapes from the text.

Further shapes

The following list contains the predefined shapes and corresponding short commands:

- Square: \squareshape and \squarepar
- Circle: \circleshape and \circlepar
- Circle with a hole: \CDlabshape and \CDlabel. The latter command fits text to a compact disc or DVD; attention: the package manual currently calls the shape \CDshape
- Diamond: \diamondshape and \diamondpar (like a rhomboid)
- Heart: \heartshape and \heartpar
- Five-point star: \starshape and \starpar
- Hexagon: \hexagonshape and \hexagonpar
- Hexagon with a hole: \nutshape and \nutpar (like a nut for a bolt)
- Rectangle: \rectangleshape{height}{width} (no short version)

The rectangle shape doesn't provide a short command version. You can use it as follows:

```
\shapepar{\rectangleshape{40}{20}} text
```

Use it without the units for the length, as it internally uses the `scale length`, as noted above. So, `height` and `width` basically define the aspect ratio of the rectangle.

The mentioned holes in the shapes above are circular.

Cutting out shapes

For text cutouts, the `\shapepar` command has a companion that allows you to create cutouts using a specific shape:

```
\cutout {side} (horizontal offset, vertical offset)
    settings \shapepar ...
```

It cuts out the text with the specified shape from the following text. The `side` option can be `l` for left or `r` for right. You can use offsets for shifting. Optionally used `settings` would be local to that instance. It can contain commands such as modifying `\cutoutsep`, which is the separation between outer text and shaped text, 12 pt by default.

For further details, please consult the package's manual. Here's an example that cuts out a circle from a paragraph with blind text and fills it with a few words:

```
\cutout{l} (5ex,2\baselineskip) \setlength{\cutoutsep}{8pt}
    \shapepar{\circleshape} a few words of text\par
\blindtext
```

This will generate the following output:

Lorem ipsum dolor sit amet, consectetuer adipiscing elit. Etiam lobortis facilisis sem. Nullam nec mi et neque pharetra sollicitudin. Praesent
a few   imperdiet mi nec ante. Donec ullamcorper, felis non sodales com-
words of modo, lectus velit ultrices augue, a dignissim nibh lectus placerat
text   pede. Vivamus nunc nunc, molestie ut, ultricies vel, semper in, velit.
Ut porttitor. Praesent in sapien. Lorem ipsum dolor sit amet, consectetuer adipiscing elit. Duis fringilla tristique neque. Sed interdum libero ut
metus. Pellentesque placerat. Nam rutrum augue a leo. Morbi sed elit sit amet
ante lobortis sollicitudin. Praesent blandit blandit mauris. Praesent lectus tellus, aliquet aliquam, luctus a, egestas a, turpis. Mauris lacinia lorem sit amet
ipsum. Nunc quis urna dictum turpis accumsan semper.

Figure 2.16 – A circular cut-out

Creating a pull quote

To capture readers' interest in a text, we can present a brief and appealing excerpt as a quotation. We can pull out some text. In a two-column layout, it looks nice to put the quotation into a window at the center of the page between the two columns, with the regular text flowing around it. It's also an excellent way of embedding images.

How to do it...

One approach is to use the shapepar package to cut out space from the text, like in the previous recipe. However, doing it twice, once for each column, would take some work.

The pullquote package provides a solution. It can typeset a balanced two-column text layout with a cut-out window. This can be filled with text or an image. The shape is arbitrary.

We will use placeholder text and highlight a quote by Donald Knuth, the creator of TeX.

1. Download the file pullquote.dtx from https://bazaar.launchpad.net/~tex-sx/tex-sx/development/view/head:/pullquote.dtx.

2. Click on "browse files" and download also pq-alice.jpg, pq-duck.pdf, and pullquote_test.tex, to have filler images and a sample file. The image files are used by pullquote.dtx so you need them for compiling it.

3. Compile pullquote.dtx with pdfLaTeX. Do it twice for correct references. It will generate a pullquote.sty file and the documentation file pullquote.pdf. Place the files where your LaTeX can find them or simply in the document's folder.

4. Start with a document class, load the lipsum package for dummy text, and load the pullquote package:

```
\documentclass{article}
\usepackage{lipsum}
\usepackage{pullquote}
```

5. Create a command that prints your quote in a paragraph box:

```
\newcommand{\myquote}{%
  \parbox{4cm}{
    \hrule\vspace{1ex}
    \textit{I can't go to a restaurant and order food
      because I keep looking at the fonts on the
        menu.}

    \hfill Knuth, Donald (2002)%
    \vspace{1ex}
    \hrule
  }%
}
```

6. In the document, use a `pullquote` environment with the self-defined macro in the argument and dummy text, as follows:

```
\begin{document}
\begin{pullquote}{object=\myquote}
   \lipsum[1]
\end{pullquote}
\end{document}
```

7. Compile and have a look:

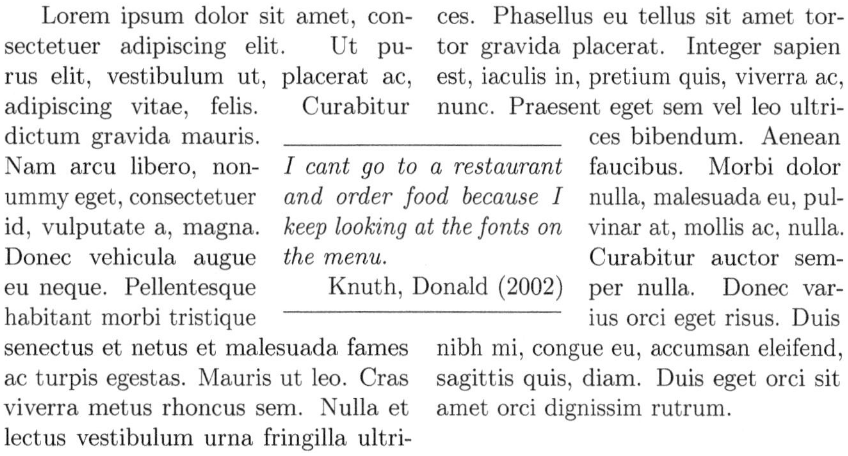

Lorem ipsum dolor sit amet, consectetuer adipiscing elit. Ut purus elit, vestibulum ut, placerat ac, adipiscing vitae, felis. Curabitur dictum gravida mauris. Nam arcu libero, nonummy eget, consectetuer id, vulputate a, magna. Donec vehicula augue eu neque. Pellentesque habitant morbi tristique senectus et netus et malesuada fames ac turpis egestas. Mauris ut leo. Cras viverra metus rhoncus sem. Nulla et lectus vestibulum urna fringilla ultri-

I cant go to a restaurant and order food because I keep looking at the fonts on the menu.

Knuth, Donald (2002)

ces. Phasellus eu tellus sit amet tortor gravida placerat. Integer sapien est, iaculis in, pretium quis, viverra ac, nunc. Praesent eget sem vel leo ultrices bibendum. Aenean faucibus. Morbi dolor nulla, malesuada eu, pulvinar at, mollis ac, nulla. Curabitur auctor semper nulla. Donec varius orci eget risus. Duis nibh mi, congue eu, accumsan eleifend, sagittis quis, diam. Duis eget orci sit amet orci dignissim rutrum.

Figure 2.17 – A pull quote with text

How it works...

We loaded the `lipsum` package, which gives us **Lorem Ipsum** Latin filler text. Then, we loaded the `pullquote` package. We defined a macro, which prints the quote.

For our example, we made a paragraph box with lines above and below, printing italic text and the author's name. To avoid undesired white space, we commented out the line breaks at some places by a % sign at the end.

In the document, we made a `pullquote` environment with that macro as a pulled object within the argument and dummy text to fill the space around.

`pullquote` finished the rest for us. It handles the following tasks:

- Putting the object into a box
- Measuring its height and width

- Adding space for the distance
- Normalizing the total height to be an integral multiple of the value specified for the `\baselineskip` command to match several text lines
- Calculating the vertical position
- Determining the shape of the paragraph
- Balancing the text columns according to the specified shape
- Organizing and printing the entire construct

There are some limitations. Ideally, the text within the environment should consist of simple paragraphs of text. This means that lists such as `itemize`, displayed math, section headings, and modified vertical spacing, in general, are undesirable. Such non-simple elements may trouble the calculation. However, it's already great for images and text boxes.

There's more...

The `key=value` list in the argument of the `pullquote` environment supports further parameters. In addition to the default rectangular shape, there's a circular shape. We can specify it via the `shape` option. The following example will illustrate it. We will create a TikZ picture to have an actual circled element as a quote. So, we need to load the `tikz` package as well.

You can test this functionality with the following code, similar to the previous example:

```
\documentclass{article}
\usepackage{lipsum}
\usepackage{pullquote}
\usepackage{tikz}
\newcommand{\mylogo}{%
  \begin{tikzpicture}
    \node[shape=circle, draw=gray!40, line width=3pt,
      fill={gray!15}, font=\Huge] {\TeX};
  \end{tikzpicture}%
}
\begin{document}
\begin{pullquote}{shape=circular, object=\mylogo}
  \lipsum[1]
\end{pullquote}
\end{document}
```

The code will produce this layout:

Lorem ipsum dolor sit amet, consectetuer adipiscing elit. Ut purus elit, vestibulum ut, placerat ac, adipiscing vitae, felis. Curabitur dictum gravida mauris. Nam arcu libero, nonummy eget, consectetuer id, vulputate a, magna. Donec vehicula augue eu neque. Pellentesque habitant morbi tristique senectus et netus et malesuada fames ac turpis egestas. Mauris ut leo. Cras viverra metus rhoncus sem. Nulla et lectus vestibulum urna fringilla ultrices. Phasellus eu tellus sit amet tortor gravida placerat. Integer sapien est, iaculis in, pretium quis, viverra ac, nunc. Praesent eget sem vel leo ultrices bibendum. Aenean faucibus. Morbi dolor nulla, malesuada eu, pulvinar at, mollis ac, nulla. Curabitur auctor semper nulla. Donec varius orci eget risus. Duis nibh mi, congue eu, accumsan eleifend, sagittis quis, diam. Duis eget orci sit amet orci dignissim rutrum.

Figure 2.18 – A pull quote with an image

TikZ is a highly versatile graphics package. You can read more about it in *Chapter 6, Creating Graphics*. We could also have used an external image using \includegraphics. To learn more about this method, refer to the recipe *Shaping an image like a circle* in *Chapter 5, Working with Images*.

For arbitrary shapes specified by shape functions, consult the package manual. It also explains image inclusion support with the shape=image option. Then, the cut-out dimensions would be calculated from the image dimensions. To utilize this feature, the free **ImageMagick** program would need to be installed on the system since it would then be called internally.

3
Adjusting Fonts

When LaTeX was young, documents looked quite similar, since there was little choice of fonts. Over time, many new fonts have been created and gained support in LaTeX.

To find the perfect fonts for your documents, visit the **LaTeX Font Catalogue** at https://tug.org/FontCatalogue.

In this chapter, we will see how to choose fonts globally and adjust them within the document. We will specifically cover the following:

- Using standard font commands
- Choosing a document font
- Locally switching to a different font
- Importing just a single symbol of a font
- Printing font tables
- Writing bold mathematical symbols
- Getting sans-serif fonts for mathematics
- Writing double-stroke letters as if on a blackboard
- Enabling the searching and copying of ligatures
- Suppressing ligatures
- Adding a contour

Using standard font commands

Before we start, let's look at some standard LaTeX commands to switch between fonts. Experienced LaTeX users can skip this section. We will keep this very short, as other introductory texts usually cover font commands in detail. Specifically, the *LaTeX Beginner's Guide* covers fonts in *Chapter 10, Using Fonts*, which is an excellent place to start.

Fonts for text have five main attributes:

- **Family**: This denotes the style of a font, whether it has serifs or not, and whether it's **proportional** or **monospaced**. The latter is also called the **typewriter** style. You can switch to a family using one of these commands:

  - `\rmfamily`: This switches to a Roman font, where the characters have **serifs**. It is the default font family.

  - `\sffamily`: This command changes to a **sans-serif** font.

  - `\ttfamily`: This switches to a typewriter font.

- **Encoding**: We covered this in the previous chapter and concluded that T1 encoding is usually a good choice for common Latin text, which the following command can activate:

  ```
  \usepackage[T1]{fontenc}
  ```

- **Series**: This denotes how heavy a font is. Use the following commands to change the weight:

  - `\bfseries`: This command activates the bold font.

  - `\mdseries`: This switches to medium font, which is the default.

- **Shape**: This stands for the overall design style of a font. A font family can contain several shapes:

  - `\upshape`: This command chooses upright text, which is the default.

  - `\slshape`: This makes text slanted, where characters appear inclined to the right.

  - `\itshape`: This switches to an italic font style, which is also inclined to the right but with particular design and aesthetics, making it very different from the upright shape.

  - `\scshape`: This switches to small capitals. In this style, lowercase letters look like capital letters, only smaller. This is a popular choice for an elegant appearance.

- **Size**: A document has a specific base font size. That size is specified as an option for the document class, as we did in the first chapter. Then, the following commands can be used to switch to a different size in the document or within a macro:

  - In increasing order, we get a larger text size using one of the `\large`, `\Large`, `\LARGE`, `\huge`, and `\Huge` commands

  - In decreasing order, we get a smaller text size using any of the `\small`, `\footnotesize`, `\scriptsize`, and `\tiny` commands

  - We can switch back to the regular size using the `\normalfont` command

You can limit the effect of these commands using environments. You can also limit the impact using curly braces – for example, `{\bfseries ... }`.

There's another consistent syntax to modify short pieces of text, using the following commands:

- `\textrm{...}` switches the argument to Roman text, `\textsf{...}` switches it to sans-serif, and `\texttt{...}` switches it to typewriter text

- `\textbf{...}` makes the argument bold, and `\textmd{...}` makes it medium weight

- `\textit{...}` switches the argument to italic style, `\textsl{...}` makes it slanted, `\textsc{...}` applies the small caps style to it, and `\textup{...}` chooses the upright style for it

There's no such command for font size with text as an argument. It's unusual anyway to manually change the font size within the surrounding text. Just think of calculating the interline distance for the paragraph, which is calculated from the font size.

There's more...

Classes and packages use these font commands to define consistent styles. As the author, we state elements such as section headings, footnotes, subscripts, and emphasized snippets, while LaTeX chooses the corresponding size, shape, and series.

What if you wanted to use those commands yourself? It's perfect practice to use such font commands only in the preamble, in macro definitions, and not in the document body text. For example, instead of scattering `\textbf{...}` commands all over the text for bold author names, you should define an author name style – for example, like this:

```
\newcommand{\authorname}[1]{\textbf{#1}}
```

This allows you to implement easy and consistent changes in a single place, the preamble, such as when you would later decide to use lowercase or italics instead.

A macro for each required formatting brings logic into the text, and you can modify all occurrences simultaneously by changing a single macro in the preamble.

Choosing a document font

The default font has the name **Computer Modern** and is of excellent quality. It's a whole font family containing bold, italic, sans-serif, typewriter, and more font versions. All the fonts are well-composed to fit together.

If you want to change a font, use a complete bundle or carefully select font families based on shape and size. That's because, besides giving an excellent appearance to the document overall, it is essential that all font families are compliant with each other when they are used together.

This recipe will look at some font sets and recommended combinations.

Getting ready

The files for the fonts you would like to use should already be installed on your TeX system. If necessary, install them. Use the package manager of your LaTeX distribution, such as the MiKTeX package manager if you use MiKTeX on Windows, or the TeX Live manager tool called tlmgr.

If you have TeX Live installed, it offers the possibility to install entire font collections so that you can run the tlmgr tool at the command line:

```
tlmgr install collection-fontsrecommended
tlmgr install collection-fontsextra
```

If sufficient hard disk space is available, installing all fonts or even all packages of the TeX distribution could save you some headaches later, ensuring you would not miss any fonts.

TeX Live installs only free fonts without restrictions, distributed by the supplier. There's a tool called getnonfreefonts to download and install further fonts. For documentation and downloads, visit https://www.tug.org/fonts/getnonfreefonts.

How to do it...

Fonts with LaTeX support often come with a package. As the author, you can load the package, and that package takes care of loading and activating the fonts.

So, commonly, these steps would be followed in the preamble:

1. Switch to the required font encoding. Most modern fonts work with T1, as explained in *Chapter 2, Tuning the Text*:

    ```
    \usepackage[T1]{fontenc}
    ```

2. Load the font package:

```
\usepackage{fontname}
```

The `fontname` argument is the name, or the shortcut to the name, of a font that you need to know, for example, by visiting the LaTeX Font Catalogue.

3. If your default document font should be sans-serif, you can switch to that:

```
\renewcommand{\familydefault}{\sfdefault}
```

In the following recipe, you will see another method of choosing a font that works locally. Here, we will continue with a document-wide font choice.

There's more...

Let's take a look at some good alternative fonts and their combinations. It's essential to have a set of serif, sans-serif, mono-spaced, and math fonts that match each other in size and appearance.

Use each code given next together with the setting `\usepackage[T1]{fontenc}`.

We will take a look at the sample output so that you can compare the font selections. Note that you may see a lower quality than in a LaTeX document, as the production of this book may require images in bitmap format, particularly with the Kindle and EPUB formats. Depending on the print or screen resolution, this can result in blurry or pixelated output.

You can see the code of the following examples also at `https://latex-cookbook.net/chapter-03`, with a preview and online compiling.

To demonstrate this, we will revisit our very first example from the first chapter, only with some of the code reduced. We will see how Roman, sans-serif, italic, and typewriter fonts harmonize.

Latin Modern

Latin Modern is very similar to the default Computer Modern font. It is of excellent quality. This font bundle covers the usual requirements, such as having serif, sans-serif, typewriter, and symbol fonts. Load the fonts using the following command:

```
\usepackage{lmodern}
```

Latin Modern gives us the following appearance:

1 Some maths

To see the math font design, we will look at an integral approximation of a function $f(x)$ as a sum with weights w_i. Key commands are \int, \approx and \sum.

$$\int_a^b f(x)\,\mathrm{d}x \approx (b-a)\sum_{i=0}^{n} w_i f(x_i) \tag{1}$$

Figure 3.1 – Latin Modern

It is still similar to the default font we saw in our very first recipe.

Kepler fonts

The **Kepler fonts** are a complete and well-designed set of fonts in various shapes. There are upright and slanted Greek letters, bold math symbols, old-style numbers, and several weights, from light to bold extended. Even slanted small caps are available. You can get the whole set using this command:

```
\usepackage{kpfonts}
```

The appearance of our sample changes to the following:

1 Some maths

To see the math font design, we will look at an integral approximation of a function $f(x)$ as a sum with weights w_i. Key commands are \int, \approx and \sum.

$$\int_a^b f(x)\,\mathrm{d}x \approx (b-a)\sum_{i=0}^{n} w_i f(x_i) \tag{1}$$

Figure 3.2 – Kepler fonts

The typefaces harmonize well. They are not very heavy. For example, the typewriter code matches the grayness of the standard text better, since it doesn't look as heavy as in the previous sample.

Font combinations

Some fonts exist only as text fonts, math fonts, or in a specific shape. Combining different fonts regarding taste and scaling can be challenging. Here are some examples that work fine together:

```
\usepackage{libertine}
\usepackage[libertine,cmintegrals,cmbraces,
  vvarbb]{newtxmath}
\usepackage[scaled=0.95]{inconsolata}
```

Together, they give us this appearance:

1 Some maths

To see the math font design, we will look at an integral approximation of a function $f(x)$ as a sum with weights w_i. Key commands are \int, \approx and \sum.

$$\int_a^b f(x)\,\mathrm{d}x \approx (b-a)\sum_{i=0}^n w_i f(x_i) \tag{1}$$

Figure 3.3 – Libertine with nextxmath font and Inconsolata typewriter font

We loaded the **Linux Libertine** font. It is less dense than a **Times** font but denser than Computer Modern. Then, we added the newtxmath font, which is a Roman math font, but told it to use the **Libertine** font when appropriate and use Computer Modern integral and braces symbols. The last option tells the newtxmath package to use another good blackboard font with \mathbb. Try this selection and see whether you like it; omit options to compare it with the default settings. For details and further features, refer to the newtx manual via texdoc or at https://texdoc.org/pkg/newtx.

Finally, we loaded the excellent mono-spaced font **Inconsolata** for a typewriter shape and scaled it to match our text font.

Now, let's try another combination:

```
\usepackage[sc,osf]{mathpazo}
\usepackage[T1,small,euler-digits]{eulervm}
\usepackage[scaled=0.86]{berasans}
\usepackage[scaled=0.84]{beramono}
```

You can see the difference, such as a more upright shape, for integral and summation signs and variables:

1 Some maths

To see the math font design, we will look at an integral approximation of a function $f(x)$ as a sum with weights w_i. Key commands are `\int`, `\approx` and `\sum`.

$$\int_a^b f(x)\,dx \approx (b-a)\sum_{i=0}^n w_i f(x_i) \tag{1}$$

Figure 3.4 – The Mathpazo font with Euler virtual math and Bera for a typewriter style

We loaded the `mathpazo` package, which gives us a **Palatino** text font. We replaced its Palatino italic-like math font with the **Euler Virtual Math** font. It's basically the Euler font, with missing symbols taken from Computer Modern, which is why it's called *virtual*.

In addition, we loaded the **Bera** sans-serif font and the mono-spaced Bera shape for the typewriter text; both are appropriately scaled.

You may have noticed the `sc` and `osf` options for `mathpazo`, and for Palatino, which gives us a genuine small caps font and uses old-style figures as default.

Now, you have some excellent suggestions for a fine font selection. Using any of them, your document will look professionally designed but still different from a LaTeX standard document.

Locally switching to a different font

A typographically good document with a consistent appearance commonly uses just a few fonts, each with a purpose. Common font choices are as follows:

- Serif body text
- Sans-serif for headings
- Monospaced for source code

Each font family is defined in the preamble, usually implicitly done by packages. There are LaTeX commands to switch between families, shapes, and weights, but what if you also wanted to use a completely different font, such as a second serif font? This recipe will help to achieve that.

How to do it...

We will take a look at two ways to switch to a completely different font:

- Defining a command
- Defining an environment

In each case, we need to know the shortcut code for the font. The code is based on Karl Berry's naming scheme; you can read about it by running `texdoc fontname` at the command line or online at `https://texdoc.org/pkg/fontname`. You don't need to study this guide; just look at the documentation for the font package you are using. For your convenience, here is a selection of frequently used font families and their code terms:

- Avant Garde: `pag`
- Bookman: `pbk`
- Charter: `bch`
- Computer Concrete: `ccr`
- Computer Modern Roman: `cmr`
- Computer Modern Sans Serif: `cmss`
- Computer Modern Typewriter: `cmtt`
- Courier: `pcr`
- Garamond: `mdugm`
- Helvetica: `phv`
- Inconsolata: `fi4`
- Latin Modern: `lmr`
- Latin Modern Sans Serif: `lmss`
- Latin Modern Typewriter: `lmtt`
- New Century Schoolbook: `pnc`
- Palatino: `ppl`
- Times: `ptm`
- Utopia: `put`
- Zapf Chancery: `pzc`
- Zapf Dingbats: `pzd`

We will use the Zapf Chancery font for our recipe.

A command to change the font

To avoid the repetition of command sequences within a document, we will define a macro to change the font. This ensures consistent future adjustments.

Define a simple macro for the change. Write it into your preamble:

```
\newcommand{\zapf}{\fontfamily{pzc}\selectfont}
```

In your document, use it to switch the font. *Group* the command with the text to be affected. Consider ending the paragraph before you end the group, which can be done using an empty line or the \par command.

You can group commands using curly braces:

```
{\zapf Text in Zapf Chancery\par}
```

Another way to change the font, which may be a better choice to understand the code clearly, is the following:

```
\begingroup
\zapf
Text in Zapf Chancery
\par
\endgroup
```

An environment for changing the font

Creating an environment is an even more explicit way of restricting the effect of the change. Add the following command to your preamble:

```
\newenvironment{zapfenv}{\fontfamily{pzc}\selectfont}{}
```

Now, you can use it in your document:

```
\begin{zapfenv}
Text in Zapf Chancery
\par
\end{zapfenv}
```

You can save some work by moving the final paragraph break to the environment definition. This way, you don't always need to type the \par command before closing the environment. The definition will be as follows:

```
\newenvironment{zapfenv}{\fontfamily{pzc}\selectfont}{\par}
```

How it works...

At first, we chose the font family, which has yet to affect the font. We need to use the `\selectfont` command to apply the change.

Both grouping and the use of an environment keep the change local. This means that after ending the group or environment, the following text will have the same font as earlier.

The font properties at the end of the paragraph determine how TeX formats a paragraph, especially its line spacing. That's why we break the paragraph *within* the group or environment, not directly afterward. Otherwise, for example, in case of switching to a bigger font, we could have a paragraph with a big font but with a small line spacing from the outer font.

There's more...

If you want to use several different font families within a document, you can make the macro and the environment more variable by introducing an argument. The definitions can be changed to the following:

```
\newcommand{\setfont}[1]{\fontfamily{#1}\selectfont}
\newenvironment{fontenv}[1]{\fontfamily{#1}%
  \selectfont}{\par}
```

The usage with this command changes to the following:

```
{\setfont{pzc} Text in Zapf Chancery\par}
```

Using the environment, it changes to this:

```
\begin{fontenv}{pzc}
Text in Zapf Chancery
\end{fontenv}
```

There's also a command to switch back to the default font family. You can use it to reset to the default font family of the document explicitly:

```
\normalfont
```

You can change more parameters of the chosen font. In such cases, you can define some macros for several purposes, such as various heading fonts. Look at this example:

```
\newcommand{\latin}{\fontencoding{T1}\fontfamily{lmr}%
  \fontshape{sl}\fontseries{b}\fontsize{16pt}{20pt}
  \selectfont}
```

Here, we switch to T1 encoded Latin Modern Roman with a slanted shape and bold weight. Furthermore, we set a font size of 16 pt and a line spacing of 20 pt. For detailed information, refer to the *LaTeX2e font selection* guide, accessible at the command line with the `texdoc fntguide` command and available for download at `https://texdoc.org/pkg/fntguide`.

As with all physical font settings, such changes should not be directly called within a document. They are useful within global formatting commands. For example, to use the Zapf Chancery font in KOMA-Script chapter headings, use this command:

```
\setkomafont{chapter}{\normalcolor\zapf\Huge}
```

Generally, once you know how to adjust the font, you can use those commands within your own macros, such as to define the appearance of keywords, code, or hyperlinks.

Printing font tables

The last recipes showed how to print text in a particular font. This gives you a visual representation immediately. In addition, you may want to see the entire set of characters and symbols in a font. You can let LaTeX print a font table for you to achieve this.

> **Note**
> We will use the term **glyph** when we refer to the graphic representation of a particular character or symbol in a font.

How to do it...

The `fonttable` package can print the character set of a font in the shape of a table. It's straightforward, as follows:

1. In your document's preamble, load the `fonttable` package:

    ```
    \usepackage{fonttable}
    ```

2. In the document's body, use the following command to display the character table of the **Zapf Dingbats** font:

    ```
    \fonttable{pzdr}
    ```

3. Compile, and then you will see the following table in your document:

	'0	'1	'2	'3	'4	'5	'6	'7	
'04x	32	33	34	35	36	37	38	39	"2x
'05x	40	41	42	43	44	45	46	47	
'06x	48	49	50	51	52	53	54	55	"3x
'07x	56	57	58	59	60	61	62	63	
'10x	64	65	66	67	68	69	70	71	"4x
'11x	72	73	74	75	76	77	78	79	
'12x	80	81	82	83	84	85	86	87	"5x
'13x	88	89	90	91	92	93	94	95	
'14x	96	97	98	99	100	101	102	103	"6x
'15x	104	105	106	107	108	109	110	111	
'16x	112	113	114	115	116	117	118	119	"7x
'17x	120	121	122	123	124	125	126	127	
'24x	160	161	162	163	164	165	166	167	"Ax
'25x	168	169	170	171	172	173	174	175	
'26x	176	177	178	179	180	181	182	183	"Bx
'27x	184	185	186	187	188	189	190	191	
'30x	192	193	194	195	196	197	198	199	"Cx
'31x	200	201	202	203	204	205	206	207	
'32x	208	209	210	211	212	213	214	215	"Dx
'33x	216	217	218	219	220	221	222	223	
'34x	224	225	226	227	228	229	230	231	"Ex
'35x	232	233	234	235	236	237	238	239	
'36x	240	241	242	243	244	245	246	247	"Fx
'37x	248	249	250	251	252	253	254	255	
	"8	"9	"A	"B	"C	"D	"E	"F	

Figure 3.5 – The Zapf Dingbats character table

How it works...

The \fonttable command prints a table showing all the symbols of the font. Each cell contains the decimal position in the character set, while columns and rows show the hexadecimal and octal numbering.

There's more...

The \xfonttable command prints a table of font characters with particular properties. It takes four arguments – encoding, family, series, and shape. For example, you can print the character table of the T1 encoded Zapf Chancery medium italic font with the following command:

```
\xfonttable{T1}{pzc}{m}{it}
```

You will get the following output:

	'0	'1	'2	'3	'4	'5	'6	'7	
'00x	\ 0	' 1	^ 2	~ 3	" 4	" 5	° 6	ˇ 7	"0x
'01x	˘ 8	‾ 9	˙ 10	, 11	¸ 12	, 13	‹ 14	› 15	
'02x	" 16	" 17	„ 18	« 19	» 20	– 21	— 22	23	"1x
'03x	■ 24	ı 25	▌ 26	ff 27	fi 28	fl 29	ffi 30	ffl 31	
'04x	␣ 32	! 33	" 34	# 35	$ 36	% 37	& 38	' 39	"2x
'05x	(40	) 41	* 42	+ 43	, 44	- 45	. 46	/ 47	
'06x	0 48	1 49	2 50	3 51	4 52	5 53	6 54	7 55	"3x
'07x	8 56	9 57	: 58	; 59	< 60	= 61	> 62	? 63	
'10x	@ 64	A 65	B 66	C 67	D 68	E 69	F 70	G 71	"4x
'11x	H 72	I 73	J 74	K 75	L 76	M 77	N 78	O 79	
'12x	P 80	Q 81	R 82	S 83	T 84	U 85	V 86	W 87	"5x
'13x	X 88	Y 89	Z 90	[91	\ 92	] 93	^ 94	_ 95	
'14x	' 96	a 97	b 98	c 99	d 100	e 101	f 102	g 103	"6x
'15x	h 104	i 105	j 106	k 107	l 108	m 109	n 110	o 111	
'16x	p 112	q 113	r 114	s 115	t 116	u 117	v 118	w 119	"7x
'17x	x 120	y 121	z 122	{ 123	| 124	} 125	~ 126	- 127	
'20x	Ă 128	Ą 129	Ć 130	Č 131	Ď 132	Ě 133	Ę 134	Ğ 135	"8x
'21x	Ĺ 136	Ľ 137	Ł 138	Ń 139	Ň 140	■ 141	Ő 142	Ŕ 143	
'22x	Ř 144	Ś 145	Š 146	Ş 147	Ť 148	Ţ 149	Ű 150	Ů 151	"9x
'23x	Ÿ 152	Ź 153	Ž 154	Ż 155	IJ 156	İ 157	đ 158	§ 159	
'24x	ă 160	ą 161	ć 162	č 163	ď 164	ě 165	ę 166	ğ 167	"Ax
'25x	ĺ 168	ľ 169	ł 170	ń 171	ň 172	■ 173	ő 174	ŕ 175	
'26x	ř 176	ś 177	š 178	ş 179	ť 180	ţ 181	ű 182	ů 183	"Bx
'27x	ÿ 184	ź 185	ž 186	ż 187	ij 188	ı 189	¿ 190	£ 191	
'30x	À 192	Á 193	Â 194	Ã 195	Ä 196	Å 197	Æ 198	Ç 199	"Cx
'31x	È 200	É 201	Ê 202	Ë 203	Ì 204	Í 205	Î 206	Ï 207	
'32x	Đ 208	Ñ 209	Ò 210	Ó 211	Ô 212	Õ 213	Ö 214	Œ 215	"Dx
'33x	Ø 216	Ù 217	Ú 218	Û 219	Ü 220	Ý 221	Þ 222	SS 223	
'34x	à 224	á 225	â 226	ã 227	ä 228	å 229	æ 230	ç 231	"Ex
'35x	è 232	é 233	ê 234	ë 235	ì 236	í 237	î 238	ï 239	
'36x	ð 240	ñ 241	ò 242	ó 243	ô 244	õ 245	ö 246	œ 247	"Fx
'37x	ø 248	ù 249	ú 250	û 251	ü 252	ý 253	þ 254	ß 255	
	"8	"9	"A	"B	"C	"D	"E	"F	

Figure 3.6 – The Zapf Chancery italic font character table

You can also use the `fonttable` package to get an impression of how the font looks in regular text. The `\fonttext` command prints some example sentences in the chosen font. Give the font name as an argument, as follows:

```
\fonttext{pzcmi7t}
```

Now, you get some regular text, where you can see the shape and appearance of the font. Apart from regular text, it also shows ligatures, umlauts, and accents, which are characters with diacritical marks. This allows you to evaluate the completeness of the character set and whether it's suitable for your purpose. This is such a piece of text:

¿But aren't Kafka's Schloß and Æsop's

Œuvres often naïve vis-à-vis the dæmonic

phœnix's official rôle in fluffy soufflés?

Figure 3.7 – Text using the Zapf Chancery font, with ligatures, umlauts, and diacritical marks

You can try the full code examples at `https://latex-cookbook.net/chapter-03`.

For more information, run `texdoc fonttable` at the command line or visit `https://texdoc.org/pkg/fonttable` to see the entire package documentation.

Importing just a single symbol of a font

There are many packages that provide symbols. You often get the new commands for additional symbols by simply loading a package, using the `\usepackage` command. However, name conflicts can exist if other packages already use the same command name. It can result in an error or silently overwriting the command.

In this recipe, we will see how to choose one or more specific symbols from a package and access them, without loading the whole package.

We will choose a binary relation symbol from the `mathabx` package. This will be a symbol for *less or equal*. Later, we will import its negation.

Getting ready

In this recipe, we need to take a look at the source code of the symbol package to imitate part of what it does, so prepare yourself:

- Locate the `mathabx.sty` file and open it. At the command prompt, the `kpsewhich mathabx.sty` command gives you the location, but you can also use your file manager to search for it.

- In `mathabx.sty`, you can see `\input mathabx.dcl`. There are symbol declarations. Open this file as well. It is in the same folder, but the `kpsewhich mathabx.dcl` command will find it.

- Type `texdoc fntguide` to open the *Guide to LaTeX2e font selection*. This is optional, but the manual can help you to understand it.

How to do it...

We will copy the required lines of code from the font package to our document. Follow the following steps:

1. From the `mathabx.sty` file, copy all the necessary font declarations to your document preamble:

```
\DeclareFontFamily{U}{matha}{\hyphenchar\font45}
\DeclareFontShape{U}{matha}{m}{n}{
    <5> <6> <7> <8> <9> <10> gen * matha
    <10.95> matha10 <12> <14.4> <17.28> <20.74>
    <24.88> matha12
    }{}
\DeclareSymbolFont{matha}{U}{matha}{m}{n}
\DeclareFontSubstitution{U}{matha}{m}{n}
```

2. From the `mathabx.dcl` file, copy all the required font declarations to your document preamble:

```
\DeclareMathSymbol{\leq}{3}{matha}{"A4}
\DeclareMathSymbol{\nleq}{3}{matha}{"A6}
```

3. Test those declarations in the document body:

```
If $A \leq B$, then $B \nleq A$.
```

4. Take a look at the output:

$$\text{If } A \leq B, \text{ then } B \nleq A.$$

Figure 3.8 – The redefined relation symbols

Compare this to the symbols in the default font without our redefinition, using the `\leq` and `\not\leq` commands for the relation symbols:

$$\text{If } A \leqslant B, \text{ then } B \nleqslant A.$$

Figure 3.9 – The default relation symbols

You can see the rationale for changing the look of such a specific symbol, regarding parallel lines, writing habits, and vertical centering.

How it works...

By simply copying and pasting, we copied the behavior of the symbol package. We chose only the relevant symbols. The commands are described in detail in the aforementioned *Guide to LaTeX2e font selection*; refer to it for more information. Here, we primarily need to copy the commands from the package source code.

We redefined the original \leq command, since we don't need to have two versions, as it's recommended to decide on only one for consistency. However, you can freely choose a name, such as the following:

```
\DeclareMathSymbol{\myleq}{3}{matha}{"A4}
```

Writing bold mathematical symbols

There are several ways to get bold mathematical symbols. LaTeX directly provides a classic method. Take a look at this code:

```
\boldmath $y=f(x)$\unboldmath
```

It works like this:

1. In text mode, we switch to bold math alphabets.

2. We enter math mode, in which bold symbols are always chosen, if available.

3. We leave math mode.

4. While in text mode, we switch the math alphabet back to normal – non-bold.

However, this makes all symbols a formula bold. This kind of emphasis is somewhat rare today, as it destroys the uniform grayness of the text from a typographer's point of view.

A more common requirement is to get bold versions of certain symbols. For example, bold symbols are often used for vectors and number systems.

In this recipe, we will take the most recommendable approach to get bold symbols.

How to do it...

We will use the bm package, as follows:

1. Load the bm package in your preamble. Do this *after* all packages, which define symbol fonts, because the package works on a higher level. If you are not sure about this, add the following line *below* all font packages:

    ```
    \usepackage{bm}
    ```

2. Declare a command for each bold symbol:

```
\bmdefine{\balpha}{\alpha}
\bmdefine{\bX}{X}
```

3. Use the new macros in your document within math mode.

How it works...

The bm package does the following for us:

- Determines the available bold math fonts and uses them if available
- Defaults to the so-called **poor man's bold** if no bold version can be found, which means overprinting with slight offsets
- Keeps the correct spacing of the symbol
- Respects the meaning of symbols, such as delimiters

As math mode was made for math symbols, the new bold symbols can only be used in that mode.

There's more...

There are alternative ways to write bold symbols. Let's take a look at some of these.

Standard LaTeX

One standard command is `\mathbf{argument}`, which prints the argument in bold. However, there are a few drawbacks:

- It switches from italics to an upright shape. So, what originally had the look of a variable now gets the appearance of an operator.
- It doesn't support many special characters – for example, `\mathbf{\alpha}` prints a regular non-bold Greek alpha letter.

AMS-LaTeX and amsmath

The amsmath bundle, specifically its amsbsy package, provides the `\boldsymbol{argument}` command, which also prints its argument in bold. It works for many more symbols, such as Greek letters. Even if there's no bold version available, you can use `\pmb{argument}`, which provides a *poor man's bold* version of the argument.

Comparing the bm and amsmath packages

This recipe recommends the bm package, which produces a look similar to what \boldsymbol from amsmath does because it takes exceptional care of meaning and spacing in math mode. For a visual comparison, let's build a formula with many bold symbols to see the effects.

Add the following example to your LaTeX editor:

```
\documentclass{article}
\usepackage{bm}
\bmdefine{\bX}{X}
\bmdefine{\bi}{i}
\bmdefine{\bMinus}{-}
\bmdefine{\bSum}{\sum}
\bmdefine{\bLeft}{(}
\bmdefine{\bRight}{)}
\begin{document}
\[ \sum_{i} ( - X_{i} ) \]
\[ \bSum_{\bi} \bLeft \bMinus \bX_{\bi} \bRight \]
\end{document}
```

Compile that example so that we can compare the regular and bold versions:

$$\sum_{i}(-X_i)$$

$$\bm{\sum_{i}(-X_i)}$$

Figure 3.10 – A comparison of regular and bold symbols

Now, we switch to the amsmath version:

```
\documentclass{article}
\usepackage{amsmath}
\newcommand{\bX}{\boldsymbol{X}}
\newcommand{\bi}{\boldsymbol{i}}
\newcommand{\bMinus}{\boldsymbol{-}}
\newcommand{\bSum}{\boldsymbol{\sum}}
\newcommand{\bLeft}{\boldsymbol{(}}
\newcommand{\bRight}{\boldsymbol{)}}
\begin{document}
\[ \sum_{i} ( - X_{i} ) \]
\[ \bSum_{\bi} \bLeft \bMinus \bX_{\bi} \bRight \]
\end{document}
```

The output is as follows:

$$\sum_i (-X_i)$$

$$\sum_i (-\boldsymbol{X}_i)$$

Figure 3.11 – A comparison of regular and bold symbols with amsmath

You can see what happened:

- The summation symbol is not bold

- The summation index has moved to another position

- The spacing between the parenthesis and the minus sign has become too wide

- The italic correction after the X is lost because the kerning is too high – that is, the index is too far right now

If you already work with the amsmath package and the \boldsymbol command, switching to the bm package is easy – simply add \usepackage{bm} after \usepackage{amsmath}. The bm package redefines the \boldsymbol command to become its own version. This way, all flaws in the previous amsmath example will immediately be fixed.

Getting sans-serif mathematics

There are situations where a sans-serif font is required for documents. It can be, for example, a requirement by a university or institute. It may even be a design decision – for example, presentation slides often use a sans-serif font. It's the default behavior of the LaTeX beamer class.

You can switch to sans-serif for the default text font family using this command:

```
\renewcommand{\familydefault}{\sfdefault}
```

In such a case, it's desirable to print math formulas in sans-serif as well to get a consistent design. The beamer class already does this.

In this recipe, we will do that for an arbitrary class. We will change all math formulas to have a sans-serif font.

How to do it...

We will use the `sfmath` package. Follow these steps to get sans-serif math formulas:

1. Load the `sfmath` package. Do it after font packages or commands that change `\sfdefault`:

    ```
    \usepackage{sfmath}
    ```

2. If you use the default font – that is, Computer Modern – additionally load the `sansmathaccent` package:

    ```
    \usepackage{sansmathaccent}
    ```

3. In your document, write math formulas as usual. For example, copy this formula from *Chapter 1, Exploring Various Document Classes*:

    ```
    \[
        \int_a^b f(x)\,\mathrm{d}x \approx (b-a)
        \sum_{i=0}^n w_i f(x_i)
    \]
    ```

4. Compile the document. Take a look at the appearance of the output:

$$\int_a^b f(x)\, dx \approx (b-a) \sum_{i=0}^n w_i f(x_i)$$

Figure 3.12 – The formula with the sans-serif math font

The math formulas are now written in sans-serif. Looking closer, you can see that the sum operator still has serifs, however.

How it works...

The `sfmath` package switches to sans-serif math for the whole document. It automatically detects the available sans-serif font. That's why loading it after any change to `\sfdefault` by another package is essential. For example, if you use Helvetica, write `\usepackage{helvet}` and then write `\usepackage{sfmath}` afterward.

There's an issue with math accents. For example, with the default Computer Modern font, math accents such as `\tilde`, `\dot`, and `\hat` may be slightly misplaced, since the Computer Modern sans-serif font doesn't provide the positioning information. The `sansmathaccent` package comes to the rescue. It corrects that behavior in the specific case of the `sfmath` package, together with the Computer Modern font. That's why we loaded that too.

There's more...

Instead of automatic font selection, you can let the `sfmath` package explicitly use a particular font using a package option:

- `cm`: This is for Computer Modern sans-serif
- `lm`: This selects Latin Modern sans-serif
- `helvet`: This is used for Helvetica
- `cmbright`: This sets the CM-Bright font
- `tx`: This chooses the `txfonts` Times font bundle with a Helvetica-like sans-serif font
- `px`: This selects the `pxfonts` Palatino font bundle, which also has a Helvetica-like sans-serif font

Using one of the following options, you can gain even more control over the font:

- `T1experimental`: This is used to get a T1 encoded math font. It is experimental and required if you use the Latin Modern font.
- `AlphT1experimental`: This is for using T1 encoding for the \mathrm, \mathbf, \mathit, and \mathsf commands.
- `mathrmOrig`, `mathbfOrig`, `mathitOrig`, and `mathsfOrig`: These are used to preserve the original behavior of the \mathrm, \mathbf, \mathit, and \mathsf commands, respectively. Otherwise, the \mathrm command would also use, for example, a sans-serif font.
- `slantedGreek`: Use this to get slanted uppercase Greek letters.

So, loading the `sfmath` package could look like this:

```
\usepackage[helvet,slantedGreek]{sfmath}
```

An alternative approach

Instead of the `sfmath` package, you can load the `sansmath` package:

```
\usepackage{sansmath}
```

Now, you can switch on sans-serif math using the `sansmath` command.

To end this setting, you can use the \unsansmath command to stop it. There's even a `sansmath` environment that switches to sans-serif math inside. So, this package provides a finer approach in a situation when you don't need consistent sans-serif math throughout the entire document.

Sans-serif fonts with direct math support

The easiest way is to switch to a sans-serif font that directly supports mathematics. Of course, this depends on whether you like that font at all. Here are two possibilities.

Arev Sans

Bitstream Vera Sans, designed as a sans-serif screen font, has been extended to include Greek, Cyrillic, and a lot of mathematical symbols. The result is the `arev` package. All you need for sans-serif math and text is to load the package:

```
\usepackage{arev}
```

The previous equation now becomes this:

$$\int_a^b f(x)\,dx \approx (b-a) \sum_{i=0}^{n} w_i f(x_i)$$

Figure 3.13 – Sans-serif math with the arev package

Where does the name **Arev** come from? Read the word backward.

Kepler fonts

We already talked about the Kepler font bundle in the first recipe of this chapter. This complete font set also supports sans-serif math. This is a complete font set that also supports sans-serif math. You can get sans-serif formulas using the following command with options:

```
\usepackage[sfmath,lighttext]{kpfonts}
```

The previous example with Kepler fonts now looks like this:

$$\int_a^b f(x)\,dx \approx (b-a) \sum_{i=0}^{n} w_i f(x_i)$$

Figure 3.14 – Sans-serif math with the Kepler fonts

Writing double-stroke letters like on a blackboard

Mathematicians need a lot of symbols for variables, constants, vectors, operators, sets, spaces, and many other objects. So, they use small and big Latin and Greek letters, calligraphic letters, or write upright, italic, or bold so that they can be distinguished from each other in the same document.

When writing on a blackboard or a whiteboard in a lecture, it's challenging to write bold letters. So, double-stroke letters were invented. A typographer may prefer these, as they don't destroy the grayness of text, in contrast to bold symbols.

How to do it...

We will use the `dsfont` package. Follow these steps to get double-stroke letters:

1. Load the `dsfont` package:

   ```
   \usepackage{dsfont}
   ```

2. In your document, use the `\mathds` command:

   ```
   \[
     \mathds{N} \subset \mathds{Z} \subset
     \mathds{Q} \subset \mathds{R} \subset \mathds{C}
   \]
   ```

3. Compile; the output will be the following:

$$\mathbb{N} \subset \mathbb{Z} \subset \mathbb{Q} \subset \mathbb{R} \subset \mathbb{C}$$

Figure 3.15 – Double-stroke letters

How it works...

The `dsfont` package provides double-stroke capital letters for the whole alphabet; lowercase letters are not supported. That's a design decision. The symbols for 1, h, and k have been added at some stage.

There's more...

There are alternative font packages – `amssymb`, `bbold`, and `bbm`. They provide similar symbols. I selected the `dsfont` package because it matches the style I know from my math studies.

Such symbols, and thousands more, can be found in the **Comprehensive LaTeX Symbol List**. You can use the `texdoc symbols` command at the command line or open it online at `https://texdoc.org/pkg/symbols`.

Enabling the searching and copying of ligatures

Sometimes, two or more consecutive characters are joined to a single glyph. This is called a **ligature**. Depending on the font, LaTeX commonly does it for ff, fi, fl, ffi, ffl, and so on. That's because font makers designed specific glyphs for certain character combinations.

While it looks fine in print and on screen, there is a caveat – if you copy text from the produced PDF file into another document, such as a text or a Word file, the ligatures may appear broken.

Another problem is searching for words containing ligatures in PDF files, which can fail, as the ligature ff differs from the letter combination ff.

We will now tackle both challenges.

How to do it...

We will stick to the commonly used pdfLaTeX. There are several possible ways to fix it. The first way is this:

1. Input the `glyphtounicode.tex` file into your document's preamble:

   ```
   \input{glyphtounicode}
   ```

2. On the next line, activate the required pdfTeX feature:

   ```
   \pdfgentounicode=1
   ```

How it works...

The `glyphtounicode.tex` file is part of pdfTeX and should already be installed on your computer. You can find it using the `kpsewhich glyphtounicode.tex` command at the command line. However, if you use the `\input` command, LaTeX will also find it. That file contains proper translations for alphabetic presentation, such as the following:

```
\pdfglyphtounicode{ff}{0066 0066}
\pdfglyphtounicode{fi}{0066 0069}
\pdfglyphtounicode{fl}{0066 006C}
\pdfglyphtounicode{ffi}{0066 0066 0069}
\pdfglyphtounicode{ffl}{0066 0066 006C}
```

By setting `\pdfgentounicode=1`, we enabled the translation.

There's more...

The `cmap` package also enables you to search for and copy characters to make PDF files. Just load it like this:

```
\usepackage{cmap}
```

The `mmap` package is an extension of the `cmap` package, which also works with math symbols. You can load it instead of `cmap`, as follows:

```
\usepackage{mmap}
```

If these methods don't work with a particular font or encoding and you still need to fix it, refer to the following recipe.

Suppressing ligatures

A ligature is a combination of several letters in a single glyph. Ligatures improve the readability and visual quality of text, and thus, we should retain them. However, there may be a reason to disable them – for example, in verbatim text, such as source code.

Furthermore, it's possible that searching or copying ligatures in a PDF file would fail, which we discussed in the previous recipe.

How to do it...

We will now see how to deactivate ligatures. We will use the `microtype` package:

1. Load the `microtype` package:

    ```
    \usepackage{microtype}
    ```

2. Disable ligatures entirely:

    ```
    \DisableLigatures{encoding = *, family = * }
    ```

3. If you would like to restrict that feature to a certain font, you can specify it instead, such as the following:

    ```
    \DisableLigatures{encoding = T1, family = tt* }
    ```

4. You can even suppress just selected ligatures using the following command. Specify the letter that starts the ligature:

    ```
    \DisableLigatures[f]{encoding = *, family = * }
    ```

How it works...

Suppressing ligatures is one of the many features of the `microtype` package. You can switch off some or all the ligatures using the aforementioned interface. However, be aware that the text may not look so nice anymore. Even the kerning of the font is disabled.

Besides the well-known letter ligatures, LaTeX knows a lot more, such as double quote marks, guillemots, and wide dashes, done by -- and ---. So, it can be a good idea not to turn off all ligatures. When all are turned off, there are still commands to write those ligatures, such as \textendash and \textemdash for the wide dashes.

Adding a contour

When text is printed over a background, it is much more with a contour present to overprint the background. This contour may be white. This way, there would be a nice clearance around the text.

Another utilization would be to improve the visibility of text with very light colors for better reading on a white background.

Let's see how to achieve that.

How to do it...

Our example will use the color yellow for chapter headings in a book. This is hardly readable, so we will add a black contour to improve the readability:

1. We will use the `scrbook` class, which supports chapter headings, so start your document with the following:

    ```
    \documentclass{scrbook}
    ```

2. Load the `contour` package. Use the `outline` option to print a real outline; otherwise, copies of the original text will be used to create a contour. Specify the thickness of the contour as a length, as follows:

    ```
    \usepackage[outline]{contour}
    \contourlength{1.5pt}
    ```

3. Define a macro for the new chapter font style of our chapter headings:

    ```
    \newcommand{\chapterfont}[1]{%
      \protect\contour{black}{\textcolor{yellow}{#1}}}
    ```

4. Apply that style to the chapter headings:

    ```
    \setkomafont{chapter}{\Huge\chapterfont}
    ```

5. Now, your chapter headings will be yellow with a black contour. You can verify this by completing the code in a small compilable document. Add the following to your document:

    ```
    \begin{document}
    \chapter{Introduction}
    Text follows.
    \end{document}
    ```

6.   Compile, and take a look at the output:

1   Introduction

Text follows.

Figure 3.16 – Characters with a contour around them

How it works...

The `contour` package creates a contour by placing copies of the text around it. The thickness of this contour can be specified as seen in the preceding figure.

The `\setkomafont` command can use a macro at the end, which takes an argument. In this case, this will be the heading text handed over to our newly defined macro.

A vector font is required, which is recommendable in any case. This should be a so-called **Type 1 font**. With pdfLaTeX, **TrueType** fonts are supported too.

If your engine supports it, you can even let contour generate a real outline of the text instead of using copies, which should result in better quality. For example, with pdfTeX, you can add package options to enable it, as follows:

```
\usepackage[pdftex,outline]{contour}
```

Without those two options, the contour package would auto-detect the engine and create the contour, by printing text copies behind the original text.

See also

With **XeLaTeX** and **LuaLaTeX**, you can use even system fonts such as **TrueType** fonts and feature-rich **OpenType** fonts. That's LaTeX based on the new engines called **XeTeX** and **LuaTeX**.

The TeX User Group has a good page to start with XeLaTeX: `https://www.tug.org/xetex/`.

LuaLaTeX is a good choice for additional programming features, since it adds the **Lua** programming language. You can read more about it at `https://www.luatex.org`.

4
Creating Tables

In this chapter, you will find recipes for crafting aesthetically pleasing tables. Specifically, this chapter covers the following topics:

- Designing a legible table
- Positioning tables
- Merging cells
- Splitting a cell diagonally
- Adding footnotes to a table
- Aligning numeric data
- Coloring a table
- Importing data from an external file

With LaTeX, we can create and print complex tables. In this chapter, we will first focus on achieving good readability. We will then continue to explore helpful design elements.

We assume you know the basics of tabular environments from an introduction to LaTeX such as *LaTeX Beginner's Guide, Second Edition, Packt Publishing, Chapter 6, Creating Tables*. You can find the code examples of that chapter online at `https://latexguide.org/chapter-06`.

While the recipes are based on standard LaTeX `tabular` environments, you can use them similarly with `tabular*`, `tabularx`, `tabulary`, and related environments. Let's have a brief look at them:

- The `tabular*` environment, a standard LaTeX environment, achieves a desired table width by adjusting the spacing between columns. The table width is given as an additional argument to the environment. The syntax and usage are explained here: `https://latex2e.org/tabular.html`.

- The `tabularx` environment comes from the package with the same name. It also spans the table to a given width. It's probably the most popular and highly recommendable tool for this purpose. In contrast to the `tabular*` environment, which adjusts inter-column space, it achieves that by automatically calculating column widths, trying to distribute the available space evenly. Read more about it using `texdoc tabularx` at the command line or access it online at `https://texdoc.org/pkg/tabularx`.

- The `tabulary` environment from the `tabulary` package also balances column widths but tries to give more space to columns that have more content. This sophisticated approach introduces new column types with a width proportional to the width of the most extended entry in each column. You can consult the manual using `texdoc tabulary` or find it online at `https://texdoc.org/pkg/tabulary`.

- The `array` environment works similarly to the `tabular` environment but is designed for use in math mode.

Now, let's look at good table design.

Designing a legible table

When we learn how to write tables with LaTeX, we learn how to write in rows and columns and draw lines between cells and borders around the table. However, indiscriminately applying borders can result in a table that looks like the following one:

*	1	2	3
1	1	2	3
2	2	4	6
3	3	6	9

Figure 4.1 – A table with vertical and horizontal lines

Such a habit may arise from using **WYSIWYG** (which stands for **What You See Is What You Get**) software such as Excel or Word to write tables. However, while such a grid helps enter data, reading is challenging.

Well-crafted books feature more legible tables. Let's take a look at how to create a reader-friendly table.

How to do it...

We will use the `booktabs` package, written with an emphasis on good design. In particular, it enhances the lines within tables. It pays specific attention to horizontal lines with improved spacing and adjustable thickness.

For our example, we will sketch a table displaying the availability of certain structuring features in LaTeX's base classes. Here's how to do this:

1. Specify the class. You could use the `article` class for now:

   ```
   \documentclass{article}
   ```

2. Load the `booktabs` package:

   ```
   \usepackage{booktabs}
   ```

3. Load the `bbding` package, which provides a checkmark symbol:

   ```
   \usepackage{bbding}
   ```

4. Set up a `table` environment within the document body and create the `tabular` layout. For convenience, here's the complete remaining code to copy:

   ```
   \begin{document}
   \begin{table}
     \centering
     \renewcommand{\arraystretch}{1.6}
     \begin{tabular}{lccccc}
       \toprule
       Class   & Part page  & Chapters   & Abstract   &
                           Front-/Backmatter & Appendix name
       \\
       \cmidrule(r){1-1}\cmidrule(lr){2-2}
       \cmidrule(lr){3-3}\cmidrule(lr){4-4}
       \cmidrule(lr){5-5}\cmidrule(l){6-6}
       article &            &            & \Checkmark \\
       book    & \Checkmark & \Checkmark &            &
                 \Checkmark & \Checkmark                 \\
       report  & \Checkmark & \Checkmark & \Checkmark &
                 & \Checkmark                 \\
       \bottomrule
     \end{tabular}
     \caption{Structuring differences between standard
               \LaTeX\ classes}
     \label{comparison}
   \end{table}
   \end{document}
   ```

5.   Compile the document and review the outcome:

Class	Part page	Chapters	Abstract	Front-/Backmatter	Appendix name
article			✓		
book	✓	✓		✓	✓
report	✓	✓	✓		✓

Table 1: Structuring differences between standard LaTeX classes

Figure 4.2 – A table with only horizontal lines

How it works...

We used a `table` environment to generate a table with a caption. This is the standard container for producing tables with captions that can also be referenced. The `table` and `tabular` environments are explained in introductions to LaTeX such as *LaTeX Beginner's Guide*. Please consult such a book to learn the basics if needed.

Now, let's focus on the actual structure and the line improvements. In a nutshell, an ampersand symbol (&) ends a column, and a double backslash (\\) completes a row.

While you can end a row at any time using \\, it's good practice to use all column separators (&), even if the cells are empty. It makes inserting values in cells easier and helps align subsequent rows and their respective columns.

Ending a line in the source code after \\ is also a good idea. Additionally, align ampersands, if possible, as this enhances code readability and makes filling the correct columns easier. Remember that several consecutive spaces are treated as one, so additional spacing won't negatively impact your document's appearance.

The `booktabs` package provides commands for horizontal lines, also called **rules**. This term originates from the British typesetting tradition. The key distinctions between the `booktabs` package and standard LaTeX `tabular` lines are the following:

- There is more space above and below a line by default
- There are several kinds of rules with customizable thickness

In particular, the commands are as follows:

- `\toprule`: This command is used for a thick line at the top by default

- `\midrule`: This command prints a line within the table, which is by default thinner than a top or bottom line

- `\bottomrule`: This command prints a line at the bottom of the table, having the same thickness as the top line by default

- `\cmidrule`: This command is used for a line spanning over one, two, or more columns and has the same thickness as the `\midrule` command

The last command has a more intricate syntax, as follows:

```
\cmidrule[thickness](trim){a-b}
```

The `thickness` argument is optional and can specify your desired thickness, such as `1pt`.

The `trim` argument is also optional and lets you specify horizontal trimming: `r` for right and `l` for left. Both can be combined, as we did in the preceding example.

The mandatory `a-b` argument defines that the line will span from column a to column b.

All commands understand an optional argument for thickness; for instance, you could also write the `\toprule[1pt]` command to generate a top line with a width of 1 pt.

While the fundamental use can be seen in our example, the package manual explains more options for tweaking, such as changing the default thickness for each kind of rule and adjusting trimming. You can read the manual by running `texdoc booktabs` at the command line or visiting `https://texdoc.org/pkg/booktabs`.

There's more...

In addition to using excellent tools such as the `booktabs` package, well-considered design is the key to great tables. So, let's sum up valuable advice given by typographers:

- Respect the reading direction. This means you should always design with the following principles in mind:

  - Write text horizontally

  - Never use vertical lines

  - A few horizontal lines can support reading in the structure, such as below the header or between groups of content

These rules can be changed for tables when columns are expected to be read from top to bottom.

If you create a very wide table and choose to print it rotated by 90 degrees, such as by using the `sidewaystable` environment from the `rotating` package, you have a new reading direction, and text and lines should follow it as indicated in the preceding instructions.

- Minimize what doesn't belong to the information, such as lines, dividers, boxes, colors, and font changes. Consequently, don't use double lines.

- Leave white space around the table. Then, you may not need top and bottom lines.

Generally, white space gives invisible support to the structure, so we increased the default `\arraystretch` value of 1 to 1.6. In the upcoming recipe, the impact of structuring with white space becomes even more apparent.

Here's some final advice for optimizing the table layout:

- Align text for optimal readability

- Align decimal values at the decimal point for easier comparison

- Instead of repeatedly using units within individual cells, place the unit in the column header

- Instead of repeating values, consider merging neighboring cells

The recipes later in this chapter will support us regarding these points.

Finally, let's look at the positioning of the caption. Traditionally, captions for figures are positioned below the figure, so you first see the visual content and then receive an explanation and additional context. Standard LaTeX treats tables in the same fashion.

However, as tables can often contain complex and data-rich content, consider placing the caption before the table. This allows you to explain the content and context, so the reader understands it before studying the data within the table. That's a widely followed convention. Take a look at the TeX FAQ at `https://texfaq.org/FAQ-destable` to learn about table design with captions at the top. We will do this in the *Adding footnotes to a table* recipe later in this chapter, so you also have a proper example.

Positioning tables

Tables can get quite big. If there's insufficient free space on a page to accommodate the table, that table will be pushed to the next page. This would leave white space at the end of the page. You could manually move some text to compensate. But imagine having a large document with many tables; manually moving images to balance page breaks can become cumbersome. Fortunately, LaTeX offers an automated solution for managing this.

How to do it...

This is the standard way of including tables:

1. Use a `table` environment.

2. Center the content, if desired, using the `\centering` command.

3. Write a caption.

4. Add a label for cross-referencing.

5. Write the table content using a `tabular` environment.

A typical code sequence looks like this:

```
\begin{table}[htbp!]
   \centering
   \caption{A description}
   \label{tab:name}
   \begin{tabular}{...}
      ...
   \end{tabular}
\end{table}
```

You can reference the table number in your document using the `\label{tab:name}` command.

How it works...

That automatic process is known as **floating**. This principle applies to `table` and `figure` environments when you include images, which we'll discuss in the following chapter. When you use a `table` environment, its content can float within the text to find the next available location while allowing the text to occupy the page space optimally. For instance, if a page runs out of space, a table can move to the top of the following page. Text, which comes after the table in the document code, would be repositioned before the table or figure to fill the page. This might seem a bit perplexing initially, but it ultimately aids in optimizing page breaks.

In case you find that a table has moved too far away from its intended location, you can add placement options. We used the `htbp!` option in the preceding code. These characters allow placement *here* (if space allows), *top*, *bottom*, or on a dedicated *page*. The exclamation mark relaxes some default typographical constraints to ensure tables don't float too far ahead. All options together cause the table's output to be as close as possible to the position in the code. Omit an option to disallow certain places. For example, without the b option, a table would not float to the bottom but may float to the top of a page.

The \caption command at the beginning sets text above the table and gives it a number. If you use the \label command for cross-referencing, ensure it comes after the \caption command to obtain the correct number. The tab: prefix has been used because it's a good practice in code writing to indicate types of cross-references, such as fig: for figures and eq: for equations.

There's more...

If the automated positioning of tables or figures isn't the best fit for your document, there are methods to restrict or temporarily deactivate it. We will look at these options now.

Limiting floating

Floating tables and figures don't cross chapter borders. However, they may go to a later section within the same chapter. If you would like to limit the floating behavior so tables and figures remain within the same section, load the placeins package in your preamble with the section option:

```
\usepackage[section]{placeins}
```

You can also load the placeins package without the option. It gives you the new \FloatBarrier command, which you can use to prevent floating beyond this point.

> **Note**
> The \clearpage command ends a page and forces the output of all floating tables and figures that still need to be placed.

Fixing the position of a table or figure

Sometimes, tables or figures should stay at a certain position. Disabling floating is straightforward: don't use a table or figure environment. However, if you would like to use the same syntax as the preceding, just without floating, you can achieve it using the float package. Add the following command to your document preamble:

```
\usepackage{float}
```

Then, start a table environment with the H option:

```
\begin{table}[H]
```

Merging cells

As suggested in the table design advice in the first recipe of this chapter, instead of duplicating identical values in adjacent cells, you can leave the other cells empty if it's evident to the reader that the same values apply.

We can support the meaning by merging cells and centering the cell value over the new width or height.

How to do it...

Merging and centering can be done horizontally, vertically, or both combined. We will start with the horizontal method, spanning cells over multiple columns. This is often used for table headers that apply to several columns. So, in this recipe, we will combine header texts.

As modeling clay, we will take the differences between various LaTeX compilers. While the LaTeX format remains the same, the underlying TeX engine causes differences. We will arrange them now. Follow these steps:

1. Specify the class; you could use the `article` class for now:

    ```
    \documentclass{article}
    ```

2. Load the `array` package, which provides useful commands:

    ```
    \usepackage{array}
    ```

3.   Load the `booktabs` package to get nicer lines:

    ```
    \usepackage{booktabs}
    ```

4. Load the `metalogo` package to write TeX logos:

    ```
    \usepackage{metalogo}
    ```

5. Define how you would like to stretch the table row spacing:

    ```
    \renewcommand{\arraystretch}{1.6}
    ```

6. To get the table, copy the following code into your editor; an explanation follows. For completeness, this is the whole remaining document body:

    ```
    \begin{document}
    \begin{tabular}{@{}p{1.5cm}p{1.6cm}
                    >{\raggedleft}p{1cm}
                    >{\raggedright}p{1.6cm}r@{}}
        Compiler & \multicolumn{2}{c}{Input}
                 & \multicolumn{2}{c}{Output} \\
        \cmidrule(r){1-1}\cmidrule(lr){2-3}
        \cmidrule(l){4-5}
                 & Encoding & Images  & Fonts & Format \\
        \cmidrule(lr){2-2}\cmidrule(lr){3-3}
        \cmidrule(lr){4-4}\cmidrule(l){5-5}
        \LaTeX & utf8, ascii, applemac, latin1, \ldots
    ```

```
      & EPS & Type 1, Type 3 & DVI \\
   pdf\LaTeX & utf8, ascii, applemac, latin1, \ldots
      & PDF PNG JPG & Type 1, Type 3 & PDF \\
   \XeLaTeX, \LuaLaTeX & utf8 & PDF PNG JPG & Type 1,
         Type 3, OpenType, Graphite, TrueType & PDF\\
\end{tabular}
\end{document}
```

7. Compile the document and take a look at the output:

Compiler	Input		Output	
	Encoding	Images	Fonts	Format
LaTeX	utf8, ascii, applemac, latin1, ...	EPS	Type 1, Type 3	DVI
pdfLaTeX	utf8, ascii, applemac, latin1, ...	PDF PNG JPG	Type 1, Type 3	PDF
XeLaTeX, LuaLaTeX	utf8	PDF PNG JPG	Type 1, Type 3, Open-Type, Graphite, TrueType	PDF

Figure 4.3 – A table with merged header cells

How it works...

We will take a minute to look at the `tabular` column specifier options:

*   `@{code}`: This option inserts the given code instead of the column separation space. The code can be a command, such as a symbol or a space macro. Here, we set it to be empty, thus achieving left alignment with the lines.

*   `p{width}`: This option specifies that cells have a specific width and have line breaks. The p stands for paragraph.

- >{code}: This option inserts code before a cell of the column, while <{code} does it afterward. This comes from the array package and is documented in the manual. Here, we use it to insert the \raggedleft command to avoid the default full justification. Full justification isn't so nice in table cells because, in narrow columns, it could lead to excessive space between words that are hard to hyphenate.

- r, l, and c: These options stand for right-aligned, left-aligned, and centered, respectively.

Now, look at the Input cell, which spans over two columns. We used the following command:

```
\multicolumn{number of columns}{formatting}{text}
```

Here, we set 2 as the number of columns to span, c for centered formatting, and finally, the cell text follows.

> **Note**
>
> In addition to cell merging, the \multicolumn command is an easy way to alter the formatting of a single cell. The \multicolumn{1}{formatting}{text} command defines the formatting of a single cell independently of the table's global column formatting.

We used very few lines for this table to convey its structure, which is nevertheless clearly visible thanks to the spacing.

There's more...

As mentioned, we can also span cells over multiple rows. When dealing with an odd number of rows to span, we could simply fill the row in the middle. So, let's look at a case where we need centering by merging.

Compile this short example showing selected classes of major LaTeX bundles:

```
\documentclass{article}
\usepackage{booktabs}
\usepackage{multirow}
\begin{document}
\begin{tabular}{cc}
  Bundle & Main classes \\
  \cmidrule(lr){1-1}\cmidrule(lr){2-2}
  \addlinespace
  \multirow{4}{*}{\LaTeX\ base} & article  \\
        & book      \\
        & report    \\
        & letter    \\
  \addlinespace
```

```
    \multirow{4}{*}{KOMA-Script}  & scrartcl \\
        & scrbook  \\
        & scrreprt \\
        & scrlttr2 \\
    \end{tabular}
    \end{document}
```

This code will produce the following table:

Bundle	Main classes
LaTeX base	article book report letter
KOMA-Script	scrartcl scrbook scrreprt scrlttr2

Figure 4.4 – A table with vertically merged cells

We loaded the multirow package and used this command:

```
\multirow{number of rows}[struts]{width}[correction
    value]{text}
```

Here, the number of rows argument may even be negative, in which case the spanning would reach backward. The optional correction value argument can be a positive or negative LaTeX length added for fine-tuning.

The other optional struts argument is only interesting if you insert so-called \bigstrut commands. A **strut** is an invisible vertical rule matching the full height of a line of text; see also https://latex2e.org/_005cstrut.html. A big strut shall match a table row height, including the \hline space. Here, you may specify their number. If you want to explore this, please consult the multirow manual, in the *Using bigstrut* section. Open it via texdoc multirow at the command line or find it at https://texdoc.org/pkg/multirow.

While you can define a width value for the text, we wrote * to use the natural text width of the cells' text.

Splitting a cell diagonally

If we need a header for the first column but also for the entries of the first row, the top-left cell can be split to contain both header entries, separated by a diagonal line.

How to do it...

We will use the `slashbox` package. It is part of **MiKTeX** but not part of **TeX Live**. Users of TeX Live can download it from **CTAN** at `https://ctan.org/pkg/slashbox`.

In this recipe, we will build a timetable. It's intended to be filled out by hand later, so we use vertical lines for delimiting fields. Follow these steps:

1. Use any document class; here, we use the `article` class:

    ```
    \documentclass{article}
    ```

2. Load the `slashbox` package:

    ```
    \usepackage{slashbox}
    ```

3. Within the document body, create the `tabular` layout:

    ```
    \begin{document}
    \renewcommand{\arraystretch}{1.8}
    \begin{tabular}{|l|c|c|c|c|c|}
        \hline
        \backslashbox{Time}{Weekday} & Monday    & Tuesday
                        & Wednesday    & Thursday & Friday \\
        \hline
        8--10   & & & & & \\
        10--12  & & & & & \\
        12--14  & & & & & \\
        14--16  & & & & & \\
        \hline
    \end{tabular}
    \end{document}
    ```

4. Compile and take a look:

Time \ Weekday	Monday	Tuesday	Wednesday	Thursday	Friday
8–10					
10–12					
12–14					
14–16					

Figure 4.5 – A diagonally split header cell

How it works...

We used vertical lines because the table should be read by day, that is, by column. The `slashbox` package provides these two commands:

- `\slashbox[width][trim]{left top text}{right bottom text}`
- `\backslashbox[width][trim]{left bottom text}{right top text}`

The optional arguments are for adjusting when the automatic calculation doesn't fit your needs. You can specify the width of the slashed column. You can choose trimming of the default left and right column separation space by stating `l`, `r`, or `lr` for left trim, right trim, or cutting at both sides, respectively.

The diagonal line can run from the upper-left to the lower-right corner, like a backslash, or from the lower-left to the upper-right corner, like a slash symbol.

Adding footnotes to a table

It's advisable to keep entries concise in tables, especially row header text; otherwise, the table is more complicated to read. For example, long headers could make it harder for our eyes to follow a row with short entries but wide spaces. One approach to adding necessary details while keeping the table short and crisp is using footnotes.

Rather than placing the notes at the foot of the page, adding them directly at the foot of the table is a good idea. We also call them **table notes**. These are some reasons for and benefits of this approach:

- Tables are usually self-contained objects for reference.
- While commonly footnotes are written at the bottom of the page to retain the text flow, it's enough to move a table note below the table so as not to disturb the table content. There's no need to push notes further down to the bottom of the page.
- Tables can be repositioned to achieve better page breaks; in such cases, their notes should remain together with that table.
- Table notes can be independent of text footnotes. This saves headaches about keeping footnote numbering in order.

Footnotes in `minipage` environments already work this way, so you could wrap your table in a `minipage` environment as a first possibility. In this recipe, we will take a more sophisticated approach.

How to do it...

Let's first quickly look at the caption. We placed it above the table so the reader knows what data comes next. We used the `tablecaptionabove` option of the `scrartcl` class to get proper caption spacing. That's because conventional LaTeX caption spacing is designed for captions below a table, not above it. Take a look at `https://texfaq.org/FAQ-destable` for information and alternative ways.

We are using the `threeparttable` package, which can generate footnotes below tables with the same width as the table body. With a normal `tabular` or related environment, which may be inside a `table` environment, take the following steps:

1. Load the `threeparttable` package in your document preamble:

   ```
   \usepackage{threeparttable}
   ```

2. Surround your original `tabular` environment with a `threeparttable` environment. In other words, place the `\begin{threeparttable}` command before the `tabular` environment and put the `\end{threeparttable}` command after the `tabular` environment.

3. Within a table cell, add table notes using the `\tnote{symbol}` command, where the `symbol` argument is mandatory and can be any number, letter, or symbol you choose. Here's an example:

   ```
   … & cell text\tnote{1} & …
   ```

4. Right before the end of the `threeparttable` environment, which means right before the `\end{threeparttable}` command, insert a `tablenotes` environment. There, insert your footnotes in the form of a list:

   ```
   \begin{tablenotes}
     \item[1] Your first remark
     \item[2] Another remark
   \end{tablenotes}
   ```

Let's apply this to the first recipe of this chapter, as follows:

1. Take the full recipe code and insert commands as described in the preceding steps. For our example, we will add three notes. We will use the `scrartcl` class together with the `tablecaptionabove` option because we place the caption above the table. The code now becomes the following:

   ```
   \documentclass[tablecaptionabove]{scrartcl}
   \usepackage{booktabs}
   \usepackage{bbding}
   \usepackage{threeparttable}
   \begin{document}
   \begin{table}
   ```

```
\centering
\renewcommand{\arraystretch}{1.6}
 \caption{Structuring differences between standard
        \LaTeX\ classes}
\label{comparison}
\begin{threeparttable}
  \begin{tabular}{lccccc}
    \toprule
    Class   & Part page  & Chapters
      & Abstract\tnote{1}
      & Front-/Backmatter\tnote{2}
      & Appendix name\tnote{3} \\
    \cmidrule(r){1-1}\cmidrule(lr){2-2}
    \cmidrule(lr){3-3}\cmidrule(lr){4-4}
    \cmidrule(lr){5-5}\cmidrule(l){6-6}
    article &               &                & \Checkmark\\
    book    & \Checkmark & \Checkmark &               &
             \Checkmark & \Checkmark                \\
    report  & \Checkmark & \Checkmark & \Checkmark &
                        & \Checkmark                \\
    \bottomrule
  \end{tabular}
  \begin{tablenotes}
    \item[1] An environment: \verb|\begin{abstract}|
            \ldots \verb|\end{abstract}|
    \item[2] Commands: \verb|\frontmatter|,
            \verb|\mainmatter|, \verb|\backmatter|
    \item[3] The \verb|article| class provides the
            \verb|\appendix| command without
            ``Appendix'' prefix.
  \end{tablenotes}
\end{threeparttable}
\end{table}
\end{document}
```

2. Compile that code and examine the changes:

Table 1: Structuring differences between standard LaTeX classes

Class	Part page	Chapters	Abstract[1]	Front-/Backmatter[2]	Appendix name[3]
article			✓		
book	✓	✓		✓	✓
report	✓	✓	✓		✓

[1] An environment: \begin{abstract} ... \end{abstract}
[2] Commands: \frontmatter, \mainmatter, \backmatter
[3] The article class provides the \appendix command without "Appendix" prefix.

Figure 4.6 – Table notes

How it works...

In contrast to the conventional \footnote command, using the threeparttable package requires additional manual effort. We need to do the following:

- Choose symbols or numbers
- Take care of the numbering order ourselves
- Write the list of notes manually with the correct symbol or number

Like a tabular environment, a threeparttable environment takes an optional argument for vertical placement, which can be t for top, b for bottom, or c for centered alignment. Top alignment is the default. That environment doesn't float. However, you can put the threeparttable environment into a table environment as usual, with a caption and a label for referencing so that it can float.

The behavior of threeparttable notes can be customized by options. They can be globally given to the \usepackage command or locally applied to a tablenotes environment. These are as follows:

- para: Table notes will subsequently be printed without line breaks in between
- flushleft: There will be no hanging indentation for table notes
- online: Instead of superscript, table note symbols will be printed by the \item command in standard size at the line base
- normal: This is the default formatting, which means superscript symbols, hanging indentation, and line breaks between table notes

Further commands for fine-tuning are provided and are described in the package manual. You can open it by typing `texdoc threeparttable` at the command line or on the internet at `https://texdoc.org/pkg/threeparttable`.

Aligning numerical data

Standard alignment options in table columns are left, right, and centered. However, we may need more precise alignment options when dealing with numerical values. The most effective way to compare number magnitudes is by aligning digits at specific positions, such as decimal points. Integers can simply be right aligned. Numbers with decimal fractions could be filled up with zeroes to get decimal points aligned, but that would add vacuous noise. Adding zeroes also could lead to a wrong impression of accuracy.

In the case of fractions, it's good to align at the decimal points directly. In this recipe, we will implement this.

How to do it...

The `siunitx` package is primarily intended for typesetting values with units consistently. It provides a `tabular` column type for aligning at decimal points as an additional benefit. We will use this now as follows:

1. Load the `siunitx` package in your preamble:

   ```
   \usepackage{siunitx}
   ```

2. Use `S` as the column specifier for a column with alignment at decimal points like this:

   ```
   \begin{tabular}{lSS}
   ```

3. Within a table cell, simply write the number. For good legibility, insert some spaces in the source code to get decimal points aligned. Repeating space characters doesn't hurt, though it's not required.

4. To avoid this special alignment, such as in the case of row headers, enclose the cell text in curly braces, like this:

   ```
   ... & {atomic mass} & ...
   ```

Let's try it with a concise but complete example. We will use the siunitx package described just now, as well as the chemformula package. The chemformula package makes typing chemical formulas easier. We will see more of this package in *Chapter 11, Using LaTeX in Science and Technology*. Follow these steps:

1. Put this code into your LaTeX editor:

```
\documentclass{article}
\usepackage{booktabs}
\usepackage{siunitx}
\usepackage{chemformula}
\begin{document}
  \begin{tabular}{lSS}
    \toprule
              & {atomic mass} & {total mass} \\
    \midrule
    \ch{C}    &    12.011     & 12.011       \\
    \ch{H}    &    1.00794    & 6.04764      \\
    \ch{C2H6} &               & 30.06964     \\
    \bottomrule
  \end{tabular}
\end{document}
```

2. Compile that example and take a look at the outcome:

	atomic mass	total mass
C	12.011	12.011
H	1.007 94	6.047 64
C_2H_6		30.069 64

Figure 4.7 – A table with values aligned at the decimal point

How it works...

By default, an S column places the numbers so that the decimal points are in the center of the cell and horizontally aligned to each other.

You can customize the alignment of numbers in an S column. Proper alignment implies reserving space for the numbers. You can specify the number of integers, decimal places, and alignment type by using the \sisetup command of the siunitx package, as follows:

```
\sisetup{table-format = 2.5,
    table-number-alignment = right}
```

Here, the table-format parameter will be parsed so that the siunitx package knows we reserve space for two integer figures and five decimal places.

The format string can be even more sophisticated. Look at this string:

```
table-format = +2.5e+2
```

It additionally reserves space for an exponent with two decimals, an exponent sign, and a mantissa sign. This is useful for numbers such as -22.31442 x 10^{-10}.

The package manual describes further options. It is worth reading since the siunitx package is an excellent choice when you need to print numbers with units. You can read the manual by typing texdoc siunitx at the command line or at https://texdoc.org/pkg/siunitx.

We will meet this package again in *Chapter 11, Using LaTeX in Science and Technology*.

There's more...

Further packages can be used for the same purpose, namely dcolumn and rccol. Both provide tabular column types for the proper alignment of numbers. They are the classics, but siunitx is a capable, innovative, and very actively maintained package that even impelled LaTeX3 development, so you can safely use it for future work.

Coloring a table

Sometimes, we see **zebra-striped** tables with alternating row colors. This design is intended for supporting horizontal reading without the need for separating lines.

While some people like that design, some find it harder to read. For example, while looking at a table, the eye may scan one color first and then jump back, scanning the rows with the other color. So, when we decide to go for this design, we should consider the following:

- Make the color variation small to prevent the eye from jumping across even or odd rows. The information should be visually stronger than the distinction between those two layers.

- Keep a good contrast between color and text. For example, black text with a dark gray background is hardly readable.

- Have a different color for the header to emphasize it.

How to do it...

We will use the `xcolor` package for this task. The sample data for this table, which we will also use in later recipes, has been taken from `https://distrowatch.com`. It measures the interest in Linux distributions based on page hits over a year in 2023.

Let's work on an example as follows:

1. Start with a document class:

    ```
    \documentclass{article}
    ```

2. Load the `xcolor` package with the `tables` option for table support:

    ```
    \usepackage[table]{xcolor}
    ```

3. Declare alternating row colors:

    ```
    \rowcolors{2}{gray!30}{white}
    ```

4. Define a macro for the table header appearance:

    ```
    \newcommand{\head}[1]{%
      \textcolor{white}{\textbf{#1}}}
    ```

5. Enlarge the default `tabular` line spacing:

    ```
    \renewcommand{\arraystretch}{1.5}
    ```

6. In the actual `tabular` environment, use the `\rowcolor{color}` command to color any row and the `\head{text}` command for cells with header commands. Here is the code for the table within the remaining document body:

    ```
    \begin{document}
    \begin{table}
      \centering
      \sffamily
      \begin{tabular}{rlr}
        \rowcolor{black!75}
            & \head{Distribution} & \head{Hits} \\
         1 & MX Linux     & 2717 \\
         2 & Mint         & 2097 \\
         3 & EndeavourOS  & 2055 \\
         4 & Manjaro      & 1382 \\
         5 & Debian       & 1316 \\
         6 & Ubuntu       & 1083 \\
         7 & Pop! OS      & 1063 \\
         8 & Fedora       & 1056 \\
    ```

```
      9 & openSUSE      & 748   \\
     10 & Lite          & 685
   \end{tabular}
\end{table}
\end{document}
```

	Distribution	**Hits**
1	MX Linux	2717
2	Mint	2097
3	EndeavourOS	2055
4	Manjaro	1382
5	Debian	1316
6	Ubuntu	1083
7	Pop! OS	1063
8	Fedora	1056
9	openSUSE	748
10	Lite	685

Figure 4.8 – A zebra-striped table

How it works...

The `xcolor` package implicitly loads the `colortbl` package, the standard package for coloring tables. The `colortbl` package provides three main commands:

- `\columncolor[color model]{color name}[left overhang][right overhang]`: This command has an optional `xcolor` model argument, which can be `rgb` or `cmyk`. The mandatory `color name` argument can be any color name supported by the `xcolor` package. The remaining two optional arguments define the overlap to the left and the right. Only the color name is mandatory. The `\columncolor` command is intended for placing within tabular column definitions by the `>{...}` syntax.

- `\rowcolor`: This command has the same arguments. The command has to be at the beginning of the first cell in the row and is valid for the entire row.

- `\cellcolor[color model]{color name}`: This command colors a single cell.

Using these commands, you can color tables in any way you want.

The xcolor package provides another useful command, which we used in our example:

```
\rowcolors[commands]{start row number}{odd-row}{even-row}
```

This command colors odd and even rows with alternating colors, starting from a given row number. Optionally, you can supply commands executed at each row. Examples of such commands are \hline and \noalign{...}.

In our example, we used just one \rowcolor command for the header and one \rowcolors command for the remaining rows. We used white for the text color for better readability within a header row with a darker color. Alternatively, with the black text color, you could choose a color that keeps the text readable, such as with the \rowcolor{gray} command.

Both the colortbl and xcolor package manuals explain further commands and details, accessible via texdoc, at https://texdoc.org/pkg/xcolor and https://texdoc.org/pkg/colortbl, respectively.

Importing data from an external file

It can be convenient to fetch the data for the row entries from an external file. This is particularly useful for large datasets, especially when the data originates from an external data source or application, such as an Excel spreadsheet. Such applications often provide an export feature, particularly exporting to a **Comma-Separated Values (CSV)** file. Such files have plain text format with a simple tabular structure, with each line representing a table row and commas separating the cells.

Only a few lines are needed to import such a CSV file into a LaTeX table.

How to do it...

We will load the datatool package, let it import data from a comma-separated file, sort it, and print it. Follow these steps:

1. Store your data in the same folder as your main tex document. Here, we will use the data from the previous recipe, stored in a file named linux.csv:

    ```
    Distribution,Hits
    MX Linux,2717
    Mint,2097
    EndeavourOS,2055
    Manjaro,1382
    Debian,1316
    Ubuntu,1083
    Pop! OS,1063
    ```

```
Fedora,1056
openSUSE,748
Lite,685
```

2. Start with a document class, such as the `article` class, and load the `booktabs` package for improved `tabular` layout and the `datatool` package for data handling:

```
\documentclass{article}
\usepackage{booktabs}
\usepackage{datatool}
```

3. With the following `datatool` commands, load the data from the file and sort it:

```
\DTLloaddb{Linux}{linux.csv}
\DTLsort{Hits=descending}{Linux}
```

4. Start the document and set up a `tabular` environment:

```
\begin{document}
\begin{tabular}{rlr}
  & Distribution & Hits \\
  \cmidrule(lr){2-2}\cmidrule(lr){3-3}
```

5. Use this command to iterate through the data, building `tabular` rows:

```
\DTLforeach{Linux}{%
   \distribution=Distribution, \hits=Hits}{%
      \theDTLrowi & \distribution & \hits \\}
```

6. End the `tabular` environment and the document:

```
\end{tabular}
\end{document}
```

7. Compile and take a look at the output:

	Distribution	Hits
1	MX Linux	2717
2	Mint	2097
3	EndeavourOS	2055
4	Manjaro	1382
5	Debian	1316
6	Ubuntu	1083
7	Pop! OS	1063
8	Fedora	1056
9	openSUSE	748
10	Lite	685

Figure 4.9 – Displaying imported data

How it works...

The `datatool` package is a powerful tool for working with external data. Here, we read in a file, sorted it by a chosen key, and printed it.

Let's review the steps we took:

1. We loaded the `datatool` package using the `\usepackage` command.

2. We loaded the `linux.csv` file into a database with the name `Linux`. The command syntax is as follows:

    ```
    \DTLloaddb[options]{database name}{file name}
    ```

    Here, `options` may contain the following settings:

    *   `omitlines=n`: This option specifies an integer number of *n* lines to skip at the start.

    *   `noheader=true` or `noheader=false`: This option indicates whether the file contains a header. By default, the presence of a header is assumed. If you specify `noheader` without a value, `true` is assumed.

    *   `keys={key1,key2,…}`: This option specifies the keys for the database; it would override values from an existing header.

    *   `header={header1,header2,…}`: This specifies the headers; it would override a header from the file. For example, these header entries would be used in easy printing with the `\DTLdisplaydb{database name}` command.

3. By default, it's assumed that commas separate the data. You can change this using the `\DTLsetseparator{character}` command to use any character or by calling the `\DTLsettabseparator` command without an argument to choose tab as the separator.

4. We sorted the database using this command:

    ```
    \DTLsort[replacement keys]{sort criteria}{database
        name}
    ```

    Here, the `sort criteria` argument is a list of keys with an optional order, which can be set to `descending` or `ascending`. The latter is the default if you just list keys. If the current key is empty, the optional list of replacement keys is used in the given order.

5. While we could simply print all using the `\DTLdisplaydb{database name}` command or the `\DTLdisplaylongdb{database name}` command, when using the `longtable` package, we iterated through the database for maximum flexibility:

    ```
    \DTLforeach[condition]{database name}{assign
        list}{text}
    ```

The result of this macro is text for each row, which can include commands but with replacements done with the `assign list` argument values in the form of a `command=key` list, as in our recipe. We did not use the optional `condition` argument, which is a Boolean value that can be calculated using the `\ifthenelse` command and related commands. This value, which is by default true, decides whether to use `text` for the current row.

The manual is comprehensive and worth reading. We just saw a short example here, but you can do a lot more. As with most packages, you can access the `datatool` manual by typing `texdoc datatool` at the command line and reading it online at `https://texdoc.org/pkg/datatool`.

5
Working with Images

In LaTeX, you can easily include external images in your documents. This chapter begins with essential pointers for including images and then explores helpful techniques for arranging and adjusting them.

Specifically, we will cover the following:

- Including images with optimal quality
- Customizing images
- Adding a frame to an image
- Cutting an image to get rounded corners
- Shaping an image like a circle
- Drawing over an image
- Aligning images
- Arranging images in a grid
- Stacking images

LaTeX supports a limited range of image file formats. First, we will speak about supported formats and their practical differences in usability and quality. Then, we will explore methods to enhance the decorative aspects of images, particularly photos.

Finally, we will arrange images with alignment, in a grid, or layering.

While this chapter is about *using* images, you can read about *creating* images in *Chapter 6, Creating Graphics.*

Starting from this chapter, we'll streamline the content to focus on necessary commands without reiterating the `\documentclass` command at the start and the `\end{document}` command at the end of each example. You can access, edit, compile, and download the code examples for this chapter at `https://latex-cookbook.net/chapter-05`.

Including images with optimal quality

First, it's crucial to ensure that your images are of good quality initially.

Bitmap images, such as JPG/JPEG and PNG files, possess a fixed number of pixels, so they may become blurry or pixelated when scaled.

Vector images, in contrast, maintain quality even when scaled. You can zoom in and out, and they keep looking fine. An example of this is the **Scalable Vector Graphic** (**SVG**) format. LaTeX does not natively support it. However, SVG images can be converted to **Portable Document Format** (**PDF**) and **PostScript** (**PS**), which are also vector formats, though they can contain bitmap images.

SVG images can also be converted to TiKZ images. We will speak about TikZ in *Chapter 6, Creating Graphics*. In any case, opting for vector formats over bitmap formats is advisable.

Today, the **pdfLaTeX** compiler is the most widely used. It allows the direct inclusion of PDF images. Furthermore, it supports the mentioned bitmap formats, JPG/JPEG and PNG. Classic LaTeX, which generates **Device Independent** (**DVI**) format files, only supports the **Encapsulated PostScript** (**EPS**) format. This PostScript format has some limitations; for example, it cannot span several pages. It's intended to be embedded in documents. To simplify usage, an EPS file contains additional dimension information.

Getting ready

When creating diagrams or drawings through an external program, always try to export them in a vector format. Often, programs can export to PDF or PS format. There are also printer drivers, which generate PDF or PS files based on **GhostScript**, a widely used PostScript language interpreter.

If your images are initially bitmap images, such as photos or screenshots, there's usually nothing to gain by simply converting to PDF or EPS format. Situations in which images can be vectorized by interpolating with a tool are pretty rare and are for relatively simple images. For example, the **Inkscape** graphics program has a so-called **tracing feature** for vectorizing bitmaps.

So, for different types of images, we should prepare differently:

- **Drawings and diagrams**: Save them in a scalable format such as PDF or EPS.
- **Photos**: Capture them with high resolution. If the camera saves as JPG, you can directly include them. However, change them to PNG format if you want to edit them. That's because PNG provides lossless compression, unlike JPG, where you may lose quality whenever you save it.
- **Screenshots**: Save these in PNG format and not as JPG. It's a bitmap anyway, but PNG preserves the original quality without lossy compression. You can obtain high-resolution screenshots of smaller dialog windows if you switch to a larger system font and use the highest screen resolution.

Don't resize the images before including them. The PDF viewer or printer driver will do the scaling based on the device's resolution.

How to do it...

The graphicx package serves as our primary tool. Follow these steps:

1. Select a supported format. If necessary, convert your image to a compatible format. With classical LaTeX, which produces DVI output, use the EPS format. With pdfLaTeX, use PDF, JPG/JPEG, or PNG formats.

2. Load the graphicx package in the document preamble:

   ```
   \usepackage{graphicx}
   ```

3. At the place in the document where the image should appear, insert the following command:

   ```
   \includegraphics{filename}
   ```

   If you need to fit a certain width or height, add it as an argument, as follows, using, for example, half of the width of the text:

   ```
   \includegraphics[width=0.5\textwidth]{filename}
   ```

   Note that you can use absolute values with units such as cm, mm, or in, like this:

   ```
   \includegraphics[width=5cm, height=3cm,
       keepaspectratio]{filename}
   ```

   Here, the keepaspectratio option ensures image proportions remain intact. The width and height options are the maximum bounds, so the image will not exceed any of those two dimensions.

4. For bitmaps, you may enable interpolation as follows:

   ```
   \includegraphics[interpolate]{filename}
   ```

How it works...

The \includegraphics command has a mandatory argument: the image's filename. The name can be used without a filename extension. In that case, pdfLaTeX would first look for a .pdf file with that name; if it cannot find it, it tries .png, then .jpg, and then .PDF, .PNG, and .JPG, in that order. That's for convenience; you can use the full name with an extension if ambiguity arises.

Moreover, the \includegraphics command understands numerous options in the key=value format. This way, we specified width and height. Additional options are shown in the following recipe.

The interpolate option activates the interpolation for bitmaps, which PDF supports. If you zoom in on a raster image, you won't see big pixels. Instead, a capable PDF reader would apply a smooth transition between adjacent color values.

There's more...

In the previous chapter, in the *Positioning tables* section, we talked about automatic table placement and using captions and labels for referencing. That mechanism, which we call **floating**, works the same with images.

The code of a floating figure looks like the following:

```
\begin{figure}[htbp!]
  \centering
  \includegraphics{filename}
  \caption{Some text}
  \label{fig:name}
\end{figure}
```

The explanation of the htbp! options and how floating works in general are in the previous chapter.

There's an extensive document about using imported graphics in LaTeX. It includes a thorough explanation of the concept of floats. You can find it on CTAN at https://mirrors.ctan.org/info/epslatex/english/epslatex.pdf.

Customizing images

Before you add an image such as a photo to your document, it's best to preprocess it using graphics software. LaTeX isn't designed for image post-processing. However, there are some basic ways to customize how an image is included.

How to do it...

The graphicx package allows customization via simple options:

- You can scale an image by specifying a scaling factor, such as the following:

  ```
  \includegraphics[scale=0.5]{filename}
  ```

- You can resize an image to a fixed width using width and height options, as in the previous recipe.

- You can rotate an image by specifying an anti-clockwise rotation angle, like so:

  ```
  \includegraphics[angle=90]{filename}
  ```

- You can rotate around a particular origin by adding a key, such as c for the center, B for the baseline, and l, r, t, and b for left, right, top, and bottom, respectively. A combination would be understood, such as tl for the top-left corner. The default rotation point is the center of the image:

  ```
  \includegraphics[angle=90,origin=c]{filename}
  ```

- You can trim and clip, such as in this example, where we cut 1 cm off the left, 2 cm off the bottom, 3 cm off the right, and 4 cm off the top:

  ```
  \includegraphics[trim=1cm 2cm 3cm 4cm,clip]{filename}
  ```

For a comprehensive understanding, read the details in the package manual, which is accessible by typing texdoc graphicx at the command line or by visiting https://texdoc.org/pkg/graphicx.

Adding a frame to an image

One way to add a basic frame to an image or to text is by using one of the following commands: \frame{...}, \framebox{...}, or \fbox{...}. However, these commands generate a plain box with thin black lines and a certain distance to the content. How about changing the color, line thickness, or distance? The classic way to do the latter is by changing the LaTeX lengths, \fboxrule and \fboxsep. It can be a bit cumbersome, particularly when dealing with varying lengths. Fortunately, there's an easier way to accomplish that.

How to do it...

We will load the adjustbox package. It provides several handy commands for modifying boxes. It implicitly loads the graphicx package and exports its own features to the \includegraphics command. Follow these steps:

1. Load the xcolor package:

   ```
   \usepackage{xcolor}
   ```

2. Load the adjustbox package together with the export option:

   ```
   \usepackage[export]{adjustbox}
   ```

3. At the place in your document where the image is to be placed, use the \includegraphics command, as in the previous recipe. This time, add the cframe option:

   ```
   \includegraphics[width=10cm,
       cframe=red!50!black 5mm]{filename}
   ```

4. Compile the document, as I did with a photo of my dog. Now, you can see a frame fitting right around the image:

Figure 5.1 – A photo with a frame

How it works...

The xcolor package provides commands for specifying colors by name and blending different colors. Here, we used the syntax red!50!black, which means we've selected a color that's a 50:50 percent mix of red and black.

The adjustbox package can export some of its features. We activated that export; now, we can use additional options with the known \includegraphics command. We chose the cframe option for a colored frame, which has this syntax:

```
cframe=color thickness separation margin
```

The color parameter is mandatory and requires the xcolor package. The other values are optional lengths but are understood in this order. So, we chose a frame thickness of 5 mm and kept the default zero inner separation and outer margin.

A similar frame option works without the color value and up to three lengths given for thickness, separation, and margin.

The cfbox and fbox options work in a similar war. They internally rely on the \fbox command instead of the \frame command. In other words, they use a default thickness of the \fboxrule value and, for content separation, the \fboxsep value.

Cutting an image to get rounded corners

In the previous recipe, we obtained an image with sharp corners. However, there might be instances where you'd prefer rounded corners. Let's see how to achieve this neat effect.

How to do it...

We will use a few features of a very modern (La)TeX graphics package called **TikZ**. People usually spell it that way. Its name and features are explained in *Chapter 6, Creating Graphics*, where we will talk much more about it. Follow these steps:

1. Load the `tikz` package in your preamble:

    ```
    \usepackage{tikz}
    ```

2. Declare a box for storing the image:

    ```
    \newsavebox{\picbox}
    ```

3. Define a macro that allows us to use our recipe repeatedly:

    ```
    \newcommand{\cutpic}[3]{
      \savebox{\picbox}{\includegraphics[width=#2]{#3}}
      \tikz\node[draw, rounded corners=#1, line width=4pt,
        color=white, minimum width=\wd\picbox,
        minimum height=\ht\picbox, path picture = {
          \node at (path picture bounding box.center) {
            \usebox{\picbox}};
      }] {};}
    ```

4. Use the new macro within your document to include an image:

    ```
    \cutpic{1cm}{8cm}{filename}
    ```

5. Compile the document to see the effect:

Figure 5.2 – A photo with a frame and rounded corners

How it works...

After loading the TikZ package, we created a box for storing the image. We defined a macro; its first task is to put our image into the box using the \savebox command.

The new \cutpic macro takes three arguments:

- A length value for the rounded corners
- The width of the image
- The filename of the image

The \tikz command is an abbreviation for \begin{tikzpicture} ... \end{tikzpicture}, which is handy for simple figures. Here, the figure is just a single node with some options.

The rounded corners=width option produces the shape of a rounded rectangle for the node. We chose to let it draw in white color with 4 pt thickness. At this place, you can choose any color you like.

While the node has an empty node text, we required a minimum height and width to match the size of our image. Now, our box comes into play: we measured its width and height for handing over to the node with the \wd and \ht TeX primitive commands.

Finally, we used an advanced TikZ option. The path picture=code option fills a drawing path by executing the given code. That path will clip the result of the code. So, instead of filling it with a color, a pattern, or a shade, we printed out the image using the \usebox command. For this, we encapsulated the image in its own node and placed it at the center.

There's more...

TikZ often provides multiple methods to achieve the same result. An alternative approach would be to use the current bounding box node to define a clip path or simply draw a rectangle with rounded corners in white over the image.

Using nodes has advantages, such as getting anchors for alignment, connecting by edges or arrows, naming that node and referring to it, and getting shapes and further options right away. You can also use nodes for alignment, as seen in a later recipe in this chapter.

While we'll explore several TikZ examples in *Chapter 6, Creating Graphics*, we will again use it to help us customize images in the following recipes.

Shaping an image like a circle

A circular shape can add a stylish touch to portrait photographs, an organizational chart, or photos on a website.

How to do it...

As in the previous recipe, we will define a TikZ macro for this purpose. Take a look at the following steps:

1. Load the TikZ package:

   ```
   \usepackage{tikz}
   ```

2. Define a macro so we can use it often:

   ```
   \newcommand{\roundpic}[4][]{
       \tikz\node [circle, minimum width = #2,
         path picture = {
             \node[#1] at (path picture bounding box.center){
                 \includegraphics[width=#3]{#4}};
           }] {};}
   ```

3. Use the new macro within your document to include an image:

   ```
   \roundpic[xshift=-1cm,
     yshift=-2.6cm]{5.8cm}{9cm}{filename}
   ```

4. Compile the document. When I used a photo of my dog (here using `xshift` and `yshift` to select the desired area of the photo), I got the following image:

Figure 5.3 – A photo cut into a circle

How it works...

Refer to the previous recipe to understand the TikZ node construction with the `path picture` option. This time, we used a circle for the outer node, so our image got cropped in a circular shape. We used four arguments. The first optional argument can contain node options. In our example, we used them to shift the image for better positioning in the cut window. The subsequent options are the node's width, the image's width, and, of course, the name of the image file.

There's more...

Typically, when we insert images, the baseline is at the bottom. We can change it to be at the center for positioning. In such a case, we can give the node a name and then tell TikZ to use the center of the node as the baseline for aligning the entire image, as follows:

```
\newcommand{\roundpic}[4][]{
  \tikz[baseline=(photo.center)]
    \node (photo) [circle, minimum width = #2,
      path picture = {
        \node [#1] at (path picture bounding box.center)
        {\includegraphics[width=#3]{#4}};
}] {};}
```

Then, the center of the photo would be aligned with the baseline of adjacent text. This alignment may be preferred for small images embedded within the text.

Drawing over an image

If you need to add text, arrows, or other annotations to an image, it's recommended to do so directly within LaTeX. This offers several advantages compared to using external graphics software:

- **Font consistency**: You can use the same fonts in your annotations in the image as those used throughout your LaTeX document, ensuring visual uniformity

- **Style consistency**: Styles such as line widths, colors, and arrow types adhere to the style of your other drawings

- **Scalability**: Your annotations scale seamlessly and will remain sharp and high-quality

- **Macro integration**: You can use macros from your preamble or packages in your annotations

How to do it...

We will draw with TikZ. We use the onimage package for this example. If it's not available in your TeX distribution or on CTAN, you can download it from Launchpad: https://bazaar.launchpad.net/~tex-sx/tex-sx/development/view/head:/onimage.dtx. The .dtx filename extension stands for **DocTeX**, which is used to have the package and documentation in a single file. You can read more about it at https://texfaq.org/FAQ-dtx.

Here's how to use that .dtx file:

1. Download onimage.dtx to your computer.

2. Compile onimage.dtx with pdfLaTeX. That generates several files, including a .pdf and a .sty file.

3. Read the onimage.pdf file, which is the package documentation.

4. Copy the onimage.sty file to your LaTeX document folder.

Now, follow these steps with your own LaTeX document:

1. Within the LaTeX document preamble, load the onimage package:

    ```
    \usepackage{onimage}
    ```

2. Define TikZ styles for your annotations:

    ```
    \tikzset{annotations/.style = {
      tsx/show help lines,
      every path/.append style = {very thick,
        color = yellow},
      every node/.append style = {yellow,
        font = \bfseries\sffamily}}}
    ```

3. In your document body, use the tikzonimage environment:

    ```
    \begin{tikzonimage}[width=.8\textwidth]{filename}
      [annotations]
    \draw[dashed] (0.59,0.71)    -- (0.86,0.12)
                  (0.634,0.71) -- (0.86,0.12);
    \draw[dotted] (0.56,0.85)    -- (0.86,0.12)
                  (0.66,0.85)  -- (0.86,0.12);
    \draw (0.3,0.4) edge[->] (0.68,0.4)
          (0.3,0.4) edge[->] (0.3,0.93);
    \node[rotate=90] at (0.28,0.8) {height};
    \node            at (0.62,0.35) {velocity};
    \end{tikzonimage}
    ```

4. Compile the document. To show the result, I again used a photo of my dog. You can see the additional illustrations:

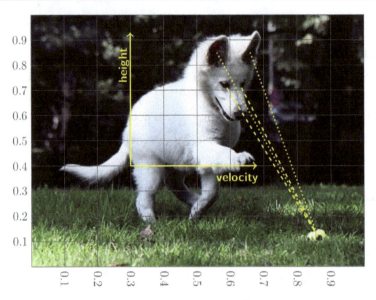

Figure 5.4 – Drawing over a photo

How it works...

Loading the onimage package automatically loaded the TikZ graphics package.

Using the \tikzset command, we defined a style named annotations to apply it at several places easily. In this style, we activated the tsx/show help lines option, which draws a grid over the image. We can use this later to get coordinates visually. For the final document, we comment out or delete this option to remove the grid.

Furthermore, we defined that every path in such annotations should be drawn yellow and very thick, and all text in nodes should have a bold sans-serif font in yellow. Since we did this only for the annotations style, other drawings won't be affected.

For the image itself, we used the tikzonimage environment. Its syntax is as follows:

```
\begin{tikzonimage}[image options]{filename}[TikZ options]
   ... your TikZ code ...
\end{tikzonimage}
```

This handy environment has the following features:

- It implicitly creates a tikzpicture environment with the given TikZ options

- It includes the image within a node, passing image options and the filename parameter to the \includegraphics command

- It provides a coordinate system with the origin at the lower-left corner of the image

- The coordinate system adjusts relative to the image size's dimensions, wherein the point $(1,1)$ denotes the upper-right corner of the image

- It draws a grid of helplines if desired

As this has already been done for us, we can focus on the actual drawing commands. We used standard TikZ syntax:

- Drawing dashed and dotted lines between coordinates in parentheses; all lines inherit the `very thick` and `yellow` style

- Drawing arrows, which are edges with an arrow shape, is done by the `->` option

- Placing a rotated node and a regular node with text, inheriting the yellow bold sans-serif font from the `annotations` style

The grid helps to get the desired coordinates for precise placement, adjust the estimated coordinates, and compile again. As the coordinates are relative, resizing the entire image does not impact their accuracy.

You can leverage additional TikZ capabilities, such as shapes, arrows, colors, fadings, and transparency. We will explore some of these functionalities in *Chapter 6, Creating Graphics*.

Aligning images

By default, the baseline of an image is at its bottom. So, adjacent images would be aligned at the bottom. There may be instances where top alignment or vertical center alignment is preferred.

How to do it...

We will use the `\height` command for shifting to get vertical centering. Take the following steps:

1. Load the `graphicx` package. For testing, or if you don't have images, add the `demo` option to use black rectangles in place of images:

   ```
   \usepackage[demo]{graphicx}
   ```

2. In your document, use the `\raisebox` command together with half of the `\height` value:

   ```
   \raisebox{-0.5\height}{\includegraphics[height=4cm,
     width=8cm]{filename1}}
   \hfill
   \raisebox{-0.5\height}{\includegraphics[height=2cm,
     width=4cm]{filename2}}
   ```

3.   Your images (in the demo case, black-filled rectangles) will be vertically aligned:

Figure 5.5 – Images with vertically-centered alignment

How it works...

The \height command returns the current height above the baseline. The \totalheight command would include the height below the baseline, which, in our case, doesn't exist.

We raised each box by minus half its height to get vertical centering. Even text before or after would be aligned to the middle because we lowered all the boxes.

Writing the following command would give us top alignment of the images:

```
\raisebox{-\height}{\includegraphics{...}}
```

The adjustbox package provides many more commands for aligning boxes with text or images.

Instead of black-filled rectangles as placeholder images, LaTeX provides example images. We will use them in the final recipe of this chapter.

Arranging images in a grid

The \includegraphics command could load a more extensive set of photos, plots, or diagrams with some space in between, for example, positioned using minipage environments. A \foreach loop may help if the filenames can be generated programmatically.

In this recipe, we will produce a grid of aligned images with arbitrary names, which will be easy to arrange.

How to do it...

We will use a tabular environment for positioning. That's no surprise yet. However, we will read in the tabular cell content, which we will then use as filenames for inclusion. The collcell package provides the required feature. Follow these steps:

1.   Load the graphicx package and the collcell package:

```
\usepackage{graphicx}
\usepackage{collcell}
```

2. Define a command for including an image with a chosen width and height:

```
\newcommand{\includepic}[1]{%
  \includegraphics[width=3cm,height=2cm,
  keepaspectratio]{#1}}
```

3. Define a new column type that uses that new command in its column specification. We use the letter i for an image:

```
\newcolumntype{i}{@{\hspace{1ex}}
  >{\collectcell\includepic}c<{\endcollectcell}}
```

4. In your document, use a `tabular` environment with the new column type. Again, photos of my dog will serve as an example. The cells contain the basic filename – that is, `meadow` for `meadow.jpg`, and so on:

```
\begin{tabular}{iii}
  meadow  & sea     & beach \\
  blanket & tunnel  & tired \\
  pond    & chewing & halfasleep
\end{tabular}
```

5. Compile the document and check out the result:

Figure 5.6 – A gallery of photos

How it works...

To streamline our code, we used the \newcolumntype command of the array package. This package is implicitly loaded by the collcell package. The @{\hspace{1ex}} expression is the code for changing the inter-column space to 1ex, which is helpful in adjusting the tabular spacing. The array syntax >{...} inserts code before a cell, while the <{...} syntax inserts code afterward.

However, we cannot simply write code such as >{\includegraphics{} and <{}}, just to enclose the filename in the \includegraphics{...} command. The compiler interprets the curly braces literally, mixing array syntax with the \includegraphics command argument braces.

The collcell package comes to the rescue. Its \collectcell command starts reading the cell content. Its \endcollectcell command states the end of that content, which will be provided to the user's macro. The latter is the argument for the \collectcell command; in our case, it's the \includepic command. We defined this macro to encapsulate the \includegraphics command and our desired options, including the image width.

With this column type in use, we can effortlessly input image file names in the cells. Of course, it can be combined with conventional column types as needed.

Stacking images

We can also stack images on top of one another, such as for a fancy photo collage. This can be combined with previous recipes such as rotating and framing. Let's focus on stacking here.

How to do it...

The stackengine package allows things to be placed above each other. It can handle text and math as well as images. Let's try it with the latter, using sample images. Here's how to proceed:

1. In your document preamble, load the mwe package. It provides dummy images and automatically loads the graphicx package, which we otherwise load ourselves, as before:

    ```
    \usepackage{mwe}
    ```

2. Load the stackengine package:

    ```
    \usepackage{stackengine}
    ```

3. In the document body, use the \stackinset command. It takes six arguments. This sounds like a lot of work, but it allows flexible positioning. The syntax is as follows:

    ```
    \stackinset{horizontal alignment}
        {horizontal offset}
        {vertical aligment}
        {vertical offset}
        {image above}{image below}
    ```

In our recipe, we use right and top alignment and shift by 2 cm horizontally and vertically:

```
\stackinset{r}{2cm}{t}{2cm}{%
    \includegraphics{example-image}}{%
    \includegraphics[angle=-10]{example-image}}
```

4. Compile, and we get the following:

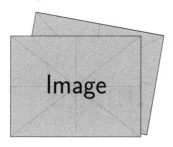

Figure 5.7 – Stacked images

How it works...

Let's look at the specifics of the earlier syntax:

- Horizontal alignment can be l for left, c for center, or r for right aligned. In the case of right alignment, the offset means shifting to the left by this length, otherwise to the right.

- Vertical alignment can be t for top, c for center, or b for bottom alignment. In the case of top alignment, the offset means shifting down by this length, otherwise, upward.

You can also specify negative lengths or leave it empty for zero offset.

Apart from images, you can use \stackinset for stacking letters and symbols, for example, the following:

```
\stackinset{c}{}{c}{}{$\star$}{O}
```

This produces a big letter O with a star inside as follows:

Figure 5.8 – Stacked symbols

You can mix images and text. This way, you could place any annotation over an image, such as by using commands such as the following:

```
\stackinset{l}{1em}{t}{1em}{Inside annotation}{%
  \includegraphics[width=5cm]{example-image}}
```

This results in the following:

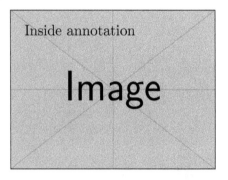

Figure 5.9 – An image with an annotation

You can nest multiple \stackinset commands to add several annotations or stack several images together.

To see all features in detail, look at the stackengine manual. You can access it using the texdoc stackengine command at the command line or open it at https://texdoc.org/pkg/ stackengine.

6

Creating Graphics

In this chapter, we will explore LaTeX's extensive graphic capabilities. You will learn to create impressive graphics of various kinds.

This chapter covers the following topics:

- Building smart diagrams
- Constructing a flowchart
- Growing a tree
- Building a bar chart
- Drawing a pie chart
- Drawing a Venn diagram
- Putting thoughts into a mind map
- Generating a timeline

A picture is worth a thousand words. Presenting a single image can significantly simplify the understanding of complex concepts. Diagrams, in particular, help to distill pertinent information, showcase relationships and process sequences, and facilitate quantity comparisons.

In this chapter, you will primarily find recipes for various diagram types, complemented by further valuable graphic recipes.

All the recipes in this chapter are based on the highly capable graphics package **pgf/TikZ**. **pgf** stands for **Portable Graphics Format**, serving as the backend, while **TikZ** is the name of the frontend. That name is an abbreviation for "TikZ ist kein Zeichenprogramm," which translates as "TikZ is not a drawing program." The following recursive acronym, created in the tradition of GNU, should tell potential users what to expect – no WYSIWYG, which means you cannot see the output during creation but after compiling. Nonetheless, TikZ offers all the advantages of TeX, including high quality, macros, reusability, and access to a wealth of libraries and packages.

Another capable graphics package for LaTeX is **PSTricks**, which has a rich history and numerous features, is built on PostScript, and works with conversion tools to generate PDF documents.

In this chapter, we opt for TikZ due to its highly readable syntax, comprehensive documentation, and compatibility with all TeX engines (pdfTeX, XeTeX, and LuaTeX) and formats (LaTeX, plain TeX, and ConTeXt). Finally, our choice is influenced by TikZ's increasing popularity in the LaTeX community over the years.

We won't cover drawing basic shapes such as rectangles or circles; the TikZ manual already covers this. Instead, we'll begin by exploring modern packages designed for specific purposes, enabling the creation of comprehensive and functional graphics.

For learning TikZ, I recommend my book *LaTeX Graphics with TikZ, Packt Publishing, 2023*. It covers many details, including drawing and aligning nodes, edges, and arrows, and using colors, transparency, styles, coordinate calculations, and transformations. Visit `https://tikz.org` to learn more about the book.

Getting ready

To compile the recipes in this chapter, ensure you have TikZ installed. Note that while TikZ is the common name, the actual package name is `pgf`, which you can locate in your LaTeX installation's package manager. To work with this book, you need version 3.0 or later.

Many of the recipes also utilize additional packages alongside TikZ. Be sure to have each mentioned package installed when starting a recipe. In any case, I recommend a complete TeX installation.

To provide numerous complete and usable recipes in this graphics chapter, we won't delve into the basics of TikZ commands. You can always refer to the reference manual to learn about them. I assume you have some familiarity with nodes, edges, and styles, but feel free to consult the manual when you need a deeper understanding of these concepts. However, I will provide detailed explanations of how the recipes function.

For more in-depth customization and understanding, keep the TikZ manual readily available. You can easily access it by typing `texdoc tikz` or `texdoc pgf` at the command line. This also applies to the other packages used in this chapter.

If you're reading the book without access to a TeX installation with documentation, or if you use an online LaTeX solution such as Overleaf, visit `https://texdoc.org/pkg/tikz`. The excellent website at `https://tikz.dev` provides the manual in an HTML version.

The websites `https://tikz.net` and `https://texample.net` are collections of hundreds of TikZ graphics examples, with full source code and an integrated online compiler. If you want to draw anything, an example from those websites can be an excellent start.

Building smart diagrams

At first, let's focus on a quick win – getting a diagram with minimal technical effort. So we would just need to fill in our thoughts.

The `smartdiagram` package makes building diagrams of various types very easy.

How to do it...

Once you have loaded the `smartdiagram` package, you only need a simple command. Follow these steps:

1. As always, begin with any `document` class:

   ```
   \documentclass{article}
   ```

2. Load the `smartdiagram` package:

   ```
   \usepackage{smartdiagram}
   ```

3. Start the document:

   ```
   \begin{document}
   ```

4. Define the diagram. An option in square brackets defines the type, and an argument in curly braces contains a comma-separated list of items:

   ```
   \smartdiagram[flow diagram:horizontal]{Edit,
       \LaTeX, Bib\TeX/ biber, make\-index, \LaTeX}
   ```

5. End the document:

   ```
   \end{document}
   ```

6. Compile, and take a look at the output:

Figure 6.1 – A horizontal flow chart

How it works...

We generated the image with a straightforward call to the `\smartdiagram` command and the required arguments. The syntax of the command is as follows:

```
\smartdiagram[type of diagram]{list of items}
```

We've selected a horizontal flow diagram. To obtain a vertical layout, use `flow diagram` without the `:horizontal` suffix to get a vertical layout. There is a defined set of diagram types. Instead of merely listing them, let's create some examples to observe the outcomes.

There's more...

We can change both the diagram type and the items to produce various diagrams. If there's a root or central item, it should always be the first in the list.

Circular diagram

Let's try a circular diagram. It's counter-clockwise by default. Add `:clockwise` to the option to get a clockwise order:

```
\smartdiagram[circular diagram:clockwise]{Edit,
    pdf\LaTeX, Bib\TeX/ biber, make\-index, pdf\LaTeX}
```

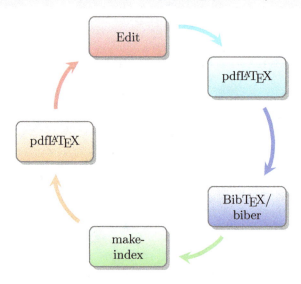

Figure 6.2 – A circular diagram

Bubble diagram

Consider using a bubble diagram for a straightforward way to present key terms in a central context. The initial item in the list resides in the center circle, while the rest are positioned in colored circles surrounding it, with slight overlapping to convey their close connection.

To get macros for further TeX logos, we will also load the `dtk-logos` package, so add to the preamble the following:

```
\usepackage{dtklogos}
```

You can download this package at `https://github.com/dante-ev/dtk-bibliography` and put it in your `document` folder.

Alternatively, you could use the `metalogo` package, available at `https://ctan.org/pkg/metalogo`, which provides logo commands such as `\XeTeX`. Another option is combining strings, such as writing Lua`\TeX`, to achieve the same effect.

The `smartdiagram` call becomes the following:

```
\smartdiagram[bubble diagram]{\TeX\ engines,
  \TeX\ (dvi), pdf\TeX, \XeTeX, \LuaTeX, \ConTeXt}
```

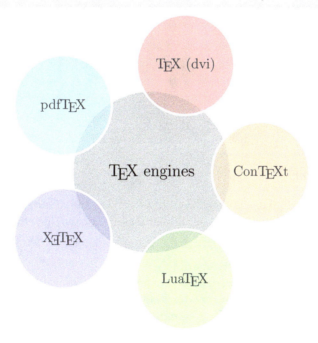

Figure 6.3 – A bubble diagram

Constellation diagram

A constellation diagram gives a slightly different form. In this, each item is in a colored circle connected to the center, which is again the first item:

```
\smartdiagram[constellation diagram]{\TeX\ software,
    Editor, Compiler, Converter, PDF Reader}
```

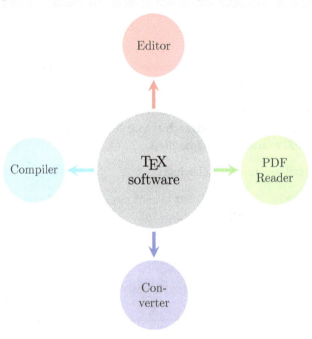

Figure 6.4 – A constellation diagram

Descriptive diagram

For nicely arranged items with a description, there's the descriptive diagram. As a consequence, the items are now a list of small lists. We use additional curly braces to hide the comma within an item so that it won't be taken as an item separator:

```
\smartdiagram[descriptive diagram]{
    {Style,{Define shapes, colors, shading,
            and line styles for nodes and arrows}},
    {Position, {Place nodes using a matrix,
                relative or absolute positioning}},
    {Relation, Insert edges or arrows
            between selected nodes},
    {Label, Add labels on edges or arrows}}
```

This gives us the following diagram:

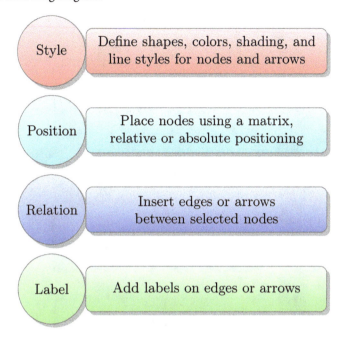

Figure 6.5 – A descriptive diagram

Also, the diagram shows some tasks related to drawing with TikZ, which will later be helpful for us.

A priority descriptive diagram

If your descriptive diagram has a certain order and you would like to emphasize that, use a `priority descriptive diagram`, such as the following:

```
\smartdiagram[priority descriptive diagram]{
   Develop a document structure,
   Choose a document class,
   Select suitable packages,
   Setup the document preamble,
   Write your document,
   Finetune the layout}
```

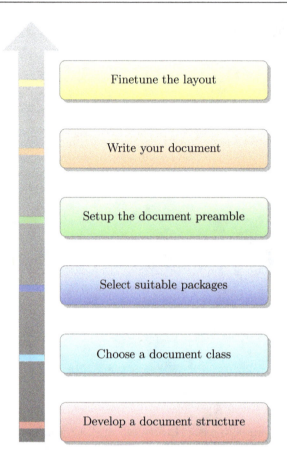

Figure 6.6 – A priority descriptive diagram

Animating a diagram

You can quickly animate such a diagram in a presentation made with the beamer class. It's as simple as the following:

- Using the beamer class
- Using a frame environment for the diagram
- Writing \smartdiagramanimated instead of \smartdiagram

This, applied to one of the preceding examples, results in the following:

```
\documentclass{beamer}
\usepackage{smartdiagram}
\begin{document}
```

```
\begin{frame}
  \smartdiagramanimated[circular diagram]{Edit,
  pdf\LaTeX, Bib\TeX/ biber, make\-index, pdf\LaTeX}
\end{frame}
\end{document}
```

The diagram will then be built step by step, frame by frame.

Further customization

Of course, you can set the colors and shapes of all elements. For details, refer to the `smartdiagram` manual, as usual via `texdoc`.

Constructing a flowchart

We used predefined chart types in the prior recipe, *Building smart diagrams*. If greater flexibility is required, creating custom diagrams from scratch is a viable option. Doing this is simple, and it's an excellent way to develop your skills in drawing with TikZ.

Just as we observed in the descriptive diagram from the first recipe, we'll do the following:

1. Define shapes and colors.
2. Place nodes using a matrix.
3. Insert labeled arrows between selected nodes.

Of course, the actions of each step can be adjusted as needed. It's common to position nodes and arrows initially and later refine the shapes and colors.

Now, let's dive into it. Follow the following steps, and refer to the graphical output to understand the purpose of each drawing task.

1. Start with a document class:

   ```
   \documentclass{article}
   ```

2. Load the `geometry` package, and specify a vertical margin so that our long chart will fit the page:

   ```
   \usepackage[a4paper,vmargin=3cm]{geometry}
   ```

3. Load the `tikz` package:

   ```
   \usepackage{tikz}
   ```

4. Load the `matrix`, `calc`, and `shapes` TikZ libraries:

   ```
   \usetikzlibrary{matrix,calc,shapes}
   ```

5. Define styles for the nodes, which is our first major step in these steps:

```
\tikzset{
  treenode/.style = {shape=rectangle, rounded corners,
                     draw, anchor=center,
                     text width=5em, align=center,
                     top color=white,
                     bottom color=blue!20,
                     inner sip=1ex},
  decision/.style = {treenode, diamond,
                     inner sep=0pt},
  root/.style      = {treenode, font=\Large,
                     bottom color=red!30},
  env/.style       = {treenode,
                     font=\ttfamily\normalsize},
  finish/.style    = {root, bottom color=green!40},
  dummy/.style     = {circle,draw}
}
```

6. Create some useful shortcuts for edge types:

```
\newcommand{\yes}{edge node [above] {yes}}
\newcommand{\no}{edge node [left]  {no}}
```

7. Begin the document:

```
\begin{document}
```

8. Begin the TikZ picture. Add the desired options; here, we declare -latex as the default arrow tip for edges:

```
\begin{tikzpicture}[-latex]
```

9. Now, we come to the second major step, which is positioning. Start a matrix with the name chart:

```
\matrix (chart)
```

10. Define options for the matrix:

```
[
    matrix of nodes,
    column sep      = 3em,
    row sep         = 5ex,
    column 1/.style = {nodes={decision}},
    column 2/.style = {nodes={env}}
]
```

11. Now, add the actual matrix contents, which will be the nodes of our flowchart. Like with `tabular`, columns are separated by &, and lines are ended by \\. This is also necessary for the last line. We modify the style for a particular node by inserting `|<style>|` before the node content. A final semicolon ends the `\matrix` command with options:

```
{
    |[root]| Formula              &                       \\
    single-line?                  & equation              \\
    centered?                     & gather                \\
    aligned at relation sign?     & align, flalign  \\
    aligned at several places?    & alignat               \\
    first left, centered,
        last right?               & multline              \\
    & & |[decision]| numbered? \\
    & & |[treenode]| Add a \texttt{*}
                                  & |[finish]| Done \\
};
```

12. And now, for the third major step, we draw arrows. Draw downwards "no" edges in the first column and "yes" edges to the right. We use `\foreach` loops to reduce the amount of code. The final edge goes to the last node in the bottom-right corner:

```
\draw
    (chart-1-1) edge (chart-2-1)
    \foreach \x/\y in {2/3, 3/4, 4/5, 5/6} {
        (chart-\x-1) \no (chart-\y-1) }
    \foreach \x in {2,...,6} {
        (chart-\x-1) \yes (chart-\x-2) }
    (chart-7-3) \no   (chart-8-3)
    (chart-8-3) edge (chart-8-4);
```

13. Draw a line back to the start:

```
\draw
    (chart-6-1) -- +(-2,0) |- (chart-1-1)
        node[near start,sloped,above] {no, reconsider};
```

14. Draw lines from the nodes in the second column to another node down in the third column:

```
\foreach \x in {2,...,6} {
    \draw (chart-\x-2) -| (chart-7-3);}
```

15. Draw a "yes" edge to the final node in the bottom-right corner:

```
\draw    (chart-7-3)  -| (chart-8-4)
    node[near start,above] {yes};
```

16. End the picture and the document:

```
\end{tikzpicture}
\end{document}
```

17. Compile and examine the output:

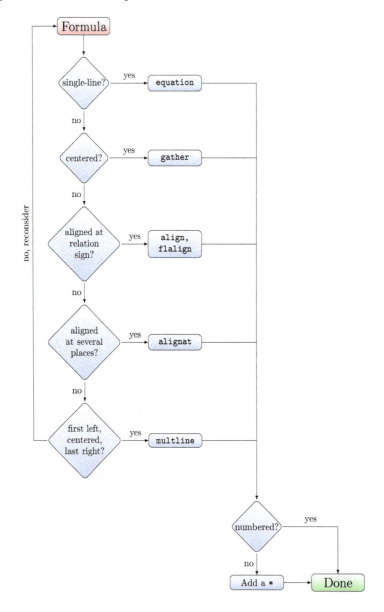

Figure 6.7 – A complex flow chart

How it works...

Precisely positioning the nodes is a critical aspect here. Manually specifying coordinates for nodes would be a cumbersome and error-prone task. An alternative is to employ the relative positioning of nodes. However, the most straightforward method is establishing a matrix, allowing us to position nodes as quickly as in a `tabular` structure. However, it necessitates a grid-like structure. TikZ offers a matrix library with a dedicated section in the manual. For a comprehensive understanding of all available options, please consult it. In this context, we've solely defined the spacing between rows and columns, as well as some column styles.

Styles can be locally defined – for instance, as options within a `tikzpicture` environment. To facilitate repeated usage, global definitions can be more desirable. To achieve this, we employed the `\tikzset` command. It takes a list of style assignments as an argument. You saw the principle:

```
thingy/.style = {list of style options}
```

You can either redefine existing styles or create your own unique styles. Now, you can effortlessly apply this new style name as an option wherever required, eliminating the need to list specific options repeatedly. This approach provides the same advantages as LaTeX macros, enhancing readability and ensuring consistency.

You can combine styles and employ them in the creation of derived styles. In this instance, we've defined a foundational style for tree nodes and developed additional styles inherited from it, while incorporating distinct attributes.

Let's return to our code – our matrix structure is as follows:

```
\matrix (name) [options] {
  entry & entry & … \\
  entry & entry & … \\
  …
};
```

Each node within the matrix now has a name assigned to it for additional drawing. We can reference a node using the `(name-row-column)` syntax, as we did with the following command:

```
\draw (chart-1-1) edge (chart-2-1);
```

This command creates a vertical edge that connects the top-left node of our chart to the node below. To define column styles, we employed the convenient `nodes={decision}` syntax, which says all nodes should have this style. We still can apply local styles, so we used the `|[style]|` shortcut at the beginning of a matrix cell.

After the matrix, we used `\draw` to draw all the edges. They are arrows in our case, since we added the `-latex` option to the `tikzpicture` environment to create this particular arrow tip.

We harnessed the power of \foreach loops to handle repetitive tasks efficiently. The simplified syntax is as follows:

```
\foreach <variables> in {<list>} { <commands> }
```

In this context, the commands can encompass variables substituted with values from the list, iterating through the entire list. The \foreach command is comprehensively covered in a dedicated section within the TikZ manual. For our recipe, familiarity with this syntax and examples involving one and two variables should be sufficient for a fundamental understanding.

A special edge is drawn using the - | syntax. This means a horizontal line and then a vertical line to the destination. | - is the counterpart that does it the other way around. For details regarding drawing syntax and available options, refer to the TikZ manual. It also contains tutorials, which are helpful for quickly diving in.

Growing a tree

A widespread type of hierarchical graph is a tree. Tree nodes have children connected by edges, usually displayed in rows when growing down or in columns when growing horizontally.

How to do it...

We will use basic TikZ without extra packages. Follow these steps:

1. Start with a document class:

    ```
    \documentclass{article}
    ```

2. Load the tikz package:

    ```
    \usepackage{tikz}
    ```

3. Start the document:

    ```
    \begin{document}
    ```

4. Begin with a TikZ picture, and specify options for it:

    ```
    \begin{tikzpicture}[sibling distance=10em,
      every node/.style = {shape=rectangle,
        rounded corners, draw, align=center,
        top color=white, bottom color=blue!20}]]
    ```

5. Draw a node and add children to it:

    ```
    \node {Formulas}
      child { node {single-line} }
    ```

```
    child { node {multi-line}
      child { node {aligned at}
        child { node {relation sign} }
        child { node {several places} }
        child { node {center} } }
      child { node {first left,\\centered,\\
                    last right} }
  };
```

6. End the picture and the document:

```
\end{tikzpicture}
\end{document}
```

7. Compile, and take a look at the output:

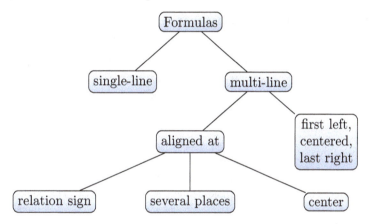

Figure 6.8 – A vertical tree

How it works...

To avoid overlapping, we defined a distance between siblings. As all the nodes are the same, we defined one style for all, using a rounded rectangle as a drawn border and a color fading from white to light blue. We did it by setting those options to `every node/.style`. This default style simplifies writing. We can still change specific node styles.

There's more...

We can play with diagram types and items to get different diagrams. If there's a root item or a central item, it's always the first in the list.

Creating a decision tree

Our recipe started with a vertical tree. We can also draw it in the horizontal direction. Let's do it this way now. We will use this occasion to introduce TikZ **styles**. A style is a set of options. Styles make drawing easier, similar to macros – we don't need to repeat the same options repeatedly. Instead, we refer to a desired style. Styles can be combined.

We will now go through the steps in detail:

1. Again, start with a document class:

   ```
   \documentclass{article}
   ```

2. Load the `tikz` package:

   ```
   \usepackage{tikz}
   ```

3. Use the `\tikzset` command to define your new styles:

   ```
   \tikzset{
     treenode/.style = {shape=rectangle, rounded corners,
                        draw, align=center,
                        top color=white,
                        bottom color=blue!20},
     root/.style     = {treenode, font=\Large,
                        bottom color=red!30},
     env/.style      = {treenode,
                        font=\ttfamily\normalsize},
     dummy/.style    = {circle,draw}
   }
   ```

4. Start the document:

   ```
   \begin{document}
   ```

5. Begin with the TikZ picture:

   ```
   \begin{tikzpicture}
   ```

6. Add options to the TikZ picture. As before, use square brackets:

   ```
   [
       grow                    = right,
       sibling distance        = 6em,
       level distance          = 10em,
       edge from parent/.style = {draw, -latex},
   ```

```
        every node/.style        = {font=\footnotesize},
        sloped
    ]
```

7. Declare the nodes and children in the tree hierarchy. If an edge needs to be labeled, add a node using the edge from parent option after the node:

```
\node [root] {Formula}
    child { node [env] {equation}
        edge from parent node [below] {single-line?} }
    child { node [dummy] {}
        child { node [dummy] {}
            child { node [env] {align\\flalign}
                edge from parent node [below]
                                    {at relation sign?} }
            child { node [env] {alignat}
                edge from parent node [above] {at several}
                                    node [below] {places?} }
            child { node [env] {gather}
                edge from parent node [above] {centered?} }
            edge from parent node [below] {aligned?} }
        child { node [env] {multline}
            edge from parent node [above, align=center]
                    {first left,\\centered,}
                node [below] {last right}}
        edge from parent node [above] {multi-line?}};
```

8. End the TikZ picture and the document:

```
\end{tikzpicture}
\end{document}
```

9. Compile, and take a look at the output:

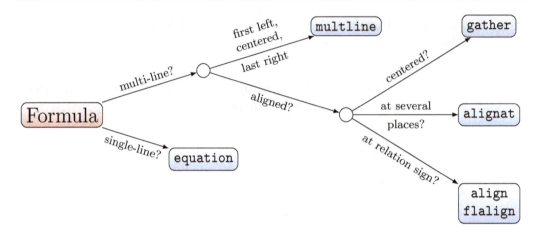

Figure 6.9 – A horizontal tree

The main difference is grow=right, used to get a horizontal tree. Besides that, we used various custom styles for nodes. After a node is connected to its parent by an edge, we use the edge from parent option to add a node with label text.

Building a bar chart

A classical way to display categories with corresponding values is a bar chart. It consists of rectangular bars that are proportional to the represented values. The primary purpose is to compare those values visually.

We can use vertical or horizontal bars.

How to do it...

We will use the pgfplots package. It's for natively plotting in LaTeX with a convenient user interface. We will use it to produce a horizontal bar chart.

Follow these steps:

1. Start with a document class:

   ```
   \documentclass{article}
   ```

2. Load the pgfplots package:

   ```
   \usepackage{pgfplots}
   \pgfplotsset{width=7cm,compat=1.18}
   ```

3. Begin the document:

```
\begin{document}
```

4. Begin a TikZ picture, which will be the container for the plot:

```
\begin{tikzpicture}
```

5. Open an axis environment:

```
\begin{axis}
```

6. Give options to the axis:

```
[
    title     = Contributions per category
                at LaTeX-Community.org,
    xbar,
    y axis line style = { opacity = 0 },
    axis x line       = none,
    tickwidth         = 0pt,
    enlarge y limits  = 0.2,
    enlarge x limits  = 0.02,
    nodes near coords,
    symbolic y coords = {LaTeX, Tools,
                        Distributions, Editors},
]
```

7. Add a plot:

```
\addplot coordinates { (57727,LaTeX) (5672,Tools)
        (2193,Distributions) (11106,Editors) };
```

8. Add another plot:

```
\addplot coordinates { (14320,LaTeX) (1615,Tools)
        (560,Distributions)  (3075,Editors)  };
```

9. Add a legend:

```
\legend{Topics, Posts}
```

10. End the `axis` environment, the TikZ picture, and the whole document:

```
\end{axis}
\end{tikzpicture}
\end{document}
```

11. Compile, and take a look at the output:

Figure 6.10 – A horizontal bar chart

How it works...

The \addplot command does the plotting work – we called it with a set of specific coordinates. In our case, we used numeric values and symbolic coordinates for the subjects.

We design the plot by adding options to the axis environment. This is the specific pgfplots environment, with a lot of options for customizing. Here's what we did:

- We provided a title.

- We set xbar as a style to get bars in the *x* direction. Specifically, this means that horizontal bars will be placed from y=0 to the x coordinate.

- Omitting unnecessary diagram parts means less distraction. This helps to focus and understand the content, so we did the following:

  - Chose a completely opaque line style for the *y*-axis so that it won't be printed

  - Hid the *x*-axis using the axis x line = none option

  - Removed the *x*-axis ticks by setting their width to zero

- We slightly enlarged the *x* and *y* limits to get a better display.

- We got nodes with values near the bars by enabling the nodes near coords option.

- We defined symbolic coordinates as y values to assign numeric (*x*) values to (*y*) subjects.

To summarize, `xbar` defined the plot style, and `symbolic y coords` let us use string values. The other axis options were just for design purposes. There are many more possible settings, so refer to the `pgfplots` manual for further customization. You can open it by entering `texdoc pgfplots` at the Command Prompt or visiting `https://texdoc.org/pkg/pgfplots`.

Drawing a pie chart

Pie charts are famous for showing proportions. Their main characteristic is that all items usually sum up to 100%. They are displayed as segments of a disc.

How to do it...

We will use the `pgf-pie` package, which builds on TikZ and is specialized in generating pie charts. Follow these steps:

1. Start with a document class:

    ```
    \documentclass{article}
    ```

2. Load the `pgf-pie` package:

    ```
    \usepackage{pgf-pie}
    ```

3. Begin the document:

    ```
    \begin{document}
    ```

4. Begin a TikZ picture, which will be the container for the pie chart:

    ```
    \begin{tikzpicture}
    ```

5. Draw the pie chart using this command:

    ```
    \pie [rotate = 180]
        {62/\TeX\ Live and Mac\TeX,
         32/MiK\TeX\ and Pro\TeX t, 6/Other \TeX}
    ```

6. End the TikZ picture and the whole document:

    ```
    \end{tikzpicture}
    \end{document}
    ```

7.   Compile, and take a look at the output:

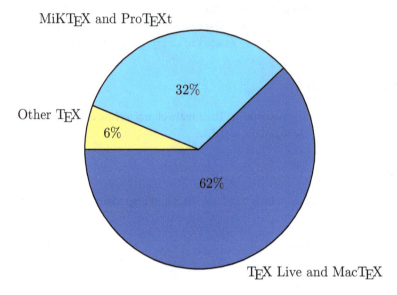

Figure 6.11 – A pie chart

How it works...

\pie is the only command of the pgf-pie package. The syntax is as follows:

```
\pie[options]{number1/text1, number2/text2, …}
```

The backslashes in our example were just because of the \TeX macro and the following space.

Let's take a look at available options with example values:

- pos = 4,6: This option positions the center at the point (4,6). The default center is (0,0).

- rotate = 90: This option turns the chart by 90 degrees.

- radius = 5: This sets the chart's radius size to 5; the default size is 3.

- color = red: This chooses a red color for all slices. We can use any color syntax that TikZ understands, such as red!80!black, for a mix of 80% red and 20% black.

- color = {red!20, red!40, red!60}: This sets a specific red color value for each of the three slices.

- explode = 0.1: This moves all the slices outwards by 0.1.

- `explode = { 0.2, 0, 0}`: This moves just the first slice of three outwards by 0.2.

- `sum = 50`: This defines the reference sum as 50 instead of the default sum of 100.

- `sum = auto`: This calculates the sum from the slice values.

- `scale font`: This scales the font size according to the slice value.

- `before number = { \$ }`: This inserts a text before the values – in this case, a dollar sign. It is empty by default.

- `after number = { percent }`: This adds a text after each value – in this case, the word "percent". With `sum = 100`, the default is the % symbol; otherwise, it is empty.

- `text = pin`: This sets the text next to the slice, connected by a short line.

- `text = inside`: This places the text within the slice.

- `text = legend`: This produces a separate legend.

- `style = drop shadow`: This adds a shadow below the chart.

There's more...

The `pie-chart` package offers further chart designs. Let's look at those and apply some of the preceding styles.

Square chart

The `square` option gives a quadratic design. Adding the `scale font` and `color` options, we arrive at the following:

```
\pie [square, scale font,
      color = {blue!10, blue!20, blue!40}] { ... }
```

With the values from our recipe, we get the following:

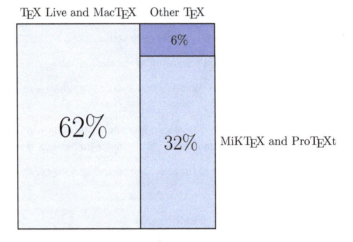

Figure 6.12 – A square chart

Polar area chart

The `polar` option changes the layout so that the slices get equal angles, but the radius represents the size. We add the `explode` and `text=legend` options:

```
\pie [polar, explode=0.1, text=legend] { ... }
```

Then, we get the following:

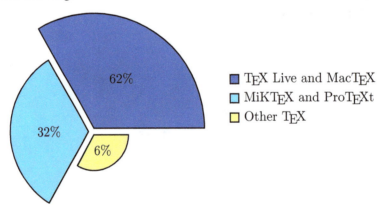

Figure 6.13 – A polar chart

Cloud chart

The cloud option produces a set of discs with a size according to the given values. This time, we put the text inside, scale it, and use a larger radius:

```
\pie [cloud, text=inside, scale font, radius=6] { ... }
```

Now, the result is as follows:

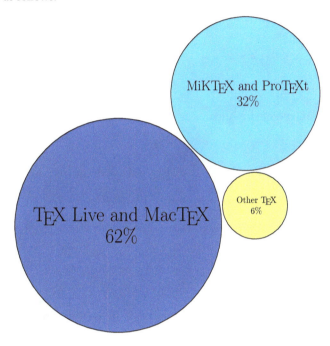

Figure 6.14 – A cloud chart

Drawing a Venn diagram

A Venn diagram displays several sets with their relationships. Commonly, these are overlapping circles. Such sets can stand for specific properties. If an element has two such properties, it would belong to an overlapping area, the intersection of the two sets.

In this recipe, we will draw a Venn diagram of three sets.

How to do it...

We will draw colored circles and apply blending to their intersections. Follow these steps:

1. Choose a document class:

   ```
   \documentclass{article}
   ```

2. Load the `tikz` package:

   ```
   \usepackage{tikz}
   ```

3. Begin the document:

   ```
   \begin{document}
   ```

4. Begin a TikZ `picture` environment:

   ```
   \begin{tikzpicture}
   ```

5. Use a `scope` environment to apply a style to a part of the drawing. Here, we apply color blending:

   ```
   \begin{scope}[blend group=soft light]
   ```

6. Draw the diagram parts, which are, in our case, just filled circles:

   ```
   \fill[red!30!white]    ( 90:1.2) circle (2);
   \fill[green!30!white]  (210:1.2) circle (2);
   \fill[blue!30!white]   (330:1.2) circle (2);
   ```

7. End `scope`. The blending effect will end at the end of the environment because environments keep settings local:

   ```
   \end{scope}
   ```

8. Add nodes with text for descriptions:

   ```
   \node at ( 90:2)       {Typography};
   \node at (210:2)       {Design};
   \node at (330:2)       {Coding};
   \node [font=\Large]    {\LaTeX};
   ```

9. End the TikZ picture and the document:

   ```
   \end{tikzpicture}
   \end{document}
   ```

10. Compile, and take a look at the output:

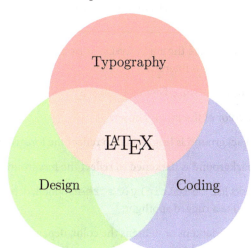

Figure 6.15 – A Venn diagram

How it works...

We created three filled circles. The center of each circle is specified in polar coordinates, with a given angle and distance from the origin. This makes radial placement easier. For example, the first circle has its center at (90:1.2), which means at 90 degrees above the origin, at a distance of 1.2. The radius of each circle is 2, so they overlap.

Normally, overlapping means that the final circle overrides what is below. We still want to look "behind" the circles to see the intersections. A classical approach is to use transparency, such as the following:

```
\begin{scope}[opacity=0.5
   ...
\end{scope}
```

This lets the background shine through. We used a `scope` environment to keep the setting local. The `opacity` value can be between 0, which means fully transparent, and 1, which means fully opaque.

Another pleasing way is using the **blend mode** feature of the PDF standard. That's what we did. It involves mixing colors in a certain way. In short, here are the possible modes:

- `normal`: Any object is drawn over the background.

- `multiply`: Color values of mixed color values are multiplied. A black factor always produces black, and a white factor doesn't cause a change. Generally, we get darker colors as the product.

- screen: This complements the color values, multiplies, and then complements again. A white factor always produces white, and a black color doesn't cause a change. Generally, we get lighter colors in such a mix.

- overlay: This mode works like the multiply or screen option, depending on the background color, resulting in an interesting overlay.

- darken: The darker one of the mixed colors is chosen.

- lighten: The lighter color of the mix is chosen.

- color dodge: The background is brightened to reflect the foreground.

- color burn: The background is darkened to reflect the foreground.

- hard light: This works like the multiply or screen option, depending on the foreground color, and gives a result like a rugged spotlight.

- soft light: This option darkens or lightens the color, depending on the foreground color, and works like a softened spotlight.

- difference: In this mode, darker colors are subtracted from lighter colors.

- exclusion: This works like the difference mode but with lower contrast.

- hue: Here, the resulting color has the foreground's hue and the background's saturation and luminosity.

- saturation: With this option, the resulting color has the saturation of the foreground and the hue and luminosity of the background.

- color: In this mode, the resulting color has the foreground hue and the background's saturation and luminosity.

- luminosity: This is like the inverse of the color mode. The resulting color has the foreground's luminosity and the background's hue and saturation.

These modes are described in the PDF standard, cited in the TikZ manual in the *Blending* section.

What seems ambitious for just overlapping colors in a Venn diagram could help overlay drawings. You can try out those modes to see what fits your needs best.

Putting thoughts into a mind map

A mind map visualizes information or ideas. Usually, there's a primary concept in the center; major concepts branch out from it. Smaller ideas start from the major concepts, so it can look like a spider web.

In this recipe, we will draw a mind map of TeX concepts.

How to do it...

We will use the TikZ `mindmap` library. Follow these steps:

1. Start with a document class:

    ```
    \documentclass{article}
    ```

2. Load the `geometry` package with the `landscape` option so that our wide map will fit the page:

    ```
    \usepackage[landscape]{geometry}
    ```

3. Load the `tikz` package and the `mindmap` library:

    ```
    \usepackage{tikz}
    \usetikzlibrary{mindmap}
    ```

4. Load the `dtk-logos` package to get additional TeX-related logo macros:

    ```
    \usepackage{dtk-logos}
    ```

5. Start the document and begin the TikZ picture:

    ```
    \begin{document}
    \begin{tikzpicture}
    ```

6. Start `path` with options:

    ```
    \path [
    ```

7. Provide the `mindmap` option, and choose a white text color:

    ```
    mindmap,
    text = white,
    ```

8. Adjust the styles for the levels of the map:

    ```
    level 1 concept/.append style =
      {font=\Large\bfseries, sibling angle=90},
    level 2 concept/.append style =
      {font=\normalsize\bfseries},
    level 3 concept/.append style =
      {font=\small\bfseries},
    ```

9. Define some styles to use for related concepts, and end the option list:

    ```
    tex/.style     = {concept, ball color=blue,
      font=\Huge\bfseries},
    engines/.style = {concept,
    ```

```
      ball color=green!50!black},
    formats/.style = {concept,
      ball color=blue!50!black},
    systems/.style = {concept,
      ball color=red!90!black},
    editors/.style = {concept,
      ball color=orange!90!black}
  ]
```

10. Now, place the central concept node and its children. The structure is similar to the tree recipe in this chapter. End the path with a semicolon:

```
node [tex] {\TeX} [clockwise from=0]
  child[concept color=green!50!black,
    nodes={engines}] {
    node {Engines} [clockwise from=90]
      child { node {\TeX} }
      child { node {pdf\TeX} }
      child { node {\XeTeX} }
      child { node {Lua\TeX} }}
  child [concept color=blue, nodes={formats}] {
    node {Formats} [clockwise from=300]
      child { node {\LaTeX} }
      child { node {\ConTeXt} }}
  child [concept color=red, nodes={systems}] {
    node {Systems} [clockwise from=210]
      child { node {\TeX Live} [clockwise from=300]
        child { node {Mac \TeX} }}
      child { node {MiK\TeX} [clockwise from=60]
        child { node {Pro \TeX t} }}}
  child [concept color=orange, nodes={editors}] {
    node {Editors} };
```

11. End the picture and the document:

```
\end{tikzpicture}
\end{document}
```

12. Compile, and examine the output:

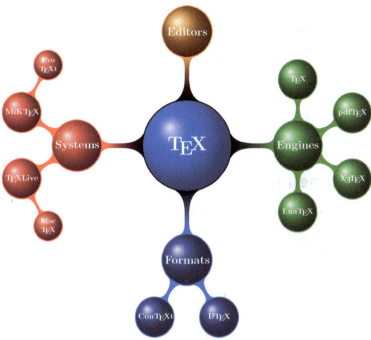

Figure 6.16 – A mind map

How it works...

The crucial component here is the `mindmap` style, which introduces additional styles and settings for implicit use, including the `concept` style for nodes. These settings mainly determine the fundamental appearance.

Initially, we refined the design by introducing style options for each sub-concept level. Consequently, we selected a bold font to enhance the legibility of white text within darker concepts, and we opted for smaller font sizes for concepts situated farther from the root. While doing this, we included a `sibling angle` value to tell TikZ the angle between significant concepts. If we were to have more concepts, we might select a smaller angle.

Additionally, we created custom styles that build upon the standard concept node style by incorporating ball shading, imparting a three-dimensional appearance. On the one hand, this serves as a demonstration of how to include additional embellishments. On the other hand, removing the ball color option to adopt a more modest style might result in a somewhat plain appearance. You can try colors and shadings provided by TikZ.

The path is just like a tree in our earlier tree recipe. Notable options are the following:

- **A start angle**: This is set using the `clockwise from = ...` syntax, where you can use the counterclockwise option as an alternative

- `nodes = {style name}`: This option applies our chosen style to all child nodes

- `concept color`: This option is for the color behind our ball shading, and it also applies to the node connections

The `mindmap` library has a dedicated section in the TikZ manual. There, you can read about alternative connections between nodes and adding annotations.

Generating a timeline

Creating a line and adding ticks, date values, and annotations is straightforward using essential TikZ functions.

Using the `timeline` library, we'll explore an alternative and colorful pre-designed approach in this recipe.

Getting ready

Until the `timeline` library becomes an official part of TikZ or becomes available on CTAN, you can download the `tikzlibrarytimeline.code.tex` file from the author's repository at https://github.com/cfiandra/timeline. You can install it in the TeX tree like any other package, but the easiest way is to put it into the same folder as your main TeX document.

How to do it...

The `timeline` library builds on TikZ but provides its own high-level commands. Follow these steps:

1. Start with a document class with a paper size that is big enough:

   ```
   \documentclass[a3paper]{article}
   ```

2. Load the `geometry` package with the `landscape` option, since our diagram will be more wide than high:

   ```
   \usepackage[landscape]{geometry}
   ```

3. Load the `tikz` package and the `timeline` library:

   ```
   \usepackage{tikz}
   \usetikzlibrary{timeline}
   ```

4. Start the document and begin the TikZ picture:

```
\begin{document}
\begin{tikzpicture}
```

5. State the number of weeks:

```
\timeline{5}
```

6. Define the time phases:

```
\begin{phases}
  \initialphase{involvement degree=3cm,
    phase color=blue}
  \phase{between week=1 and 2 in 0.4,
    involvement degree=5cm,
    phase color=green!50!black}
  \phase{between week=2 and 3 in 0.2,
    involvement degree=6cm,phase color=red!40!black}
  \phase{between week=3 and 4 in 0.5,
    involvement degree=3cm,phase color=red!90!black}
  \phase{between week=4 and 5 in 0.3,
    involvement degree=2.5cm,
    phase color=red!40!yellow}
\end{phases}
```

7. Add some text nodes as annotations on the left side:

```
\node [xshift=-0.6cm, yshift=1cm, anchor=east,
       font=\Large\bfseries] at (phase-0.180)
       {Author};
\node [xshift=-0.6cm, yshift=-1cm, anchor=east,
       font=\Large\bfseries] at (phase-0.180)
       {Publisher};
```

8. Add milestones to the upper side of the timeline:

```
\addmilestone{at=phase-0.120, direction=120:1cm,
  text={Concept}, text options={above}}
\addmilestone{at=phase-0.90, direction=90:1.2cm,
  text={Outline}}
\addmilestone{at=phase-1.110,direction=110:1.5cm,
  text={Research}}
\addmilestone{at=phase-2.100,direction=100:1cm,
  text={Writing}}
\addmilestone{at=phase-2.60,direction=90:1.5cm,
```

```
    text={First draft}}
\addmilestone{at=phase-3.90,direction=90:1.2cm,
    text={Second draft}}
\addmilestone{at=phase-4.90,direction=90:0.8cm,
    text={Approval of print draft}}
```

9. Add milestones to the lower side of the timeline:

```
\addmilestone{at=phase-0.270,direction=270:1cm,
    text={Concept Review}, text options={below}}
\addmilestone{at=phase-2.270,direction=270:1cm,
    text={First Review}}
\addmilestone{at=phase-3.250,direction=250:0.8cm,
    text={Second Review}}
\addmilestone{at=phase-3.300,direction=270:1.5cm,
    text={Approval required}}
\addmilestone{at=phase-4.260,direction=270:2.2cm,
    text={Draft for printing}}
\addmilestone{at=phase-4.300,direction=300:1cm,
    text={Publication}}
```

10. End the picture and the document:

```
\end{tikzpicture}
\end{document}
```

11. Compile, and examine the output:

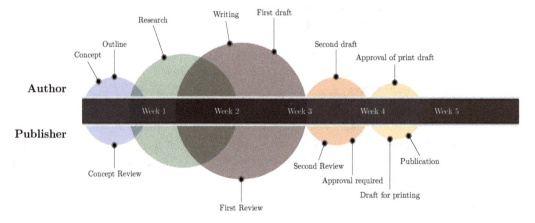

Figure 6.17 – A timeline diagram

How it works...

Using the `\timeline{5}` command, we created a filled rectangle with five weeks. Choose another number for more or fewer weeks. There's a node for each week that you can use for additional drawing; simply refer to the `(week-1)` node and so on as a named node.

Within the `phases` environment, we defined the filled circles standing for the various time phases. Let's look at sample phase arguments to understand their use:

- `between week=1 and 2 in 0.4`: This means starting at week 1 and ending at week 2, with an offset of 0.4 for fine-tuning

- `involvement degree`: This is the radius of the phase circle

- `phase color`: This is the fill color of the phase circle

That's a specific syntax for such essential elements.

Finally, we added milestones. These are text nodes connected with a line to a phase:

- `at`: This means the starting position. It's good to use relative positioning such as `phase-1.north` for above the `phase-1` node. We used the `phase-n.angle` TikZ syntax here.

- `direction`: This has been given as polar values such as `(angle:distance)`.

- `text`: This is the text within the node. We used the `text options` key to customize the placement. This option is sticky so that it will be remembered. The text has been placed above until we change `text options` to below, which is then kept.

The library offers an excellent quick start. You can use the means of TikZ for further design.

7

Creating Beautiful Designs

LaTeX also provides design concepts for non-standard documents, such as photobooks, calendars, greeting cards, colorful presentations, and fairy tale books.

This chapter explores such design ideas with a practical focus, including the following:

- Adding a background image
- Creating beautiful ornaments
- Preparing pretty headings
- Producing a calendar
- Mimicking keys, menu items, and terminal output
- Arranging topics like a puzzle
- Building a word cloud

Adding a background image

We can add background graphics such as watermarks, pre-designed letterheads, or photos to any LaTeX document. In this recipe, we will walk you through the steps to achieve this.

How to do it...

We will utilize the `background` package written by Gonzalo Medina for this task. In this recipe, you can use any LaTeX document. We will start with the `article` class and add some dummy text. You may also use a document example from another recipe for this or access this one at https://latex-cookbook.net/chapter-07.

We will insert some commands into our document preamble, which means between `\documentclass{...}` and `\begin{document}`. It takes just two steps:

1. Loading the `background` package
2. Setting up the background using the `\backgroundsetup` command with options

Here we go:

1. Load the `background` package:

   ```
   \usepackage{background}
   ```

2. Set up the background. Optionally, specify the scaling factor, rotation angle, and opacity. Provide the command for printing on the background. We will use `\includegraphics` here with a drawing of the CTAN lion from `https://latex-cookbook.net/ctanlion.pdf`, originally at `https://ctan.org/lion`:

   ```
   \backgroundsetup{scale = 1, angle = 0, opacity = 0.2,
     contents = {\includegraphics[width = \paperwidth,
     height = \paperheight, keepaspectratio]
   {ctanlion.pdf}}}
   ```

3. Compile at least twice to let the layout settle. Now, all of your pages will show a light version of the image over the entire page background, like the following:

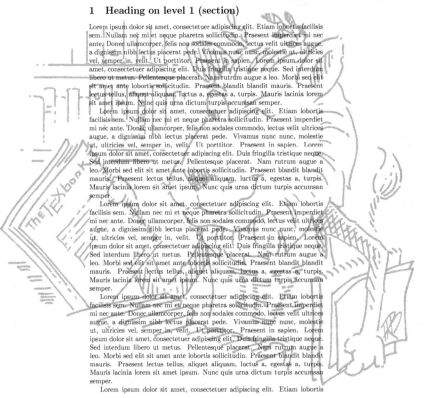

Figure 7.1 – A page with a background picture

How it works...

The background package can place any text, drawing, or image on the page background. It allows you to customize various aspects, such as positioning, color, and opacity. The example already showed some straightforward parameters, which can be specified as package options or through the \backgroundsetup command. You can use the \backgroundsetup command as often as you like to make adjustments.

The contents option contains the actual commands to be applied to the background. This can be \includegraphics, some text, or any sequence of drawing commands.

The package is built upon TikZ and the everypage package. Due to this architecture, it may require multiple compilation runs for precise positioning. This is because TikZ writes marks into the .aux file, which are then read and processed during subsequent LaTeX runs.

There's more...

Instead of images, you could display dynamic values such as the page number or the head mark with the chapter title. This can be achieved without relying on packages such as fancyhdr, or scrlayer-scrpage.

The following command places a page number in the background in the following ways:

- It's positioned at the top of the page
- It can be placed with customizable rotation, here 0 degrees
- It's scaled to four times the size of normal text
- It's colored with 80 percent of standard blue (mixed with 20 percent of white)
- It's vertically shifted downward by 2ex
- We place dashes around it

Here it goes:

```
\backgroundsetup{placement = top, angle = 0,
   scale = 4, color = blue!80,vshift = -2ex,
   contents = {--\thepage--}}
```

Here is a screenshot of the top of page 7:

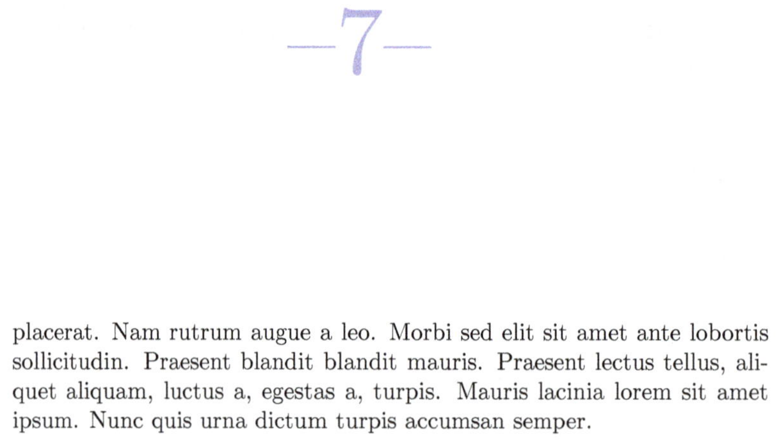

—7—

placerat. Nam rutrum augue a leo. Morbi sed elit sit amet ante lobortis sollicitudin. Praesent blandit blandit mauris. Praesent lectus tellus, aliquet aliquam, luctus a, egestas a, turpis. Mauris lacinia lorem sit amet ipsum. Nunc quis urna dictum turpis accumsan semper.

Figure 7.2 – A decorative page numbering

Let's look at an example to see how you can draw with TikZ on the background. We'll draw a rounded border and fill the interior background with a light yellow color:

```
\usetikzlibrary{calc}
\backgroundsetup{angle = 0, scale = 1, vshift = -2ex,
  contents = {\tikz[overlay, remember picture]
\draw [rounded corners = 20pt, line width = 1pt,
      color = blue, fill = yellow!20, double = blue!10]
      ($(current page.north west)+(1,-1)$)
      rectangle ($(current page.south east)+(-1,1)$);}}
```

Here, we initially loaded the `calc` library, which enabled us to perform coordinate calculations that we used later on. A TikZ image in `overlay` mode draws a rectangle with rounded corners. It features double lines with yellow in between. The rectangle's dimensions were calculated from the position of the `current page` node, representing the whole page. The final result looks like this:

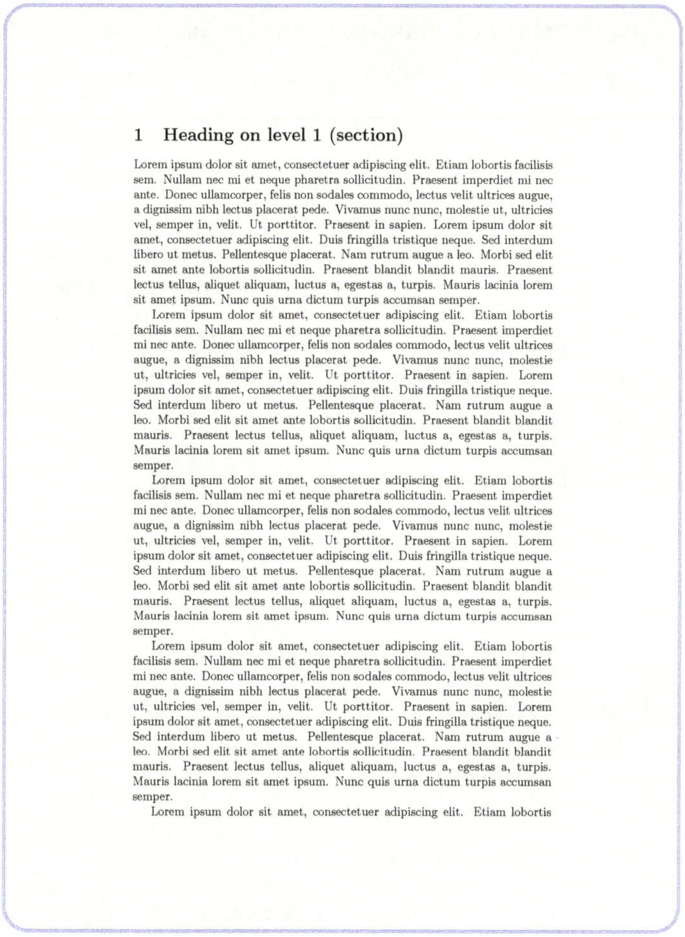

Figure 7.3 – A page with a colored background and frame

The entire code is available at `https://latex-cookbook.net/chapter-07`, too.

The next recipe will include another example, which prints ornaments at the page corners.

Here's a summary of the selected options with their default values:

- `contents`: This can be text, images, or drawing commands; `Draft` is the default text.
- `placement`: This can be `center`, `top`, or `bottom`, with `center` as the default option.
- `color`: This is a color expression that TikZ understands, with `red!45` as the default.
- `angle`: This is a value between `-360` and `360`, with `0` as the default for `top` and `bottom` and `60` for `center`.

- **opacity**: This is a value for the transparency between 0 and 1. The default is 0.5.

- **scale**: This is a positive value. The default is 8 for top and bottom and 15 for center.

- **hshift** and **vshift**: These can be any length for horizontal or vertical shifting. The default is 0 pt.

Further options for TikZ node parameters are explained in the package manual, which contains some examples. It also shows how to select just certain pages to have this background. You can open it by typing texdoc background at the command line or at https://texdoc.org/pkg/background.

More packages can do a similar task to what we showed in this recipe, for example, the watermark and xwatermark packages, and the everypage and eso-pic packages, which don't require TikZ.

Creating beautiful ornaments

Especially in older books, we find typographic ornaments such as calligraphic flowers. In this recipe, we will create a greeting card with such ornaments.

Getting ready

We will use the pgfornament package written by Alain Matthes and based on designs by Vincent Le Moign and Chennan Zhang. At the time of writing, it contains 196 high-quality vintage ornaments. It's included with TeX Live and MiKTeX; ensure you have it installed.

How to do it...

We will use a KOMA-Script class because of its arbitrary base font size. The calligra package made by Gerd Neugebauer provides a font with a hand-written style:

1. Load the document class, set paper and text dimensions, and choose a page style without the printed page number:

```
\documentclass[paper=a6,landscape,
               fontsize=30pt]{scrartcl}
\areaset{0.9\paperwidth}{0.68\paperheight}
\pagestyle{empty}
```

2. Activate T1 font encoding and load the calligra font package:

```
\usepackage[T1]{fontenc}
\usepackage{calligra}
```

3. Load the `pgfornament` package. It implicitly uses TikZ. In addition, load the `calc` library, which will be used for coordinate calculations:

```
\usepackage{pgfornament}
\usetikzlibrary{calc}
```

4. Now we write the document body:

```
\begin{document}
\centering
\begin{tikzpicture}[
  pgfornamentstyle/.style = {color = green!50!black,
                             fill  = green!80!black},
  every node/.style = {inner sep = 0pt}]
  \node [text width = 8cm, outer sep = 1.2cm,
    text centered, color = red!90!black] (Greeting)
    { \calligra Happy Birthday,\\Dear Mom!\\[-1ex]
      \pgfornament[color = red!90!black,
        width = 2.5cm]{72}};
  \foreach \corner/\sym in {north west/none,
    north east/v, south west/h, south east/c} {
      \node [anchor = \corner] (\corner)
        at (Greeting.\corner)
        {\pgfornament[width = 2cm,
        symmetry = \sym]{63}};}
  \path (north west) -- (south west)
        node [midway, anchor = east]
            {\pgfornament[height = 2cm]{9}}
        (north east) -- (south east)
        node [midway, anchor = west]
            {\pgfornament[height = 2cm,
            symmetry = v]{9}};
  \pgfornamenthline{north west}{north east}{north}{87}
  \pgfornamenthline{south west}{south east}{south}{87}
\end{tikzpicture}
\end{document}
```

5.   Compile the document and take a look at the outcome:

Figure 7.4 – A greeting card with floral ornaments

How it works...

The pgfornament package is a collection of vector ornaments that can be scaled while maintaining high quality. There are calligraphic flowers, tree leaves, and generally symbols and lines to achieve this kind of vintage design. The package's documentation contains much information on its usage and capabilities.

The fundamental command is \pgfornament [options] {number}, where the number option corresponds to the chosen ornament in the order they are listed in the package's manual. The following options can be used in a comma-separated list of expressions:

- scale: This can be a positive value, with 1 as the default

- width and height: These are LaTeX lengths

- color: This can be any color that TikZ understands

- ydelta: This can be set to shift the ornament vertically

- symmetry: This can be a value v, h, c, or none to get the ornament with vertical, horizontal, central, or no mirroring

In our example, we used the command with options in the following way:

- We set the TikZ inner sep style option to eliminate additional whitespace around nodes.

- We set the pgfornamentstyle option to be dark green and filled with lighter green.

- A node called Greeting contains the handwritten text in a dark red Calligra font. In addition, it includes ornament no. 72.

- Using the TikZ \foreach syntax, we placed ornament no. 63 at each corner with a suitable symmetry, with relative positioning to our Greeting node.

- We placed ornament no. 9 on the left and right sides. We used the midway option to put them right in the middle of the stated corners.

- Finally, we used the \pgfornamenthline command to add ornament lines no. 87 to the top and bottom edges.

There's more...

In the previous recipe, we talked about using the background package to print things on the page background. You can combine this with ornaments. This code in your preamble will print nice triangular ornaments with suitable symmetry in each corner of the page:

```
\usepackage{pgfornament}
\usepackage{background}
\backgroundsetup{angle = 0, scale = 1, opacity = 1,
  color = black!60,
  contents = {\begin{tikzpicture}[remember picture,
    overlay]
    \foreach \pos/\sym in {north west/none, north east/v,
      south west/h, south east/c} {
        \node[anchor = \pos] at (current page.\pos)
          {\pgfornament[width=2cm, symmetry=\sym]{63}};}
  \end{tikzpicture}}}
```

Lorem ipsum dolor sit amet, consectetuer adipiscing elit. Ut purus elit, vestibulum ut, placerat ac, adipiscing vitae, felis. Curabitur dictum gravida mauris. Nam arcu libero, nonummy

Figure 7.5 – Ornaments on the background of a page

We used the current page node for positioning relative to the page corners. Remember that this may require several compilation runs to achieve the final placement. You can find a complete code sample at https://latex-cookbook.net/chapter-07.

Some fonts provide typographical ornaments as glyphs; `fourier-orns`, `adforn`, and `webomints` are excellent examples.

Preparing pretty headings

This recipe will show how to bring some color into document headings.

How to do it...

We will use TikZ for coloring and positioning. Take the following steps:

1. Set up a basic document with support for filler text:

    ```
    \documentclass{scrartcl}
    \usepackage[automark]{scrlayer-scrpage}
    \usepackage[english]{babel}
    \usepackage{blindtext}
    ```

2. Load TikZ beforehand, and pass a naming option to the implicitly loaded `xcolor` package for using names for predefined colors:

    ```
    \PassOptionsToPackage{svgnames}{xcolor}
    \usepackage{tikz}
    ```

3. Define a macro that prints the heading given as an argument:

    ```
    \newcommand{\tikzhead}[1]{%
      \begin{tikzpicture}[remember picture,overlay]
        \node[yshift=-2cm] at (current page.north west)
          {\begin{tikzpicture}[remember picture, overlay]
            \path[draw=none, fill=LightSkyBlue] (0,0)
                  rectangle (\paperwidth,2cm);
            \node[anchor=east, xshift=.9\paperwidth,
                rectangle, rounded corners=15pt,
                inner sep=11pt, fill=MidnightBlue,
                font=\sffamily\bfseries] {\color{white}#1};
          \end{tikzpicture}
        };
      \end{tikzpicture}}
    ```

4. Use the new macro for the headings, printing \headmark, and complete the document with some filler text:

    ```
    \clearscrheadings
    \ihead{\tikzhead{\headmark}}
    \pagestyle{scrheadings}
    ```

```
\begin{document}
\tableofcontents
\clearpage
\blinddocument
\end{document}
```

5. Compile the document and take a look at a sample page header:

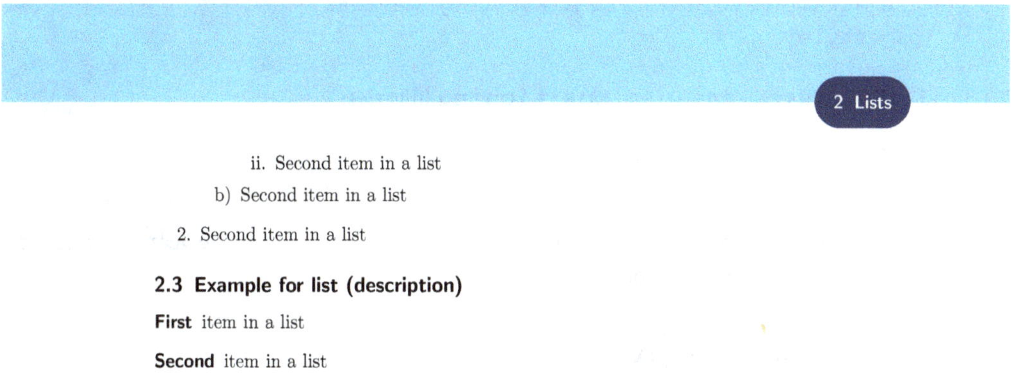

ii. Second item in a list

b) Second item in a list

2. Second item in a list

2.3 Example for list (description)

First item in a list

Second item in a list

Figure 7.6 – A fancy page header

How it works...

We've created a macro that draws a filled rectangle spanning the entire page width. We've placed a node with text inside this rectangle, shaped as a rectangle with rounded corners. This provided another brief look at TikZ's drawing syntax.

Here are the key takeaways:

- Refer to the `current page` node for positioning, as in the first recipe of this chapter
- Use the drawing macro within a header command

The rest are drawing syntax and style options described in the TikZ manual. You can read it using `texdoc tikz` at the command prompt or by visiting `https://texdoc.org/pkg/tikz`.

Producing a calendar

Self-made customized calendars can be a great gift. Also, having a personalized calendar for professional and educational purposes is helpful.

In this recipe, we'll generate a full-year calendar with all the months presented in a tabular layout. You can adjust it to print just one month below an image or for other specific needs.

How to do it...

We will use the powerful TikZ package again since it provides a calendar library:

1. Set up document class and page dimensions. Furthermore, change to the `empty` page style to not have page numbering:

```
\documentclass{article}
\usepackage[margin = 2.5cm, a4paper]{geometry}
\pagestyle{empty}
```

2. Load TikZ and its `calendar` and `positioning` libraries:

```
\usepackage{tikz}
\usetikzlibrary{calendar,positioning}
```

3. To save typing and more easily change the year, we define a macro for the year and one for calling the TikZ `\calendar` command:

```
\newcommand{\calyear}{2025}
\newcommand{\mon}[1]{\calendar[dates = \calyear-#1-01
   to \calyear-#1-last] if (Sunday) [red];}
```

4. Now, we write the document containing a TikZ picture. The month calendars are arranged in a matrix:

```
\begin{document}
\begin{tikzpicture}[every calendar/.style = {
    month label above centered,
    month text = {\Large\textsc{\%mt}},
    week list,
  }]
  \matrix (Calendar) [column sep=4em, row sep=3em] {
      \mon{01} & \mon{02} & \mon{03} \\
      \mon{04} & \mon{05} & \mon{06} \\
      \mon{07} & \mon{08} & \mon{09} \\
      \mon{10} & \mon{11} & \mon{12} \\ };
      \node [above = 1cm of Calendar, font = \Huge]
        {\calyear};
  \end{tikzpicture}
\end{document}
```

5.   Compile the document and have a look at the output:

Figure 7.7 – A year calendar

How it works...

We used a matrix to easily position the 12 month calendars; we just specified the row and column spacing.

While the given `calendar` style settings are pretty much self-explanatory, modifying them requires knowing the options. The library is extensively explained in the TikZ manual, together with some examples, at https://texdoc.org/pkg/tikz.

Based on the date calculation features and existing styles of the calendar library, you can use the bells and whistles of TikZ to get a colorful, fancy calendar. Some outstanding examples can be found in the TikZ gallery at https://www.texample.net/tikz/examples/feature/calendar-library/.

Mimicking keys, menu items, and terminal output

Technical documentation and software manuals often explain keyboard shortcuts, guide users through program menus, show terminal command output, and provide information on file locations.

This recipe helps in writing such guides.

How to do it...

We will use the `menukeys` package developed by Tobias Weh and Jonathan P. Spratte. Let's keep it concise and try out the main commands. Follow these steps:

1. Start a short document and load the `menukeys` package in it:

    ```
    \documentclass[parskip=full]{scrartcl}
    \usepackage{menukeys}
    \begin{document}
    \section*{Running \TeX works}
    ```

2. In the body text, use `\menu` for menu entries, `\keys` for keyboard combinations, and `\directory` for a path, as follows:

    ```
    In the main menu, click \menu{Typeset > pdfLaTeX}
    for choosing the \TeX\ compiler. Then press
    \keys{\cmd + T} for typesetting.
    Click \menu{Window > Show > Fonts} for seeing
    the fonts used by the document.

    Press \keys{\shift + \cmd + F} for full screen.

    The program is installed in
    \directory{/Applications/TeX/TeXworks.app}.
    \end{document}
    ```

3. Compile the document and take a look:

Running T_EXworks

In the main menu, click Typeset ⟩ pdfLaTeX for choosing the T_EX compiler. Then press ⌘ + T for typesetting. Click Window ⟩ Show ⟩ Fonts for seeing the fonts used by the document.

Press ⇧ + ⌘ + F for full screen.

The program is installed in Applications ▸ TeX ▸ TeXworks.app.

Figure 7.8 – Menu and key symbols within text

How it works...

The menukeys package provides three primary commands that parse their arguments as a list:

- \keys{combination}: This command prints a key combination given by a list of keys separated by + symbols

- \menu{sequence}: This command prints a sequence of menu entries separated by > symbols

- \directory{path} This command prints a file path in typewriter font, with components separated by / symbols

The input as separated lists follows standard conventions, and the output mimics what we expect to see on a computer screen.

Various aspects can be customized. Several predefined styles exist, such as rounded and angular menus; rounded, angular, and shadowed keys; and vintage typewriter keys. Paths can use folder symbols. If the short example whetted your appetite and you would like to modify the appearance further, have a look at the package's manual. As usual, you can read it using the texdoc menukeys command at the command line or at https://texdoc.org/pkg/menukeys.

There's more...

The sim-os-menus package written by Cédric Pierquet can draw context menus. You can use it the following way:

1. Load the package:

   ```
   \usepackage{sim-os-menus}
   ```

2. In addition, load the xfp package for floating-point calculations because the sim-os-menus package uses it internally. With TeX Live 2023 or newer, you don't need to load it:

   ```
   \usepackage{xfp}
   ```

3. Do the following when using the \ContextMenu command:

   - Use style options in square brackets

   - State menu items as a comma-separated list

   - Draw an arrow by writing (>) at the end of an item

   - Write (*) to indicate the start of a new level, just one per level

   - Use § as a separator symbol to start the next level

Here's an example:

```
\ContextMenu[Font=\sffamily]{Open, Open with(>),
   Rename, Run(>)(*), Delete §
   LaTeX, BibTeX, MakeIndex}
```

4.   Compile a document with these lines, and you'll get the following output:

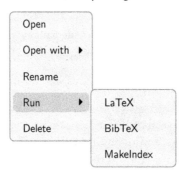

Figure 7.9 – A context menu

The menu can be customized with colors and symbols, supporting nesting up to five levels. For details, please look at the package manual by running `texdoc sim-os-menus` at the command line or at `https://texdoc.org/pkg/sim-os-menus`.

Are you interested in that package? It offers even more. It can simulate PDF viewers, image viewers, and terminal windows. In contrast to bitmap screenshots from real applications, it uses scalable TikZ graphics for better quality. Let's see what this means by looking at the terminal simulation. It works like this:

1.   Open a terminal environment, either `TermMac`, `TermUnix`, or `TermWin`, for macOS, Unix/Linux, or Windows terminal style. Leave the mandatory argument empty or choose an option; here, I've used `hbox` for automatic sizing to the content dimensions:

```
\begin{TermMac}{hbox}
```

2.   Insert your terminal window content; I've shortened it here:

```
stefan@laptop ~ % ping latex.org
...
stefan@laptop ~ % }
```

3.   End the terminal environment:

```
\end{TermMac}
```

4.   When you compile the document, you get a picture of a terminal window with text; here is my complete ping output:

```
Terminal Mac
stefan@laptop ~ % ping latex.org
PING latex.org (78.46.26.59): 56 data bytes
64 bytes from 78.46.26.59: icmp_seq=0 ttl=55 time=45.882 ms
64 bytes from 78.46.26.59: icmp_seq=1 ttl=55 time=31.600 ms
64 bytes from 78.46.26.59: icmp_seq=2 ttl=55 time=36.364 ms
^C
--- latex.org ping statistics ---
3 packets transmitted, 3 packets received, 0.0% packet loss
round-trip min/avg/max/stddev = 31.600/37.949/45.882/5.937 ms
stefan@laptop ~ %
```

Figure 7.10 – A macOS terminal window

With the `TermUnix` environment, the result looks like this:

```
Terminal UNiX
stefan@laptop ~ % ping latex.org
PING latex.org (78.46.26.59): 56 data bytes
64 bytes from 78.46.26.59: icmp_seq=0 ttl=55 time=45.882 ms
64 bytes from 78.46.26.59: icmp_seq=1 ttl=55 time=31.600 ms
64 bytes from 78.46.26.59: icmp_seq=2 ttl=55 time=36.364 ms
^C
--- latex.org ping statistics ---
3 packets transmitted, 3 packets received, 0.0% packet loss
round-trip min/avg/max/stddev = 31.600/37.949/45.882/5.937 ms
stefan@laptop ~ %
```

Figure 7.11 – A Unix terminal window

And using the `TermWin` environment, you get this picture:

```
>_ Terminal Win                                      —  □  ✕
stefan@laptop ~ % ping latex.org
PING latex.org (78.46.26.59): 56 data bytes
64 bytes from 78.46.26.59: icmp_seq=0 ttl=55 time=45.882 ms
64 bytes from 78.46.26.59: icmp_seq=1 ttl=55 time=31.600 ms
64 bytes from 78.46.26.59: icmp_seq=2 ttl=55 time=36.364 ms
^C
--- latex.org ping statistics ---
3 packets transmitted, 3 packets received, 0.0% packet loss
round-trip min/avg/max/stddev = 31.600/37.949/45.882/5.937 ms
stefan@laptop ~ %
```

Figure 7.12 – A Windows terminal window

Of course, you can customize terminal window properties, such as title, alignment, and width. Furthermore, you can choose among many options processed by the drawing commands from the `tcolorbox` package that's internally used here. You can find the details in the `sim-os-menus` package manual, as previously, and further options in the `tcolorbox` manual.

Just for a brief demonstration of how the syntax looks with options, here's a quick example:

```
\begin{TermMac}[Title = stefan - shell,
  Width=10cm]{sharpish corners}
```

Here, we have the `sim-os-menus` options in square brackets, setting the title and width of the terminal window. The `sharpish corners` option is for the underlying color box from the `tcolorbox` package and changes our round corners to sharp corners. Again, the package manuals provide a complete reference.

Arranging topics like a puzzle

Cédric Pierquet has created numerous useful and entertaining packages, often centered around graphics, including functionalities for printing playing cards, Scrabble boards, Tangram puzzles, and Wordle grids. You can find a comprehensive list of his contributions at `https://ctan.org/author/pierquet`.

Let's just try a package by him that gives a simple yet effective method to organize topics in a puzzle-like layout.

How to do it...

We will use the `thematicpuzzle` package developed by Cédric Pierquet. Additionally, we will load the `xfp` package to enable internal floating-point calculations. With TeX Live 2023 or newer, you can omit this step. Moreover, we will use the `fontawesome5` package authored by Marcel Krüger, allowing us to incorporate **Font Awesome 5** icons. Take the following steps:

1. Start with a document class. Here, we use the `standalone` class as we just want to generate a small picture:

    ```
    \documentclass[border=10pt]{standalone}
    ```

2. Load the three mentioned packages, and begin with the document:

    ```
    \usepackage{thematicpuzzle}
    \usepackage{xfp}
    \usepackage{fontawesome5}
    \begin{document}
    ```

3. Utilize the `\ThematicPuzzle` command. Here's an example where I visualize the interaction of LaTeX-related tools. I will explain the options further shortly:

```
\ThematicPuzzle[FontLabels = {\tiny\sffamily},
   Labels = { Editor, LaTeX, BibTeX,
             MakeIndex, Tools, PDF},
   BgColors = {green!90, yellow!20, red!20, blue!20,
   orange!60, yellow!30},
   IconsColor = {red!90!black}]
   { \faEdit, \faFileExport, \faBookOpen,
     \faClipboardList, \faTools,\faFilePdf }
```

4. End the document:

```
\end{document}
```

5. Compile the document and take a look:

Figure 7.13 – Arranging topics like a puzzle

How it works...

To start, we employed the `fontawesome5` package to utilize the icon font from https://fontawesome.com. That's a huge commercial icon library, where parts of it can freely be used. I anticipate the release of version 6 of the LaTeX package in 2024 since the original font is now available in version 6. The manual contains the entire list of hundreds of icon commands. You can open it through `texdoc fontawesome5` or at https://texdoc.org/pkg/fontawesome5.

The `\ThematicPuzzle` command has a mandatory argument in curly braces, representing the list of topics, one for each puzzle piece. It can be any text or symbol. We used the `fontawesome5` icons here.

We added optional style values in square brackets:

- `FontLabels`: This is the command for setting the font of the labels
- `Labels`: This is a comma-separated list of labels below the puzzle pieces
- `BgColors`: That's a list of colors for the puzzle pieces
- `IconsColor`: This determines the color of the icons and labels

That's quickly done and a nice add-on to a presentation slide.

That was a linear puzzle. You can create bigger two-dimensional puzzles using the `jigsaw` package. I demonstrated examples in the book *LaTeX Graphics with TikZ*, in *Chapter 15*, *Having Fun with TikZ*. You can find the code of my examples with output at `https://tikz.org/chapter-15`.

Building a word cloud

A visual representation of a concept can show information quickly and intuitively in a more engaging way than a textual explanation. A popular example is a **word cloud**, which displays words in different sizes based on their frequency or importance within a particular context. People like word clouds because they provide a quick and visually appealing way to grasp the most significant keywords of a topic.

So, we will define a word cloud and learn how to generate word clouds automatically from PDF or text files.

Getting ready

We will use the `wordcloud` package programmed by Maxime Chupin. It is included in TeX Live and MiKTeX, but you can also get it from `https://ctan.org/pkg/wordcloud`. The package requires **LuaLaTeX**, so choose this as the compiler in your editor. The `wordcloud` package uses Lua for parsing LaTeX commands and arguments, building lists of words from a text file, and generating **MetaPost** code. That code is interpreted by the `luamplib` package. So, you must have both packages and MetaPost installed with your TeX distribution.

How to do it...

The key is a single command with a particular argument list. Follow these steps:

1. Start a short document and load the `wordcloud` package:

    ```
    \documentclass{article}
    \usepackage{wordcloud}
    \begin{document}
    ```

2. Within the body text, use the \wordcloud command and provide a list of words and numerical weights. Their order doesn't matter. Here, we additionally demonstrate that we can wrap it in a \textsf command to use sans-serif fonts:

```
\textsf{\wordcloud[scale=1,rotate=45,margin=0.5pt,
   usecolor]{(\textrm{\LaTeX},10);(graphics,6);
   (fonts,7);(images,5);(tables,5);(bibliographies,2);
   (mathematics,3);(PDF,5);(headings,4);(paragraphs,3);
   (diagrams,3);(commands,4);(packages,5);(classes,6);
   (hyphenation,2);(macros,6);(justification,2);
   (footnotes,4);(cross-references,2);(spacing,3);
   (lines,4);(colors,5);(captions,5);(hyperlinks,3);
   (chapters,5)}}
```

3. End the document:

```
\end{document}
```

4. Compile the document, and have a look at the output:

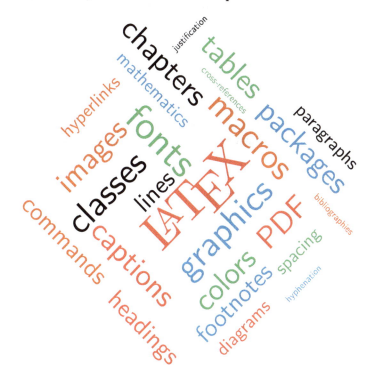

Figure 7.14 – A word cloud

How it works...

The `wordcloud` command takes a semicolon-separated list in the form `(word,weight)`. It takes optional arguments for rotating, scaling, margins, and coloring. Consult the package's manual to see all available options using the `texdoc wordcloud` command at the command line or at `https://texdoc.org/pkg/wordcloud`.

There's more...

The `wordcloud` package can read a text file, find the most used words, and display them in a cloud shape.

If your content is in PDF format, you can use the **pdftotext** tool to convert it to plain text. The pdftotext tool is part of the **Xpdf** software suite and is also available with the Poppler library, so you must have one installed. Alternatively, you can use an online conversion tool if the data is not confidential.

For our example, we will use the *Formatting information* document written by Peter Flynn, a beginner's introduction to typesetting with LaTeX. Our word cloud shall automatically show the most used words, so we have an idea of the tutorial's content, which is nearly 300 pages long. The document can be downloaded from CTAN at `https://ctan.org/pkg/beginlatex`.

Once we've converted the PDF document into a text file called `beginlatex.txt`, we can generate a word cloud with 80 words using the following command:

```
\wordcloudFile[usecolor]{beginlatex.txt}{80}
```

If you would like to omit often-used non-LaTeX words, you can exclude them from the word cloud using the following case-sensitive command with example words and re-compile:

```
\wordcloudIgnoreWords{You ,you, just, want, from, them
   for, the, same}
```

I did this for that tutorial document and got the following result:

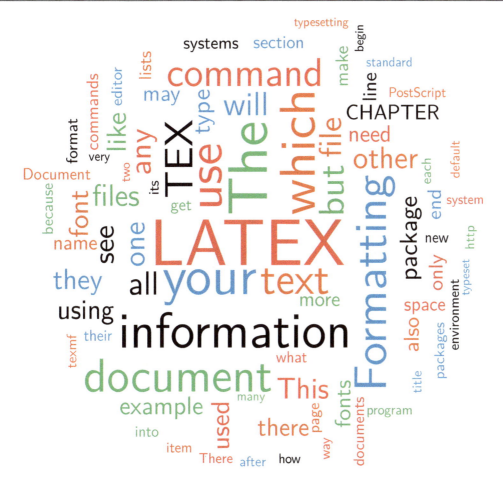

Figure 7.15 – A word cloud generated from a document

That's a mesmerizing cloud of 80 keywords easily generated from a 300-page document. The arrangement looks pretty circular. If you don't like a word arrangement, you can recompile and get a slightly different version. Personally, I like this mix of LaTeX keywords and normal words, so the brain even notices phrases in the cloud. This could be the top slide of a LaTeX introduction presentation.

8

Producing Contents, Indexes, and Bibliographies

LaTeX provides features for automatically creating tables of contents, lists of figures and tables, bibliographies, glossaries, and indexes. This chapter equips you with recipes for quickly starting and customizing such lists.

In this chapter, we will deal with the following:

- Tuning tables of contents and lists of figures and tables
- Creating a bibliography
- Adding a glossary
- Making a list of acronyms
- Generating an index

We will start with the table of contents. While it's straightforward to create one by simply using the `\tableofcontents` command, the format is pretty rigidly determined by the document class. We will see ways to modify it easily. The same can be used for the list of figures and the list of tables, which can be generated utilizing the `\listoffigures` or `\listoftables` commands, respectively.

Especially for scientific work, a list of references is essential. It's also called a **bibliography**. Using the very modern **biblatex** package, our recipe will provide a quick start.

Another recipe will show you how to create a glossary to explain scientific or technical vocabulary to the reader.

The final recipe demonstrates generating a sorted index to let your reader quickly search keywords.

Tuning tables of contents and lists of figures and tables

Especially when starting to use LaTeX, the automatic creation of a **table of contents** (**ToC**) is impressive. The ToC with section titles and page numbers is generated from your heading texts in commands such as `\part`, `\chapter`, and `\section`. The lists of figures and tables work precisely in the same way, while they use the texts in `\caption` for the list entries.

The default table of contents design follows a widely used style. In some cases, though, you might need to adjust it.

How to do it...

We will use the `tocstyle` package for customizing, which belongs to the **KOMA-Script** bundle. You can try the recipe settings in your own document or use our book example from *Chapter 1, Exploring Various Document Classes*.

Automatic correction of widths

The default widths of numbers in the ToC remain fixed, so large section or page numbers can potentially overlap with the text. It can also happen with Roman numbering, where the numbers are even broader.

Fortunately, resolving this is straightforward with the following code:

```
\usepackage[tocindentauto]{tocstyle}
```

Despite its somewhat unintuitive name, this option automatically adjusts the indentation of textual entries, preventing overlap with numbers. It's important to note that generating a ToC now requires three runs, so the widths are calculated and settled.

Printing a flat table of contents

By default, a ToC is **graduated**. This means that lower-level sectioning entries would be indented. Our book example from *Chapter 1, Exploring Various Document Classes*, has a graduated table of contents as follows:

Contents

Figure 8.1 – A standard table of contents

To have all content entries left aligned, specifically all section numbers at the left, use the `tocflat` option:

```
\usepackage[tocflat]{tocstyle}
```

Then, the ToC changes to this:

Contents

Figure 8.2 – A flat table of contents

Still, the content entries will be aligned, which means that the section numbers will be set in a box of equal width. You can omit this, pushing everything to the left, using the `tocfullflat` option:

```
\usepackage[tocfullflat]{tocstyle}
```

Now, you get this:

Contents

I. First portion	**5**
1. The beginning	**7**
1.1. A first section	7
1.2. Another section	7
II. Appendix	**11**
A. An addendum	**13**
A.1. Section within the appendix	13

Figure 8.3 – A left-aligned table of contents

The effects are even more noticeable if subsections are added to the ToC.

You can combine options by adding them, separated by commas, using `\usepackage [tocindentauto,tocflat]{tocstyle}`.

Getting KOMA-Script-like, sans-serif headings

KOMA-Script classes use a modern design of headings, which are sans-serif and bold, so they are not as heavy as the default classic serif headings. Also, bold ToC entries are sans-serif. You saw this earlier.

You can get the same behavior with other classes using the following commands:

```
\usepackage{tocstyle}
\usetocstyle{KOMAlike}
```

How it works...

You need several compiler runs to benefit from the automatic adjustments of the `tocstyle` package. Expect at least three runs:

1. In the first run, LaTeX writes all entries from commands, such as `\chapter` and `\section`, to the external table of contents file. The name of this file ends with `.toc`. The lists of figures and tables end with `.lof` and `.lot`, respectively.

2. In the following run, LaTeX can read the entries of the external file for printing the ToC. Widths are calculated and written into the `.aux` file.

3. In the next run, the ToC is produced using the known entries from the `.toc` file and the known widths from the `.aux` file. Of course, changes in section and page numbers would require running it again. That's a general consequence of straight compiling using external files: several compiler runs can be needed until things are entirely settled.

There's more...

Loading the `tocstyle` package without options produces a graduated ToC, like with standard classes. But it strongly tries to avoid page breaks between a ToC entry and its parent, automatically adjusting the widths. So, simply loading it can already be a relief.

The package provides many commands for fine-tuning the style of the ToC, which is challenging. Refer to the package manual for details, which you can open using `texdoc tocstyle` at the command line or `https://texdoc.org/pkg/tocstyle`.

Creating a bibliography

The traditional method of producing a bibliography, or a list of references, uses **BibTeX**. This is an external program for building a bibliography from a plain text database with a chosen style and citing references in the text.

LaTeX Beginner's Guide, Second Edition has a BibTeX tutorial for creating bibliographies. Refer to this guide for learning about the classic way. In our cookbook, we will use an advanced package called `biblatex`, which is generally considered to be the successor of BibTeX.

Here's why `biblatex` stands out:

*   It is a complete reimplementation of LaTeX's standard bibliographic features
*   It supports the BibTeX database format but understands further formats

`biblatex` entirely uses TeX macros for formatting. BibTeX styles, in contrast, are programmed in a postfix stack language. So, for customizing styles with `biblatex`, you don't need to learn another language. There are more benefits:

- It supports subdivided bibliographies
- You can generate multiple bibliographies within a single document
- You can have separate lists of bibliographic shorthands
- The `biblatex` package can still use BibTeX as the backend but works with a new and capable backend called **biber**

Using the `biber` backend with the `biblatex` package is highly recommended for several reasons:

- It can most notably process UTF-8 input, including accented characters and Unicode symbols. BibTeX, in contrast, requires 7-bit ASCII text.
- You can customize the sorting, such as considering capitalization and following sorting guidelines of various languages. It can automatically use your operating system locale.
- Handling names is more flexible, such as correctly citing names with prefixes.
- Multiple bibliographies in the same document, such as per chapter, can be produced in one run, while BibTeX needs one run for each chapter.
- The `biber` backend can even sort each bibliography in the document independently and differently.
- Unlike BibTeX, `biber` hardly encounters memory limitations, which can sometimes pose challenges.

How to do it...

We will start with the same small example of *LaTeX Beginner's Guide*, so that you can compare the new `biblatex` approach with the classic BibTeX way.

Follow these steps:

1. With any text or LaTeX editor, start a new document and add these bibliography entries:

```
@book{DK86,
    author = "D.E. Knuth",
    title = "The {\TeX}book",
    publisher = "Addison Wesley",
    year = 1986
}
@article{DK89,
    author = "D.E. Knuth",
```

```
        title = "Typesetting Concrete Mathematics",
        journal = "TUGboat",
        volume = 10,
        number = 1,
        pages = "31--36",
        month = apr,
        year = 1989
}
@book{Lamport,
    author = "Leslie Lamport",
    title = "\LaTeX: A Document Preparation System",
    publisher = "Addison Wesley",
    year = 1986
}
```

2. Save that document. You can choose any filename. Here, we give the name `texbooks.bib`.

3. Now, we start the LaTeX document. Begin with a document class:

    ```
    \documentclass{scrartcl}
    ```

4. Load the `biblatex` package:

    ```
    \usepackage{biblatex}
    ```

5. Add the bibliography file with the full filename, including the extension:

    ```
    \addbibresource{texbooks.bib}
    ```

6. Start your LaTeX document body. For citing references, use the `\autocite` command, which is more context-aware than the standard `\cite` command:

    ```
    \begin{document}
    \section*{Recommended texts}
    To study \TeX\ in depth, see \autocite{DK86}. For
    writing math texts, see \autocite{DK89}. The
    basic reference for \LaTeX\ is \autocite{Lamport}.
    ```

7. At the place where you would like to print the bibliography, insert this command:

    ```
    \printbibliography
    ```

8. Finish your document:

    ```
    \end{document}
    ```

9. Compile the document and take a look:

Recommended texts

To study TeX in depth, see [**DK86**]. For writing math texts, see [**DK89**]. The basic reference for LaTeX is [**Lamport**].

Figure 8.4 – A document with citations

10. Still, there's no bibliography. For the cited references, we see just the keys.

11. Run the `biber` command on the document. Click the corresponding editor button if your editor provides one or run it at the command prompt. Give the document name as an argument, but without the `.tex` extension:

```
biber filename
```

12. Recompile the document and take another look:

Recommended texts

To study TeX in depth, see [1]. For writing math texts, see [2]. The basic reference for LaTeX is [3].

References

[1] D.E. Knuth. *The TeXbook*. Addison Wesley, 1986.

[2] D.E. Knuth. "Typesetting Concrete Mathematics". In: *TUGboat* 10.1 (Apr. 1989), pp. 31–36.

[3] Leslie Lamport. *LaTeX: A Document Preparation System*. Addison Wesley, 1986.

Figure 8.5 – A list of references

How it works...

`biblatex` and `biber` support the classic bibliography file format known from BibTeX. *LaTeX Beginner's Guide*, the BibTeX reference, and the `biblatex` package manual describe the latter. Please consult the latter for complete information.

First, we need to load the package. You can specify many customizing options when loading it using the `\usepackage` command. Some of the most valuable options are the following:

- `backend`: This option can be `biber` (default), `bibtex`, `bibtex8` (8-bit version), or `bibtexu` (unsupported Unicode version)

- `style`: This option can get the name of the style for the bibliography and citation

- `bibstyle`: This option is the name of a bibliography style

- `citestyle`: This option is the name of a citation style

- `natbib`: When you choose this option, `biblatex` loads commands for citation commands of `natbib`, which is a popular package for author-year citations with BibTeX

So, you could load the `biblatex` package in the preceding example this way:

```
\usepackage[
  backend = biber,
  style   = authoryear,
  natbib  = true
]{biblatex}
```

Then you get author-year notations in both citations and the bibliography as follows:

Recommended texts

To study TeX in depth, see (Knuth, 1986). For writing math texts, see (Knuth, 1989). The basic reference for LaTeX is (Lamport, 1986).

References

Knuth, D.E. (1986). *The TeXbook*. Addison Wesley.
— (1989). "Typesetting Concrete Mathematics". In: *TUGboat* 10.1, pp. 31–36.
Lamport, Leslie (1986). *LaTeX: A Document Preparation System*. Addison Wesley.

Figure 8.6 – References in author-year style

The `\addbibresource` command loads your bibliography. It provides several options, given in the `key=value` notation. The following options are most noticeable:

- `label`: This option is a name that you can use instead of the entire resource name in a reference section in the case of multiple bibliographies.

- `location`: This option can be used for a local file (default) or remotely for an Internet address, which can be a website or an FTP server.

- `datatype`: This option declares the format of the resource. It can have one of the following values:

  - `bibtex`: This value decides, using the classic BibTeX format, which is the default

  - `ris`: This value enables the Research Information Systems format

- `zoterordfxml`: This value declares the Zotero RDF/XML format

- `endnotexml`: This value chooses the EndNote XML format

You can load several files, even directly from the internet:

```
\addbibresource{maths.bib}
\addbibresource{history.bib}
\addbibresource[location=remote,
  label=tex]{http://latex.org/texbooks.bib}
```

The `\autocite` command generates a citation like the `\cite` command but avoids double punctuation marks and takes care that, if you use footnote citations, the footnote mark is printed after the punctuation. The command's behavior can also be customized with an option in the preamble. For example, with the `autocite=plain` package option, it works like the standard `\cite` command, while the `autocite=footnote` option makes it work like the `\footcite` command, making it easy to switch.

The `\printbibliography` command handles the printing of your sorted and styled bibliography. It understands some optional parameters for customizing its appearance, which are all detailed in the manual.

Note

`\addbibresource` replaces the older BibTeX command `\bibliography`. The latter takes just the file name and is not so flexible.

There's more...

While this recipe serves as a quick start, browsing the comprehensive manual is highly recommended for customizing your bibliography. You can open it as usual by typing `texdoc biblatex` at the command line or visiting `https://texdoc.org/pkg/biblatex`. You can access the `biber` manual in the same way.

The `biblatex` manual lists further predefined styles such as numeric, alphabetical, and author-year variations.

On CTAN, there are a lot of additional `biblatex` styles available for download: `http://ctan.org/topic/biblatex`. Check whether one matches your requirements; otherwise, the manual can guide you in your final adjustment. Luckily, you can use LaTeX for that instead of the BibTeX postfix language.

> **Note**
>
> Both `biblatex` and `biber` underwent substantial development in tandem. Ensure that your versions are compatible with each other. The `biber` manual provides a compatibility matrix in its introduction section.

Adding a glossary

When your document contains terms needing clarification, a **glossary** becomes invaluable. It's an alphabetized roster of words or phrases accompanied by their explanations. Enhancing this further involves incorporating back-references, indicating where these terms are used within the text.

How to do it...

We will work with the `glossaries` package. Follow these steps:

1. Start with any document class. For our example, we decided on the `scrartcl` class because, with the `parskip` option, we don't start with a paragraph indentation. But you could use the `article` class without options as well:

    ```
    \documentclass[parskip=half]{scrartcl}
    ```

2. Load the `glossaries` package and choose the style called `long3col`:

    ```
    \usepackage[style=long3col]{glossaries}
    ```

3. Use the following command to tell the package to create a glossary:

    ```
    \makenoidxglossaries
    ```

4. Create the first glossary entry for the word **TeX**. Using a `key=value` interface, state the name and a word indicating the sort order because the name is a macro. Finally, write a description. All of them should be in curly braces:

    ```
    \newglossaryentry{tex}{
      name = {\TeX},
      sort = {TEX},
      description = {Sophisticated digital
                     typesetting system, famous for
                     high typographic quality of
                     mathematical formulae}
    }
    ```

5.   Repeat this for each glossary entry. We will do this for **LaTeX** and **TikZ**:

```
\newglossaryentry{latex}{
   name ={\LaTeX},
   sort = {LATEX},
   description = {Document markup language based on
                 \gls{tex}, widely used in academia}
}
\newglossaryentry{tikz}{
   name = {Ti\emph{k}Z},
   sort = {TikZ},
   description = {Extremely capable graphics
                 language for drawing with \gls{tex}}
}
```

6.   Start the document:

```
\begin{document}
```

7.   Write some text. When you use the words that are part of the glossary, use the \gls{label} command:

```
\gls{tikz} works with plain \gls{tex}. However,
it is mostly used with \gls{latex}.
```

8.   Use the following command to print the glossary:

```
\printnoidxglossary
```

9.   End the document:

```
\end{document}
```

10.   Compile two times and take a look at the outcome:

TikZ works with plain TeX. However, it is mostly used with LaTeX.

Glossary

LaTeX	Document markup language based on TeX, widely used in academia	1
TeX	Sophisticated digital typesetting system, famous for high typographic quality of mathematical formulae	1
TikZ	Extremely capable graphics language for drawing with TeX	1

Figure 8.7 – A glossary

How it works...

This is the basic procedure:

1. Define your terms and abbreviations. This can also be done in a separate file, which you could load using the \input command.
2. Reference those entries using the \gls command, as you would do with the \ref command to a label.
3. Display the glossary list.

The glossaries package offers impressive capabilities, including various predefined layouts known as styles. We chose long3col for a longtable design with three columns. There are further longtable and supertabular styles and several list layouts similar to the standard LaTeX description list available.

> **Note**
>
> There's a package with a similar name called glossary. This is an older version by the same author; it is now obsolete and glossaries should be used instead.

All the features of the glossaries package are explained in the user guide, which you can access by typing texdoc glossaries at the command line or by opening it online at https://texdoc.org/pkg/glossaries. If you feel overwhelmed by the amount of reference information, you could read the beginner's guide instead for a quick start. It can be opened using texdoc glossariesbegin or at https://texdoc.org/pkg/glossariesbegin.

Creating a list of acronyms

For documents with many acronyms or abbreviations, a table showing their short form and the extended version is expected. This allows for compact writing and adds convenience for the reader.

The difference to a glossary is that we don't list explanations, just the longer forms.

How to do it...

We will again use the `glossaries` package. Since the concepts of a glossary and a list of acronyms are closely related, it provides an acronym mode, too. So, we will now use it that way. Take these steps:

1. Begin with a document class. It doesn't matter which one, so we'll take the same as in the previous recipe:

   ```
   \documentclass[parskip=half]{scrartcl}
   ```

   Load the `glossaries` package and choose the `long3col` style, like in the previous recipe. For acronym support, add the `acronym` option:

   ```
   \usepackage[acronym,style=long3col]{glossaries}
   ```

2. Choose an acronym style. We take `long-sc-short` here, where `sc` stands for small caps in the short form:

   ```
   \usepackage[acronym,style=long3col]{glossaries}
   ```

3. Define a new acronym using the `\newacronym` command and three arguments: a label, the short form, and the long form. Since we use small caps anyway, writing the short form in lowercase is recommended:

   ```
   \newacronym{ctan}{CTAN}{Comprehensive
      \TeX\ Archive Network}
   ```

4. Define further acronyms as needed in the same way:

   ```
   \newacronym{tug}{TUG}{\TeX\ Users Group}
   \newacronym{dante}{DANTE}{Deutschsprachige
      Anwendervereinigung \TeX}
   ```

5. Use this command to tell the package to create defined glossaries, which also applies to a list of acronyms:

   ```
   \makenoidxglossaries
   ```

6. Start the document:

   ```
   \begin{document}
   ```

7. Write some text. Like with the glossary in the previous recipe, for acronyms, use the \gls{label} command:

```
The \gls{ctan} has been founded by members of the
\gls{tug} and of the German speaking group ``\gls{dante}''.

The \gls{ctan} project is actually independent of
\gls{tug} and \gls{dante}, but \gls{dante} is still
the main supporter.
```

8. Use this command to print the list of acronyms:

```
\printnoidxglossary[type=\acronymtype]
```

9. End the document:

```
\end{document}
```

10. Compile two times and take a look:

The Comprehensive TEX Archive Network (CTAN) has been founded by members of the TEX Users Group (TUG) and of the German speaking group "Deutschsprachige Anwendervereinigung TEX (DANTE)".

The CTAN project is actually independent of TUG and DANTE, but DANTE is still the main supporter.

Acronyms

CTAN	Comprehensive TEX Archive Network	1
DANTE	Deutschsprachige Anwendervereinigung TEX	1
TUG	TEX Users Group	1

Figure 8.8 – A list of acronyms

How it works...

It works exactly like the previous recipe about glossaries. The only substantial addition is the following command:

```
\newacronym{label}{short version}{long version}
```

This command defines each acronym.

Producing an index

In longer documents such as technical books, including an index is customary. An index comprises a comprehensive list of words alongside corresponding page numbers. It is typically positioned at the document's end, guiding readers to the occurrences of those words or phrases within the document. This compilation encompasses keywords, topics, and individuals' names, facilitating easy navigation and reference within the document.

How to do it...

Indexing is typically carried out at the very end of the writing process. While reading through the document, the \index{keyword} command should be placed for each relevant keyword occurrence. A good place can be right before that keyword appears in the text. Don't include a space between \index{...} and the indexed word.

We will use the makeidx package. We will now insert the indexing commands while writing. Follow these steps:

1. Start with a document class. We will use the same as in the previous recipes:

    ```
    \documentclass[parskip=half]{scrartcl}
    ```

2. Load the makeidx package:

    ```
    \usepackage{makeidx}
    ```

3. Use this command to generate the index:

    ```
    \makeindex
    ```

4. Begin the document:

    ```
    \begin{document}
    ```

5. Write the text; insert the \index command right before the essential keywords:

    ```
    While \index{glossary}glossary entries are simply
    printed in the text, an \index{acronyms}acronym
    is firstly fully printed with the short version
    in parentheses, later only in the short version.
    ```

6. Use this command to print the index:

    ```
    \printindex
    ```

7. End the document:

    ```
    \end{document}
    ```

8. Compile a first time.

9. Run the `makeindex` command in your editor or execute the `makeindex filename` command at the command line.

10. Compile again with LaTeX and have a look at the output. Here's how the document body looks like:

While glossary entries are simply printed in the text, an acronym is firstly fully printed with the short version in parentheses, later only in the short version.

Figure 8.9 – The document body

And here's the document index:

Index

acronyms, 1

glossary, 1

Figure 8.10 – An index of a document

How it works...

Each `\index` command generates an entry with a keyword and page number in an auxiliary file. The external `makeindex` program then processes this file. During the second run, its output is read and printed.

> **Note**
>
> The `latexmk` tools can automate this process. So, you would just need a single `latexmk` call, which calls LaTeX for you, and even `biber` or `bibtex` and `makeindex`, if required. It runs often enough to resolve cross references. You can read about it using `texdoc latexmk` at the command line or `https://texdoc.org/serve/latexmk/0`.

There's more...

Indexing is typically considered one of the final tasks in document preparation. However, creating macros can streamline the process if you prefer to add index entries as you write. An everyday use case involves defining macros like a keyword program, which displays a word in a specific style and simultaneously adds an index entry.

Index entries can have sub-entries. They are added behind the main entry, separated by an exclamation mark, such as using the following command:

```
\index{main topic:sub topic}
```

We can put those two thoughts into a sample macro for packages that does the following:

1.   Creates a sub-entry for the package topic.

2.   Establishes a sub-entry for a given topic.

3.   Prints it with some formatting.

This shall be the macro:

```
\newcommand{\package}[2]{\index{packages!\texttt{#2}}%
   \index{#1!package \texttt{#2}}\texttt{#2}}
```

Let's now extend our text so that we have more index entries to play with, even though it may look a bit overdone:

```
While \index{glossary}glossary
\index{glossary!entry}entries are
simply printed in the text, an \index{acronym}acronym
is firstly fully printed with the
\index{acronym!short version}short version in
\index{parentheses}parentheses, later only
in the short version.

A glossary can be done using one of the packages
\package{glossary}{glossaries} or
\package{glossary}{nomencl}.
For a list of acronyms, suitable are
\package{acronyms}{acronym}, \package{acronyms}{acro}
and also \package{acronyms}{glossaries}.
```

Compile twice. The output now changes to the following:

While glossary entries are simply printed in the text, an acronym is firstly fully printed with the short version in parentheses, later only in the short version.

A glossary can be done using one of the packages `glossaries` or `nomencl`. For a list of acronyms, suitable are `acronym`, `acro` and also `glossaries`.

Figure 8.11 – More document text

Index

acronym, 1
    short version, 1
acronyms
    package `acronym`, 1
    package `acro`, 1
    package `glossaries`, 1

glossary, 1
    entry, 1
    package `glossaries`, 1
    package `nomencl`, 1

packages
    `acronym`, 1
    `acro`, 1
    `glossaries`, 1
    `nomencl`, 1
parentheses, 1

Figure 8.12 – A comprehensive index

You can see the sub-entries and typewriter formatting for package names.

9

Optimizing PDF Files

Initially, LaTeX produced output in **DVI** format. This stands for **device independent file**. It is still supported; however, today there are newer page description languages, such as **PostScript** (**PS**) and the widely favored **Portable Document Format** (**PDF**).

There are converters from DVI to PS, PS to PDF, and DVI to PDF. A modern TeX compiler, called **pdfTeX**, can directly generate PDF output. Combined with the LaTeX format, this is called **pdfLaTeX**, and it's pretty much the standard today.

In this chapter, we will use LaTeX to utilize the features of the PDF format. We will cover recipes for the following tasks:

- Using hyperlinks
- Adding metadata
- Including copyright information
- Inserting comments
- Producing fillable forms
- Optimizing the output for e-book readers
- Removing white margins
- Combining PDF files
- Creating an animation

Using hyperlinks

Initially, LaTeX was used primarily to produce high-quality prints on paper. Since the output was device-independent from the beginning, the results can also be viewed on screens, tablets, and smartphones.

With electronic publishing, we gain access to convenient functionalities, most notably hyperlinks, enabling effortless navigation within documents. This recipe focuses on using LaTeX to incorporate hyperlinks into a PDF.

How to do it...

We will use the `hyperref` package, which provides a user-friendly interface for accessing numerous PDF features, particularly hyperlinks. We can test it with examples from *Chapter 1, Exploring Various Document Classes.* Here are the steps to follow:

1. Open the `book` example from the first chapter in your editor.

2. At the end of the preamble, add this line for loading the `hyperref` package:

   ```
   \usepackage{hyperref}
   ```

3. Compile at least twice so LaTeX can process the data in the `.aux` file written by the `hyperref` package.

4. Take a PDF viewer, such as the Adobe Acrobat Reader, and have a look at the table of contents:

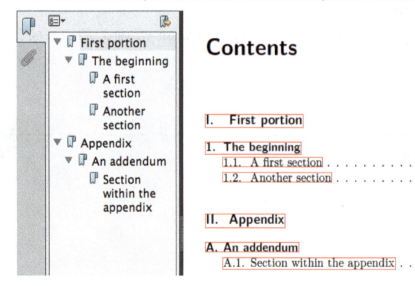

Figure 9.1 – A table of contents with hyperlinks and bookmarks

5. You can spot hyperlinks by the red borders around the entries. Each table of contents entry is a hyperlink now. Click on an entry to navigate to the corresponding chapter or section in the document body.

6. On the left, you can see bookmarks for additional navigation.

The `hyperref` package does a lot more for us. Let's sum up the most significant changes:

- All entries in the table of contents, list of figures, list of tables, and similar listings are now clickable hyperlinks, directing to their corresponding location in the body text.

- Footnote markers now serve as direct links to their respective sections, eliminating the need for manual scrolling.

- Citations are linked to their entries in the bibliography, providing easy access to referenced sources.

- References done using the `\ref` command become hyperlinks pointing to the location where the label was set. This applies, for example, to figure and table captions, headings, and equations.

How it works...

While enabling hyperlinks was easy, the internal operations of the `hyperref` package are extensive. It redefines numerous commands of classes and packages to incorporate hyperlink functionality.

Therefore, as a rule of thumb, load the `hyperref` package after all other packages to let it override their features. There are exceptions, such as the `cleveref` and `amsrefs` packages, and those reliant on the `hyperref` package, such as the `bookmark`, `hypcap`, and `hypernat` packages. A comprehensive maintained list can be found at `https://latex.net/hyperref`.

Similar to most packages, the `hyperref` package can be configured using options such as `\usepackage[linkcolor={blue}]{hyperref}`. It provides a `key=value` interface. Alternatively, after loading the package, you can set such options using the following command:

```
\hypersetup{key1 = value1,
            Key2 = value2,
            ...
}
```

In both cases, some keys can be set without a value, which would then default to `true`.

Using the `\hypersetup` command is preferable for the following reasons:

- LaTeX expands values in the package options early, which can be undesirable.

- LaTeX removes spaces in options.

- Some options, such as metadata, are better set after loading the `hyperref` package.

- While curly braces can protect the values in options, you may omit them in the `\hypersetup` command.

- If a document class already loads the `hyperref` package, as the beamer class does, or another package, you should not load it again using the `\usepackage{hyperref}` command. You can still utilize the `\hypersetup` command.

In a later recipe, *Adding metadata*, we will directly compare. Besides this, we will systematically use the \hypersetup command. The following pages provides plenty of examples.

There's more...

In addition to the default behavior, the hyperref package provides the user with commands for explicitly setting anchors and links. We can customize the link appearance. Over time, the hyperref package developed a fully fledged PDF interface. We will also explore some of its PDF-specific features.

Inserting custom hyperlinks

You can create your own anchors, assign names to them, and create links to those anchors. Additionally, you can link them directly to internet addresses.

Linking to a place within the document

Take a look at this short example:

```
\documentclass{article}
\usepackage{hyperref}
\begin{document}
See \hyperlink{mytarget}{next page}.
\newpage
\hypertarget{mytarget}{Here} starts a new page.
\end{document}
```

It works like this:

- We used the \hypertarget command to create an internal link named mytarget, which is added to a printed piece of text
- We used the \hyperlink command to link to that anchor, printing text with a hyperlink

As you can see, we can link to the target even before it has been set. That's why we need two compiler runs: LaTeX doesn't know the target in the first run before it's defined.

Linking to labeled objects

A single command is sufficient when we have already defined a label, as we can see here:

```
\begin{equation}
  \label{eq:einstein}
  E = mc^2
\end{equation}
```

Now, we can write the following:

```
Refer to the \hyperref[eq:einstein]{mass-energy
  equivalence}.
```

We got a hyperlink with text instead of a number as we would have with the \ref command. Note the following:

- We used square brackets for the label argument and curly braces for the link text.

- A common way to categorize labels is using prefixes such as eq: for equations and fig: for figures. It helps with keeping the code organized but is optional.

Linking to the internet

Let's take a quick look at some further commands. We will use samples of real-world addresses instead of placeholders for immediate understanding of the usage, as follows:

- The \href{https://latex.org}{LaTeX Forum} command prints text with a hyperlink to an address

- The \url{https://tikz.net} command prints the formatted address with a hyperlink

- The \nolinkurl{https://texdoc.org} command prints the formatted address without a link

The \hyperref command accepts more options. Here is the rather complex syntax:

```
\hyperref{address}{category}{name}{text}
```

That command prints the text and links it to address#category.name.

Let's see a sample for this command:

```
\newcommand{\baseaddress}{https://tikz.org/}
\newcommand{\chapter}{chapter-13}
\hyperref{\baseaddress\chapter}{plot}{3D}
  {Plotting in 3D}
```

The generated hyperlink points to http://tikz.org/chapter-13#plot.3D.

Generally, to avoid confusing the arguments, here's a mnemonic: the first argument is the name or label of a target, which is invisible, and the last argument, if needed, is the text that appears printed.

Changing color and shape

The default highlighting by red borders can seem a bit intrusive. You can remove them by adding the `hidelinks` option:

```
\hypersetup{hidelinks}
```

The links are still clickable. As an indication for the reader, PDF viewing software usually changes the mouse pointer when hovering over a link.

However, you can decide to color the text of hyperlinks instead of the default frames. This is an example:

```
\usepackage{xcolor}
\hypersetup{
    colorlinks,
    linkcolor = {red!75!black},
    citecolor = {green!40!black},
    urlcolor  = {blue!40!black}
}
```

Here, we loaded the `xcolor` package to use its color-mixing syntax. We get a color for internal links in the document with 75 percent red plus black. Then, we set colors for citations and external links to the internet.

Blackening the hyperlinks, that is, getting darker colors, may be less intrusive and look better in print. Colored links are actually printed, in contrast to the default borders, so you may still choose to use the `hidelinks` option for printing. Hyperlinks on regular paper don't need emphasizing.

To get a consistent link color for all kinds of links, you can set the `allcolors` option.

Getting back-references in the bibliography

To get a backlink for each bibliography item to where it has been cited, you can set the `backref` option:

```
\hypersetup{backref}
```

The section number will be printed and linked at the end of each bibliography item. Valid optional values for the `backref` key are `section`, `slide`, `page`, `none`, and `false`.

If you would like to have backlink page numbers at the end of bibliography items, use the following:

```
\hypersetup{pagebackref}
```

Hyperlinking index entries

Since an index is for looking up something, hyperlinks to the corresponding place in the text are quite natural. It's not enabled by default. However, you can switch it on using the following option:

```
\hypersetup{hyperindex}
```

Adding metadata

Standard PDFs contain concealed fields for descriptive information, such as the author's name and the document title. These fields serve archival purposes and are utilized by internet search engines, so it's advisable to use them. This recipe will demonstrate how to edit this metadata.

How to do it...

We will use the `hyperref` package interface. Let's again use our examples from *Chapter 1, Exploring Various Document Classes*:

1. Open the `book` example from the first chapter in your editor.

2. At the end of the preamble, load the `hyperref` package:

    ```
    \usepackage{hyperref}
    ```

3. Set up metadata information. Here, we use some dummy text:

    ```
    \hypersetup{pdfauthor   = The Author,
                pdftitle    = The Book,
                pdfsubject  = Draft version,
                pdfkeywords = {book, draft},
                pdfproducer = TeX version,
                pdfcreator  = LaTeX editor}
    ```

4. Compile your document.

5. Inspect the document properties using a PDF viewer such as Adobe Acrobat Reader. You can find the meta information there. It can look like this:

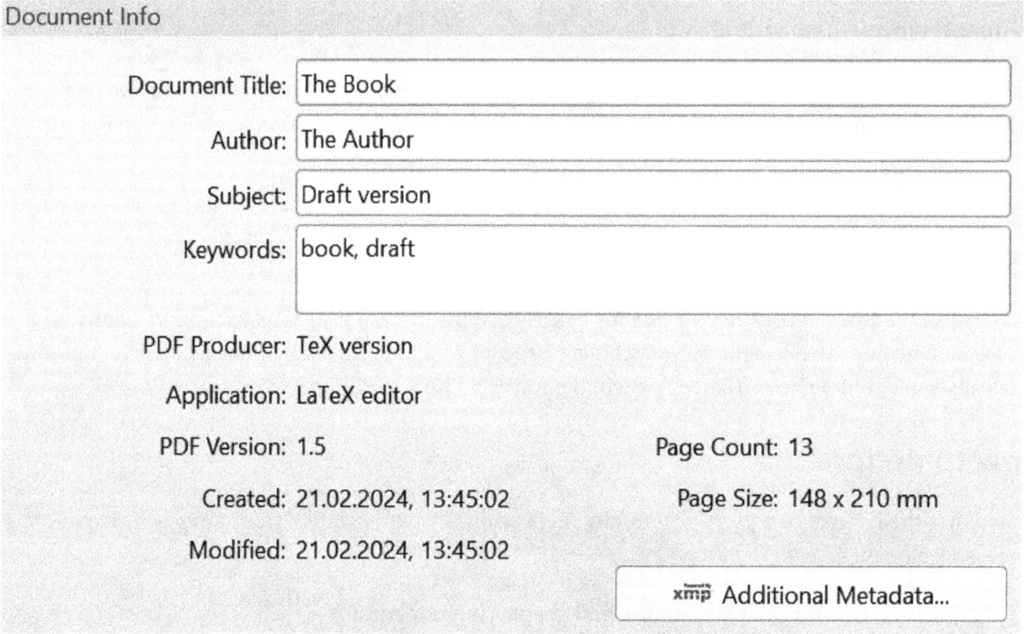

Figure 9.2 – Document properties with PDF metadata

How it works...

Some metadata is set automatically, such as the creation date and the pdfTeX compiler version as producing software. You can overwrite it and set your own data using the \hypersetup command.

Values containing commas, such as the keywords in our example, must be enclosed in curly braces since commas are otherwise used to separate options.

There's more...

In the first recipe, we explained why \hypersetup is preferable over options to \usepackage. Let's see how it looks in the latter case, especially for preserving the spaces in values:

```
\usepackage[pdfauthor   = {The\ Author},
            pdftitle    = {The\ Book},
            pdfsubject  = {Draft\ version},
            pdfkeywords = {{book, draft}},
            pdfproducer = {TeX\ version},
            pdfcreator  = {LaTeX\ editor}]{hyperref}
```

We should use curly braces for grouping to enable safe option parsing. The space with the preceding backslash is a forced space; otherwise, it would get lost. It looks a bit more complicated, especially if you were to set many more other options.

An alternative interface for setting metadata lets you even set your own keys. This is the `pdfinfo` option, which works this way:

```
\hypersetup{pdfinfo = {
            Author   = The Author,
            Title    = The Book,
            Subject  = Draft version,
            Keywords = {book, draft},
            Producer = TeX version,
            Creator  = LaTeX editor,
            Version  = 2.0,
            Comment  = Contains dummy text}}
```

We set the known data and added our own keys.

For completeness, we can declare metadata without `hyperref` by using a pdfTeX command if this compiler is used:

```
\pdfinfo{
  /Author (The Author)
  /Title (The Book)
  /Subject (Draft version)
  /Keywords (book, draft)
  /Producer (pdfTeX 1.40.0)
  /Creator (LaTeX editor)}
```

That's an unusual syntax that calls for using the `hyperref` package.

Including copyright information

We added author, producer, and creator information in the previous recipe. We can even add a field for our own copyright information. However, there's a specific place for copyright information. Even after adding metadata like we did earlier, Adobe Acrobat Reader and other PDF viewers may still display **Copyright Status: Unknown** and an empty copyright notice. We can change this.

How to do it...

The `hyperxmp` package can embed the required information. Follow these steps to add copyright information:

1. Open the `book` example from the first chapter in your editor.

2. At the end of the preamble, load the `hyperref` package:

   ```
   \usepackage{hyperref}
   ```

3. On the next line, load the `hyperxmp` package:

   ```
   \usepackage{hyperxmp}
   ```

4. Set up copyright information as follows:

   ```
   \hypersetup{
     pdfcopyright = {Copyright 2024 by Stefan Kottwitz.
       All rights reserved.},
     pdflicenseurl =
       {http://latex-community.org/license/}}
   ```

5. Compile your document.

6. Take a PDF viewer and inspect the document properties. For example, in PDF-XChange Viewer, click on **File | Document Properties | Additional Metadata**. You will see the following:

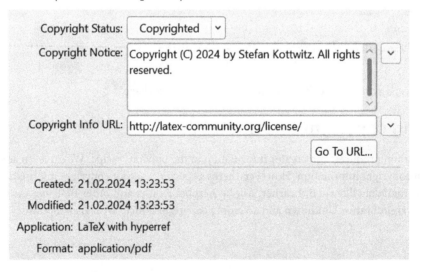

Figure 9.3 – PDF copyright information

How it works...

Adobe Systems, Inc. supports the **eXtensible Metadata Platform** (**XMP**) for embedding metadata. This method takes **eXtensible Markup Language** (**XML**) formatted attributes for inclusion within documents.

The `hyperxmp` package processes the `hyperref` package keys and adds further keys, such as those we used earlier in this chapter. So, we don't even need to deal with XML directly.

For a comprehensive overview of all options, including contact information, refer to the `hyperxmp` manual. As usual, you can access it using `texdoc hyperxmp` at the command prompt or at `https://texdoc.org/pkg/hyperxmp`.

There's more...

The `xmpincl` package is more flexible than the `hyperxmp` package but doesn't have such a handy interface. You can create a separate XML file, such as `metadata.xmp`, which can be included in the PDF:

```
\usepackage{xmpincl}
\includexmp{metadata}
```

If you want to use it, please consult the package manual for complete details and a sample xmp file, as XML markup is beyond the scope of this book, and `hyperxmp` already solves the task of our recipe.

Inserting comments

When collaborating, you may want to append notes or comments to a document, offering extra details to share with co-authors, which can later be eliminated from the final version. The PDF standard supports comments, and so does LaTeX.

How to do it...

We will insert some comments into our small document example from *Chapter 1*, *Exploring Various Document Classes*. For brevity, we will directly look at the essential commands. As with all recipes, the full source code can be downloaded. Follow these essential steps for inserting comments:

1. Load the `xcolor` package in the preamble to get color support:

    ```
    \usepackage[svgnames]{xcolor}
    ```

2. Load the `pdfcomment` package in the preamble:

    ```
    \usepackage{pdfcomment}
    ```

You could define some default settings if you wish to, such as the following. Add them when loading the `pdfcomment` package, as follows:

```
\usepackage[author={Your name}, icon=Note,
   color=Yellow, open=true]{pdfcomment}
```

3. To insert a simple comment with a marker symbol at a certain place in the document, call the `\pdfcomment` command right at that position:

```
\pdfcomment{Simple documents don't have chapters.}
```

4. You can let the comment marker appear in the margin instead:

```
\begin{equation}
   \pdfmargincomment{The equation environment produces
      a centered equation with whitespace before
      and after it.}
   ...
\end{equation}
```

5. To mark visible content while showing a comment, select it by grouping it within curly braces and use `\pdfmarkupcomment` on it. Here, we highlight and comment on the word `sections`:

```
The text will be divided into
\pdfmarkupcomment{sections}{You could additionally
   use subsections.}.
```

6. Markup comments can be tooltips that become visible when hovering the mouse pointer over it. They can be added as follows:

```
\pdftooltip{formulas}{Formulas can be inline or
   displayed in their own paragraph}
```

7. You can embrace whole environments with a sideline comment:

```
\begin{pdfsidelinecomment}[color=Red]{A bulleted list}
   \begin{itemize}
      \item ...
   \end{itemize}
\end{pdfsidelinecomment}
```

8. Furthermore, you can place free text somewhere on the document with custom dimensions, color, and transparency, like the following:

```
\pdffreetextcomment[subject={Summary}, width=7.5cm,
   height=2.2cm, opacity=0.5, voffset=-3cm]{The
   whole document is an example showing how to write
```

```
a small document.
Now we enriched it with sample comments.}
```

9. With all those comments in our small sample document, compile twice and examine the results. Here's a simple comment, a markup comment, and a sideline comment:

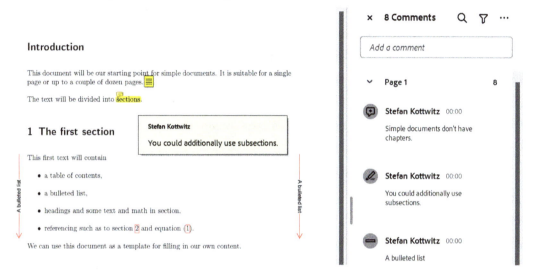

Figure 9.4 – Different styles of PDF comments

Here, you can see a tooltip, a side comment, markup comments in math mode, and a free-text comment:

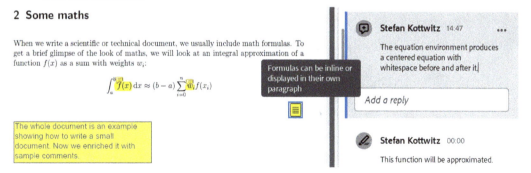

Figure 9.5 – Tooltips and comments in math mode

10. To make all comments invisible in the final published version, add the `final` option:

```
\usepackage[...,final]{pdfcomment}
```

How it works...

There are a lot of style options for customizing the appearance of comments. You saw a selection in this recipe. The complete set is described in the pdfcomment manual. As usual, you can open it by typing texdoc pdfcomment at the command prompt or visit https://texdoc.org/pkg/pdfcomment.

You can apply such options globally, as we did using the \usepackage command in the second step, or locally. In that case, use the options within square brackets as we usually do in LaTeX:

```
\pdfcomment[icon=Insert, color=red, opacity=0.5,
    author=Me]{The comment}
```

You can do it similarly with the \pdfmarkupcomment command:

```
\pdfmarkupcomment[markup=StrikeOut,
    color=red]{Text}{The comment}
```

While some options, such as width, height, and color, are self-explanatory, let's take a look at some special options.

The icon option can have these values according to the PDF standard taken from the manual:

Figure 9.6 – PDF standard icons

Adobe Acrobat Reader supports further icons, as follows:

Figure 9.7 – Adobe Acrobat Reader PDF icons

As a markup option, you can choose Highlight, Underline, Squiggly, and StrikeOut.

Producing fillable forms

PDF files can be interactive. Users can fill out forms before printing the entire document. With LaTeX, you can produce such forms. In this recipe, we will create a form.

How to do it...

Once again, we will use the `hyperref` package. We aim to produce small paper sheets for a survey as a fillable PDF form. A yellow background shall distinguish it from other papers. The format will be landscape. Let's begin the process:

1. Start a new document with A6 paper in landscape format and a small inter-paragraph space instead of paragraph indentation, as follows:

   ```
   \documentclass[a6paper,landscape,
     parskip=half]{scrartcl}
   ```

2. Set a small margin to save space on the screen:

   ```
   \usepackage[margin=0.4cm]{geometry}
   ```

3. Set the background color as 30% yellow:

   ```
   \usepackage{xcolor}
   \pagecolor{yellow!30}
   ```

4. Choose an `empty` page style, so we won't get page numbers:

   ```
   \pagestyle{empty}
   ```

5. Load the `hyperref` package:

   ```
   \usepackage{hyperref}
   ```

6. Start the document and start a `Form` environment:

   ```
   \begin{document}
   \begin{Form}
   ```

7. For positioning, we will use a `tabular` environment. Within that, we use commands for form elements, such as \TextField, \ChoiceMenu, \CheckBox, and \PushButton:

   ```
   \begin{tabular}{|lr|}\hline
     \textbf{Dear \TeX\ user, please help in
       our survey.} &
     \PushButton[width=1cm, onclick =
       {app.alert("You may use a pseudonym for the
       name.")}]{Info}\\[0.5ex] \hline
   ```

```
      & \\
      \TextField[width=5cm]{Name:} &
      \TextField[width=3cm]{Profession:} \\
      & \\
      \ChoiceMenu[radio, radiosymbol=6,
        width=0.5cm]{Software:\quad}{\TeX\ Live,
        MiK\TeX}
      &\ChoiceMenu[combo, width=3cm]{Editor:}%
      {TeXworks,TeXstudio,TeXmaker,TeXshop,
      WinEdt,Kile,Emacs,vi} \\
      & \\
      Membership in:
      \hfill\CheckBox[width=0.5cm]{TUG}\hfill
      \CheckBox[width=0.5cm]{DANTE e.V.} &
      \TextField[width=3cm]{Other:}\\ & \\ \hline
    \end{tabular}
```

8. Announce the use the remaining space for notes:

```
    \par
    \textbf{Notes:}
    \par
```

9. Provide a text field where the user may write several lines:

```
    \TextField[multiline, width=0.94\paperwidth,
      height=10\baselineskip]{ }
```

10. End the form and the document:

```
    \end{Form}
    \end{document}
```

11. Compile the document and test it by filling in some values using a capable PDF viewer such as Adobe Acrobat Reader:

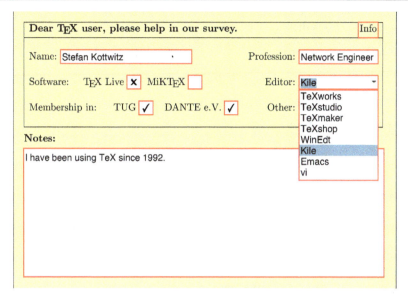

Figure 9.8 – A fillable PDF form

12. Save the PDF file, close it, and open it to verify that it keeps your data.

How it works...

We used the following three commands for fillable elements:

- \TextField[options]{label}: This gives a fillable text field

- \CheckBox[options]{label}: This prints a box that can be checked or unchecked

- \ChoiceMenu[options]{label}{list of choices}: This produces a drop-down menu where we can choose an element of a list

Some of the possible options are the following:

- width, height, and borderwidth: These are the dimensions of the element

- charsize: This is the font size of the element text

- color, backgroundcolor, and bordercolor: These are the colors of the element

- maxlen: This is the maximum allowed characters in a text field

- value: This is an initial value, such as default text in a field

- combo, radio, and popdown: This can be true or false for the type of element

- radiosymbol: This is the Zapf Dingbats symbol for the radio button
- checked: This can be true or false; it decides whether a field is selected by default

Use it as key=value syntax, like in our example. All possible options are described in the hyperref manual.

We also placed a button in our form using the following command:

```
\PushButton[onclick={app.alert(text)}]{label}
```

This command prints a button with label text on it. If clicked, it opens a pop-up window via JavaScript, displaying text. You can also add options like in *step 7* of this recipe.

You can use other JavaScript commands, for example, to let the user enter text in the pop-up window:

```
\PushButton[width=1cm, onclick =
  {app.response("What was your original motivation
  to start with LaTeX?")}]{Question}
```

An entire program can be inserted, such as for using and evaluating the input. You may also bind JavaScript code to other actions, such as onmouseover and onselect. Such actions are listed in the hyperref manual.

Form commands should only be used within a Form environment. There should be at most one Form environment in the file. However, it can be extensive.

Optimizing the output for e-book readers

A traditional book comprises a set of pages; LaTeX, too, follows this tradition. However, today, e-book reading devices, such as Kindle and iPad, and even smartphones have gained popularity for reading documents.

In this recipe, we will see how to make a document e-book-friendly.

How to do it...

We will set up a preamble for a document that could nicely be read on an electronic device such as a tablet reader. Perform the following steps:

1. Choose a suitable document class. Choose small headings and a small inter-paragraph skip instead of paragraph indentation. The latter costs too much space on an already narrow display. Use this:

```
\documentclass[fontsize=11pt,headings=small,
  parskip=half]{scrreprt}
```

2. Set a small paper size matching a common screen ratio, and choose a small margin:

    ```
    \usepackage [papersize={3.6in,4.8in},
      margin=0.2in]{geometry}
    ```

3. Choose a well-designed font that is also easily readable on the screen. Especially with a low screen resolution, a sans-serif font may be a good choice:

    ```
    \usepackage [T1]{fontenc}
    \usepackage{lmodern}
    \renewcommand{\familydefault}{\sfdefault}
    ```

4. Load the microtype package for improving justification, which is even more important for smaller screens:

    ```
    \usepackage{microtype}
    ```

5. Choose the empty page style. If chapter or part pages have their own style, set those to empty as well:

    ```
    \pagestyle{empty}
    \renewcommand{\partpagestyle}{empty}
    \renewcommand{\chapterpagestyle}{empty}
    ```

6. Use the hyperref package for easier browsing via hyperlinks. You may prefer colored links over framed appearance, as we saw in the first recipe of this chapter:

    ```
    \usepackage{hyperref}
    \hypersetup{colorlinks}
    ```

7. In your document, use relative sizes instead of absolute values, such as the following:

    ```
    \includegraphics [width=0.8\textwidth]{text}
    ```

How it works...

A tablet or smartphone differs significantly from a book, even though some reading software simulates traditional things such as page flipping. Our approach honors the difference.

We chose a document class that works in one-sided mode. There's no need to insert blank pages to let chapters start on the right-hand-side pages.

With a KOMA-Script class, we can choose smaller headings than default by setting a class option, so we chose the scrreprt class. With other classes, you could change headings and their spacing using the titlesec package.

The default paragraph indentation would make our already narrow text even harder to justify fully, so we would remove that. Setting a `parskip` option does that automatically. We even used the `half parskip` option to reduce spacing. With a non-KOMA-Script class, load the `parskip` package.

We don't need excessive margins added to the mechanical margins of the reading device, so we use the `geometry` package to get small margins.

Choosing the font is a matter of taste. Serif fonts often display poorly on low-resolution displays, so sans-serif fonts were usually preferred. However, today's screens offer a very high resolution, so the decision is up to your taste.

Furthermore, e-book reading software can already display page numbers, so we don't need to reserve space for them. The `empty` page style avoids page numbering.

There's more...

We can go even further when designing e-books. Why turn pages when we can scroll endlessly? We could forget all the challenges raised by page breaks, such as the concept of floating figures and tables. They could stay where we place them because no page break would get in the way. Boris Veytsman and Michael Ware described an approach in *Ebooks and paper sizes: Output routines made easier* in *TUGboat, Vol. 32, No.3*: `https://www.tug.org/TUGboat/tb32-3/tb102veytsman-ebooks.pdf`.

Removing white margins

To reuse the PDF output of your LaTeX document in another document, in an e-book, or on a website, it's usually a good idea to remove the margins or at least make them smaller.

Getting ready

For this recipe, you need to have installed:

- The PS interpreter software **Ghostscript**
- The programming language **Perl**
- The `pdfcrop` script

Fortunately, TeX Live automatically installs internal versions of Ghostscript and Perl, offering `pdfcrop` as a package. So, TeX Live users are lucky. You may need to install the software if you don't use TeX Live. You can find more information at `https://www.ghostscript.com`, `https://www.perl.org`, and `https://ctan.org/pkg/pdfcrop`.

How to do it...

The actual procedure is easy, given that the command line won't be an obstacle for you, as you use LaTeX. Follow these steps:

1. Go to the command line:

   - On Linux or Unix, open a **shell**
   - On Ubuntu Linux and macOS, the shell you need to open is called **Terminal**
   - On Windows, open **Command Prompt** or run the program called cmd

2. Change into the directory of your generated PDF file.

3. Given the document name is filename.pdf, execute the following command:

   ```
   pdfcrop filename
   ```

4. A file named filename-crop.pdf has been generated; open it to verify the result.

How it works...

The pdfcrop program takes the PDF file and uses Ghostscript to calculate the bounding box for each page. It produces another PDF file where the margins are removed.

The output is automatically named with -crop as the name suffix. However, you can give the output filename as a parameter. The syntax for the command is the following:

```
pdfcrop [options] filename[.pdf] [outputname]
```

You don't need to tell the program the PDF file extension for the input file.

Using the following options, you can decide to keep some margins:

- Keep a 20 PS-point margin on each side:

   ```
   pdfcrop --margins 20 input.pdf output.pdf
   ```

- Keep 10, 20, 30, and 40 PS points at the left, top, right, and bottom, in this order:

   ```
   pdfcrop --margins '10 20 30 40' input.pdf output.pdf
   ```

A PS point is 1/72 inch; in TeX, it's called a **big point**, written as 1 bp. The classical TeX point is slightly different; 1 point means 1/72.27 inch.

You can display options and information using the following command:

```
pdfcrop --help
```

There's more...

You can remove the margins that are already in the source code.

If the class doesn't matter, for example, because you are just generating a graphic, you could use the `standalone` class as follows:

- For a document without margins:

    ```
    \documentclass{standalone}
    ```

- To get a 10-point margin:

    ```
    \documentclass[border=10pt]{standalone}
    ```

- For a margin of 10, 20, 30, and 40 points at the left, right, bottom, and top:

    ```
    \documentclass[border={10pt 20pt 30pt
        40pt}]{standalone}
    ```

You can freely choose another unit, such as `in` or `cm`.

The `standalone` class provides more handy features and is well documented.

The older `preview` package does a similar job. It can extract the environments of a LaTeX document as separate graphic files.

Combining PDF files

Combining the source code of two LaTeX documents can be pretty challenging, especially if they are based on different classes. However, combining their PDF output is pretty straightforward.

How to do it...

We will use the `pdfpages` package.

We can test it with the flyer example from the first chapter together with the form example of the current chapter. Let's get going:

1. Start a document and choose any class:

    ```
    \documentclass{article}
    ```

2. Load the `pdfpages` package:

    ```
    \usepackage{pdfpages}
    ```

3. Begin the document:

```
\begin{document}
```

4. Include the first PDF file using the \includepdf command. It takes a page range as an option. Use a dash (-) for the entire page range:

```
\includepdf[pages=-]{flyer}
```

5. Include the second PDF file:

```
\includepdf[pages=-]{form}
```

6. End the document:

```
\end{document}
```

7. Compile once, and look at the newly generated file containing the flyer and the form.

How it works...

The pdfpages package is primarily for including PDF files in a LaTeX document, entirely or partially. The pages=- option means all pages. We could have specified a page range, such as pages={3-6}, and more complex choices are possible, such as pages={1,3-6,9}.

We created a new document as a container and included both source PDF files.

This way, you can combine very different files, such as an application letter, your curriculum vitae, and various scanned certificates, into a single file for an online job application.

Creating an animation

To show a developing process or visualize changes, an in-place animation can be more convenient than a series of images.

As an example application, we will draw a recursively defined fractal curve, the **Koch curve**. An animation shall present the stages of the curve, which becomes more complex with more recursions.

How to do it...

The animate package provides a simple way to generate an animation. Let's try this with the Koch curve to show growing complexity by performing the following steps:

1. Start with any document class. Here, we've chosen the standalone class, which we already mentioned earlier. So, the animation tightly fits on the page:

```
\documentclass[border=10pt]{standalone}
```

2. Load the `animate` package:

```
\usepackage{animate}
```

3. Load the TikZ package. Furthermore, load the `lindenmayersystems` library to produce fractals and the `shadings` library for filling with a shading:

```
\usepackage{tikz}
\usetikzlibrary{lindenmayersystems,shadings}
```

4. We define the fractal with the library's syntax. Don't worry about it, as it's just for having stuff to play with. The definition is as follows:

```
\pgfdeclarelindenmayersystem{Koch curve}{
   \rule{F -> F-F++F-F}}
```

5. Start the document:

```
\begin{document}
```

6. We use an `animateinline` environment. We specify options for showing control buttons, automatically starting the animation, and looping. That means that the animation restarts. The mandatory argument in curly braces is the speed, here, two frames per second:

```
\begin{animateinline}[controls,autoplay,loop]{2}
```

7. We use the `\multiframe` command to produce five frames, which we state as the first argument. The second argument is a variable, *n*, starting at 0 and incrementing by 1 in each step. Within this command, we will print the curve of order \n. Just take the TikZ curve code as it is since we are focusing on the animation:

```
\multiframe{5}{n = 0+1}{
  \begin{tikzpicture}[scale = 80]
    \shadedraw[shading = color wheel]
    [l-system = { Koch curve, step=2pt, angle=60,
                  axiom=F++F++F, order=\n }]
    lindenmayer system -- cycle;
  \end{tikzpicture}
}
```

8. End the `animateinline` environment and the document:

```
\end{animateinline}
\end{document}
```

9. Compile the document and open it in a capable PDF viewer, such as Adobe Acrobat Reader. Here are steps 2 and 5 of the animation. You can click the buttons to play backward or forward and increase or decrease the speed.

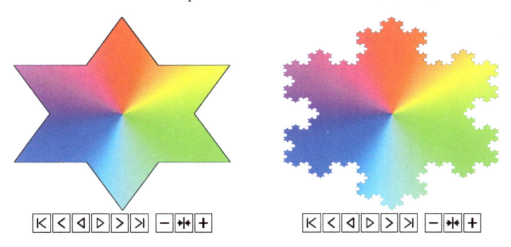

Figure 9.9 – Screenshots of a PDF animation

How it works...

We used two main features of the package:

*   The `animateinline` environment creates an animation from the environment's content, not external files. Any drawing package, such as TikZ or PSTricks, can be used. We used TikZ here.

*   The `\multiframe` command lets us build a loop around drawing commands. The syntax is as follows:

```
\multiframe{number of frames}{variable =
   initial value+increment}{drawing code
   with \variable}
```

The rest was drawing with TikZ. The `\shadedraw` command creates the actual drawing while filling it with shading. Here, we used shiny shading called `color wheel`. It provides a nice glimpse of the TikZ package while keeping our focus on animating it. You can refer to my book *LaTeX Graphics with TikZ* to learn more about that excellent package.

With the `animate` package, you can also assemble animations from existing image files. The command for this is as follows:

```
\animategraphics[options]{frame rate}{file
   basename}{first}{last}
```

Options can be used, as shown earlier. If you set `file basename` to `frame-`, `first` to 4, and `last` to 12, that command would play the sequence from `frame-4.png` to `frame-12.png`, if they exist in PNG format. The filename extension is used automatically, so with pdfLaTeX, it would look for PNG, JPG, and PDF files.

For further details, you can refer to the manual, which you can open by using `texdoc animate` or at `https://texdoc.org/pkg/animate`.

10
Writing Advanced Mathematics

LaTeX stands out for its excellent quality in typesetting formulas, making it the preferred software for mathematical writing. Beyond mathematics, LaTeX proves beneficial in various scientific fields reliant on complex formulas, which we will see in *Chapter 11, Using LaTeX in Science and Technology*.

The current chapter offers specific techniques for everyday math tasks. We assume readers possess a foundational knowledge of mathematical writing with LaTeX, but a brief tutorial is included to assist beginners. If you are already proficient in writing math, feel free to skip ahead.

This chapter covers the following topics:

- Getting started
- Fine-tuning a formula
- Automatic line breaking in equations
- Highlighting in a formula
- Writing theorems and definitions
- Drawing a commutative diagram
- Plotting functions in two dimensions
- Plotting in three dimensions
- Drawing geometry pictures
- Doing calculations

We'll explore recipes for creating graphics centered around mathematical concepts, including visualizing maps and functions and engaging in geometry exercises. At the end of this chapter, you'll find a curated list of documentation and online resources dedicated to mathematics in LaTeX.

Getting started

LaTeX utilizes a distinct syntax for mathematical expressions, requiring explicit declaration to differentiate between mathematical elements and regular text for accurate rendering. Let's explore the fundamentals of writing math!

How to do it...

We will practice the fundamentals of mathematics now. Let's craft a document together. We will go through the following steps:

1. As usual, start with a document class:

    ```
    \documentclass{article}
    ```

2. Begin the document:

    ```
    \begin{document}
    ```

3. Let's have an unnumbered section for our text:

    ```
    \section*{The golden ratio}
    ```

4. Create a statement incorporating mathematical content. Enclose each mathematical expression within parentheses, preceded by a backslash:

    ```
    The symbol for the golden ratio is the Greek
    letter \( \varphi \). Its value is the positive
    solution of \( x^2 - x - 1 = 0 \).
    ```

5. Continue the text; this time, the math content shall be displayed centered:

    ```
    It can be calculated to:
    \[
      \varphi = \frac{1 + \sqrt{5}}{2} = 1.618 \ldots
    \]
    ```

6. End the document:

    ```
    \end{document}
    ```

7.   Compile and take a look at the outcome:

The golden ratio

The symbol for the golden ratio is the Greek letter φ. Its value is the positive solution of $x^2 - x - 1 = 0$. It can be calculated to:

$$\varphi = \frac{1 + \sqrt{5}}{2} = 1.618\ldots$$

Figure 10.1 – Mathematical formulas in LaTeX

How it works...

Mathematics is composed differently than regular text. For instance, letters appear in italics by default to differentiate variables from standard text. Hence, in LaTeX, it's crucial to specify the beginning and end of the **math mode**, even for individual symbols embedded in the text.

Math styles

There are two fundamental math styles in LaTeX:

- **Inline math**: A formula is embedded within regular text. Write it as follows:

    ```
    text \( formula \) more text
    ```

- **Displayed math**: For emphasizing a formula or when its size demands better readability within its own paragraph, square brackets are used instead of parentheses as follows:

    ```
    \[ formula \]
    ```

    Such a displayed formula is centered with space before and after it. So, there should not be empty lines in the code before or after, as it would cause additional paragraph breaks, leading to more vertical space around the formula.

> **Note**
>
> The older TeX syntax $ . . . $ is available for inline math within LaTeX. It's shorter and remains popular. However, it's advised against using the other TeX syntax $$ . . . $$ for displayed math as it can result in inconsistent vertical spacing in LaTeX.

Greek letters

You observed the Greek letter phi previously. Typically, the command for a Greek letter mirrors its name preceded by a backslash. So, there are the `\alpha`, `\beta`, `\gamma`, `\delta` commands, and so on, for representing lowercase Greek letters, and `\Gamma`, `\Delta`, and so on, for uppercase Greek letters. However, Greek letters that resemble Latin letters, such as A, B, and E for capital Alpha, Beta, and Epsilon letters, don't have a default LaTeX command since they can be directly typed as regular characters and, of course, appear in italics in math mode.

Math symbols

Mathematicians are ingenious. They invented numerous math symbols, such as for operations and relations. Generations of mathematicians have used LaTeX, so nearly any math symbol we can think of is provided by LaTeX or as an additional package such as `latexsym` or `amssymb`. Load such a package as always by employing the `\usepackage` command.

However, you need to know the command for a symbol. An extensive list of more than 18.000 symbols sorted by topic provides clear tables with explanations. You can open it on your computer at the command prompt by typing `texdoc symbols` or visiting it online at `https://texdoc.org/pkg/symbols`.

Searching in that list can take a bit of time, though. The **Detexify** app comes to the rescue: it's a clever online tool that takes hand-drawn symbols, such as those drawn using the mouse or a touch screen, and gives you, in return, LaTeX commands that produce such a symbol. You can find it at `https://detexify.kirelabs.org`.

Here, you can see how it works on my poorly mouse-drawn surface integral symbol:

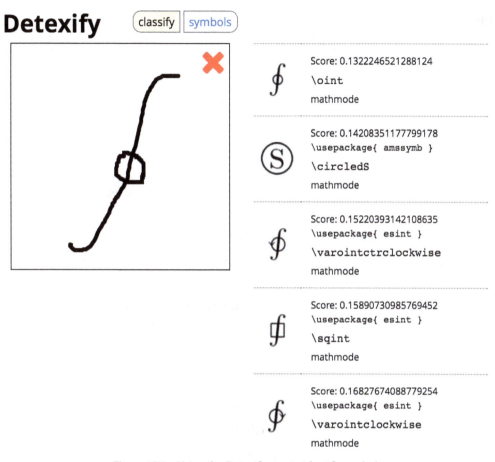

Figure 10.2 – Using the Detexify app to identify symbols

The Detexify app displays the LaTeX command, the expected output, and the required package. The list of suggestions is sorted, showcasing the best match at the top, as seen in our test case.

The Detexify app is also available as a mobile app for Apple and Android devices.

Squares and fractions

You saw further LaTeX commands in our first example:

- `\sqrt{expression}` gives a square root of the expression. There's an optional argument for other roots. For example, type `\sqrt[3]{x}` to denote the third root of x.

- `\frac{numerator}{denominator}` prints a fraction, with the numerator above the denominator, separated by a line.

> **Tip**
>
> In LaTeX, spaces within formulas are ignored, allowing you to insert as many spaces as you like. You can improve the readability of complex formulas that way.

There's more...

For writing formulas, there's quite a bit more to cover. Let's take a glance at some syntax involved.

Subscripts and superscripts

Subscripts, acting like indices, are denoted by adding them with an underscore. For example, x_1 can be written as x_1.

Superscripts, functioning as exponents, are attached using a caret. So, x^2 is written as x^2.

If a subscript or superscript should contain more than one character, enclose them within curly braces, such as in x_{ij} and y^{12}.

You can combine subscripts and superscripts by aligning them directly. Nesting them is possible, but ensure clear grouping using curly braces. For instance, consider this code illustrating different meanings due to braces:

```
\[
    x^{n_1} \neq x^n_1
\]
```

On the left side, x is raised to the power of n_1. On the right side, x_1 is introduced to the power of n:

$$x^{n_1} \neq x^n_1$$

Figure 10.3 – Comparing nested superscripts and subscripts

Even expressions with the same mathematical meaning can display variations in their appearance when printed, depending on how you set the braces:

```
\[
    {x^2}^3 = x^{2^3}
\]
```

On the left side, there are two exponents. On the right side, one exponent is nested within another, appearing in smaller font size:

$$x^{2^3} = x^{2^3}$$

Figure 10.4 – Multiple exponents

So, use braces to define the actual meaning. In particular, their inclusion becomes necessary to avoid errors when dealing with multiple superscripts or subscripts.

Operators

Usually, variables are written in italics, while mathematical functions, also called **operators**, are typically displayed in upright Roman letters because of their different meanings. Many operators are predefined, allowing you to access them simply using a backslash, such as \lim, \sin, \cos, \log, \min, and \max. Should you find an operator missing, you can define it yourself. Load the amsmath package to do this, so ensure that your preamble contains this line:

```
\usepackage{amsmath}
```

Then, you can define a new operator, "diff," in your preamble using the following command:

```
\DeclareMathOperator{\diff}{diff}
```

You will notice that subscripts or superscripts of operators in displayed equations can be positioned below or above them, respectively, as seen with \lim, for instance. You can achieve the same for your new operator if you add a star:

```
\DeclareMathOperator*{\diff}{diff}
```

We will use our own operators in one of the following recipes: *Drawing commutative diagrams*.

Numbering and referencing equations

Displayed formulas can be automatically numbered for cross-referencing purposes. Follow these steps:

1. Start an equation environment:

    ```
    \begin{equation}
    ```

2. Give it a label:

    ```
    \label{parabola}
    ```

3. Write the formula:

    ```
    y = x^2 + 1
    ```

Equations or formulas, when displayed, will receive an automatically incremented number enclosed in parentheses at the right, denoted as (1), and so forth.

4. End the `equation` environment:

```
\end{equation}
```

5. Now, you can reference it anywhere in the whole document, such as here:

```
See formula (\ref{parabola}).
```

Note that we manually included the parentheses. However, if you've loaded the `amsmath` package, which is advisable anyway, you can use its command to display the references enclosed within parentheses:

```
See formula \eqref{parabola}.
```

> **Note**
>
> For resolving references, LaTeX requires a second compiler run. The label is written to the external `.aux` file during the first run, enabling the second run to locate it there and accurately link the references.

Writing multi-line formulas with alignment

It's crucial to load the `amsmath` package, a must-have for writing mathematics with LaTeX. Add this to your preamble:

```
\usepackage{amsmath}
```

Now, you have several options.

Aligning at the relation symbol

Here's how to align equations at the relation symbol:

*   Utilize the `align` environment
*   Identify the relation symbol for alignment by inserting an ampersand symbol (`&`) immediately before it
*   Indicate line breaks using the `\\` command

So, your code will look similar to this:

```
\begin{align}
  y &= x^2 + 1 \\
  z &= 0
\end{align}
```

Now, the equations are correctly aligned at the equation sign:

$$y = x^2 + 1 \tag{1}$$
$$z = 0 \tag{2}$$

Figure 10.5 – An aligned equation system

> **Note**
>
> While browsing the internet or reviewing older documents, you might encounter the eqnarray environment used for equation alignment. It's strongly advised against using the eqnarray environment as the spacing around the relational symbols can be incorrect compared to regular equations.

Centering a block of equations

Centering a set of equations is simpler compared to the previous example:

- Use the gather environment

- Break lines using \\

So, your code will now look similar to the following:

```
\begin{gather}
    y = x^2 + 1 \\
    z = 0
\end{gather}
```

The lines are centered on each other and in the middle of the page.

Adjusting numbering

The equation, align, gather, and further amsmath environments are numbered by default. You can turn off this numbering using their respective **starred** environment version equation* (corresponding to \[... \] in standard LaTeX), align*, gather*, and so forth.

Alternatively, to suppress numbering for specific lines within these environments, append the \nonumber command at the end of a line like this:

```
\begin{gather}
    y = x^2 + 1 \nonumber \\
    z = 0
\end{gather}
```

As mentioned, you can add labels to each line you choose for referencing purposes. Note that having a number as a tag is only meaningful when accompanied by a reference. Tags primarily exist for reference, not for counting.

> **Custom tags**
>
> Instead of having numbers, you can set your own tags, such as * by inserting \tag{*} on a formula line.

The `mathtools` package provides additional assistance in this context. It shows equation numbers and tags only if there's a reference by one of the \eqref or \refeq commands (the `mathtools` reference command version). Activate this functionality as follows:

```
\usepackage{mathtools}
\mathtoolsset{showonlyrefs,showmanualtags}
```

This package offers much more, as you'll discover in the following recipe.

Fine-tuning math formulas

While LaTeX excels in typesetting formulas, there are instances where the layout may need enhancement. This recipe provides quick solutions to address such issues.

Getting ready

Let's have a look at misalignment and spacing, issues with subscripts and superscripts that can easily occur:

1. Open the following sample document with your LaTeX editor. You can take it from the code archive provided with the book or directly copy and paste it from the e-book:

    ```
    \documentclass{article}
    \usepackage{dsfont}
    \begin{document}
    \[
      \lim_{n\to\infty} \sup_{x\in\mathds{R}} f_n(x^2)
        < n \Big(\sum_{x\in\mathds{R}, n\in\mathds{N}}
        \big| f_n(x^2) \big| \Big)
    \]
    \end{document}
    ```

2. Compile and take a look at the formula:

$$\lim_{n\to\infty} \sup_{x\in\mathbb{R}} f_n(x^2) < n\left(\sum_{x\in\mathbb{R},n\in\mathbb{N}} \left|f_n(x^2)\right| \right)$$

Figure 10.6 – Regular formulas with deficiencies

Although the LaTeX code is OK, you can see that several places could benefit from refinement:

- The subscripts below the operators on the left side of the equation lack vertical alignment
- The excessive space surrounding the sum symbol should be reduced
- The exponent 2 is slightly higher than the parentheses

Let's rectify these issues.

How to do it...

The `mathtools` package offers numerous enhancements and tools for mathematical writing. It is a valuable companion to the `amsmath` package. Here's a guide on how to utilize it:

1. Add the `\usepackage{mathtools}` command to the preamble.

2. Write the `\adjustlimits` command before the `\lim` operator.

3. Insert the `\smashoperator{` command before the `\sum` and write the `}` argument closing brace after the subscript.

4. Change the `x^2` expression to `\cramped{x^2}` to lower the exponent at both places slightly. Now, your formula reads like this:

```
\[
    \adjustlimits\lim_{n\to\infty} \sup_{x\in\mathds{R}}
    f_n(\cramped{x^2})
    < n \Big( \smashoperator{\sum_{x\in\mathds{R},
    n\in\mathds{N}}}
    \big\lvert f_n(\cramped{x^2}) \big\rvert \Big)
\]
```

5. Compile the document, review the output, and compare it with the original formula:

$$\lim_{n\to\infty} \sup_{x\in\mathbb{R}} f_n(x^2) < n\left(\sum_{x\in\mathbb{R},n\in\mathbb{N}} \left|f_n(x^2)\right| \right)$$

Figure 10.7 – Improved mathematical typesetting

How it works...

Loading the `mathtools` package implicitly includes the `amsmath` package, addressing known errors within `amsmath`. Unlike `amsmath`, which is relatively static, `mathtools` has been developed to provide additional tools amassed over the years from various authors, focusing on fine-tuning mathematical layouts.

Some of the tools we've recently utilized include the following:

- `\adjustlimits`: This command aligns the limits of two consecutive operators. The syntax is as follows:

  ```
  \adjustlimits{operator1}_{limit1} {operator2}_{limit2}
  ```

- `\smashoperator`: This command ensures that the widths of subscript and superscript are disregarded.

- `\cramped`: This command enforces a more compact LaTeX style, slightly lowering exponents from their default position. This is especially advantageous for inline math, preventing undesired stretching of line spacing.

Automatic line-breaking in equations

Typically, we meticulously design formulas, especially in multiline equations, manually selecting optimal breakpoints and alignment positions. However, envision a lengthy chain of calculations, like those found in proofs or mathematical assignments. It would be incredibly beneficial if LaTeX could automatically wrap displayed formulas the way it handles regular text. And indeed, it's achievable.

How to do it...

The `breqn` package is specifically crafted for this precise purpose. This recipe will illustrate its functionality. We'll employ the `beamer` class because seminar slides typically have space limitations. Follow these steps:

1. Specify the document class:

   ```
   \documentclass[12pt]{beamer}
   ```

2. As the `beamer` class uses sans-serif math font by default, we switch to the serif math font as in regular documents:

   ```
   \usefonttheme[onlymath]{serif}
   ```

3. Load the `breqn` package:

   ```
   \usepackage{breqn}
   ```

4. Begin the document and a **frame** for a presentation slide:

```
\begin{document}
\begin{frame}
```

5. Write your mathematical formula without paragraph breaks or spaces, as you would typically construct simple math. While you can use line breaks in the editor, they're not mandatory. The crucial aspect here is to employ a dmath* environment:

```
\begin{dmath*}
    \left( \frac{f}{g} \right)^\prime(x)
        = \lim_{h \rightarrow 0}
        \left( \frac{1}{ g(x+h) g(x) } \right)
        \left[
                \frac{ f(x+h) - f(x) }{h} g(x)
                -\frac{ g(x+h) - g(x) }{h} f(x)
        \right]
        = \frac{f^\prime(x)g(x)-f(x)g^\prime(x)}{g^2(x)}
\end{dmath*}
```

6. End the frame and the document:

```
\end{frame}
\end{document}
```

7. Compile and take a look at the output:

$$\left(\frac{f}{g}\right)'(x) = \lim_{h\to 0}\left(\frac{1}{g(x+h)g(x)}\right)\left[\frac{f(x+h)-f(x)}{h}g(x)\right.$$
$$\left. - \frac{g(x+h)-g(x)}{h}f(x)\right]$$
$$= \frac{f'(x)g(x)-f(x)g'(x)}{g^2(x)}$$

Figure 10.8 – Comprehensive equations with automatic line breaking

How it works...

The key feature of the breqn package is handling excessively lengthy displayed formulas. When a formula exceeds a certain width, the package automatically breaks it at suitable points. Subsequent lines are typically indented and often commence with a relation symbol.

An implicit yet highly beneficial feature is the support for automatically scaled delimiters across line breaks. In particular, this refers to the `\left` and `\right` commands together with delimiters such as parentheses. The multi-line math environments from the amsmath package, such as the `align` and `gather` environments, would cause an error if there's one on a line but its counterpart is on another line. The standard fix is inserting the `\right.` and `\left.` commands, which produce an invisible delimiter. However, this doesn't guarantee equal measured heights for both lines, potentially resulting in delimiter pairs of different sizes. Alternatively, one might resort to manual adjustments using one of the `\big`, `\Big`, `\bigg`, or `\Bigg` commands. The breqn package effectively resolves these issues.

Giving the breqn package a try could prove beneficial. It can significantly expedite the process of writing tasks such as math homework or proofs involving extensive calculations.

> **Tip**
>
> The authors of the breqn package recommended loading the breqn package after all other math-related packages, such as amsmath, amssymb, mathpazo, or mathptmx. So, for example, the breqn package detects and uses options provided to the amsmath package, such as the leqn and fleqn options. A good rule of thumb is to load sophisticated or recently developed packages late.

Highlighting in a formula

In intricate formulas or equations, emphasizing a specific part can be incredibly useful. Methods such as color highlighting or framing can effectively achieve this emphasis and are particularly beneficial in presentations where altering the highlighted area per frame helps explain the content.

To test the effectiveness of these methods beyond simple basic math, we'll tackle more complex material using the amsmath matrices. We aim to illustrate a matrix transposition by highlighting submatrices and incorporating arrows.

How to do it...

We will use the TikZ graphics package for this. Such a comprehensive package initially seems hefty for this purpose. However, its versatility in providing consistent styles and enabling a wide range of graphical functionalities makes it an ideal choice.

Let's dive into an example, breaking down each step to showcase how TikZ can be utilized. Follow these steps:

1. Start with any document class:

   ```
   \documentclass{article}
   ```

2. Load the `amsmath` package so we can write matrices:

```
\usepackage{amsmath}
```

3. Load the TikZ package:

```
\usepackage{tikz}
```

4. In addition, load the `fit` library, which we will use for auto-fitting to nodes:

```
\usetikzlibrary{fit}
```

5. Define a macro for adding overlays:

```
\newcommand{\overlay}[2][]{\tikz[overlay,
    remember picture, #1]{#2}}
```

6. Declare a style that shall be applied for a highlighted area:

```
\tikzset{
  highlighted/.style = { draw, thick, rectangle,
                rounded corners, inner sep = 0pt,
                fill = red!15, fill opacity = 0.5
  }
}
```

7. Define a command for highlighting an area. The area shall be rectangular and will have encompassing nodes named `left` and `right`. The style from the preceding code will be applied. The name provided as an argument will be stored as the name for this area for future referencing:

```
\newcommand{\highlight}[1]{%
  \overlay{
    \node [fit = (left.north west) (right.south east),
        highlighted] (#1) {}; }
}
```

8. Define another command that prints text as a node and flags it with a name:

```
\newcommand{\flag}[2]{\overlay[baseline=(#1.base)]
  {\node (#1) {$#2$};}}
```

9. After these preparations, begin your document:

```
\begin{document}
```

10. Start a displayed equation:

```
\[
```

11. Write a matrix using the `pmatrix` environment of `amsmath`. In any cell flagged for later use, use the `\flag{name}{content}` command for the content:

```
M = \begin{pmatrix}
  \flag{left}{1} & 2 & 3 & 4 & 5 \\
  6 & 7 & 8 & 9 & 10 \\
  11 & \flag{before}{12} & \flag{right}{13} &
      14 & 15 \\
  16 & 17 & 18 & 19 & 20
\end{pmatrix}
```

12. Add the first highlighting to a sub-matrix and name it N:

```
\highlight{N}
```

13. Add some horizontal space. Write the transposed matrix with the desired flags. Again, highlight the interesting part, which is the transposed sub-matrix. We chose the name NT. Then, end the equation:

```
\qquad
M^T = \begin{pmatrix}
  \flag{left}{1} & 6 & 11 & 16 \\
  2 & 7 & \flag{after}{12} & 17 \\
  3 & 8 & \flag{right}{13} & 18 \\
  4 & 9 & 14 & 19 \\
  5 & 10 & 15 & 20
\end{pmatrix}
\highlight{NT}
\]
```

14. Now, we will add further bells and whistles. Start our `\overlay` macro:

```
\overlay{
```

15. Draw a thick, red, dotted line between interesting nodes, which we flagged previously using the names `before` and `after`:

```
\draw[->, thick, red, dotted] (before) -- (after);
```

16. Draw another such line, this time dashed, between our sub-matrices:

```
\draw[->, thick, red, dashed] (N) -- (NT)
    node [pos=0.68, above] {Transpose};
```

17. Add labels to the sub-matrices, then add the closing brace for \overlay:

```
\node[above of = N ] { $N$    };
\node[above of = NT] { $N^T$ };
}
```

18. End the document:

```
\end{document}
```

19. Compile the document twice. After the second run, our result is as follows:

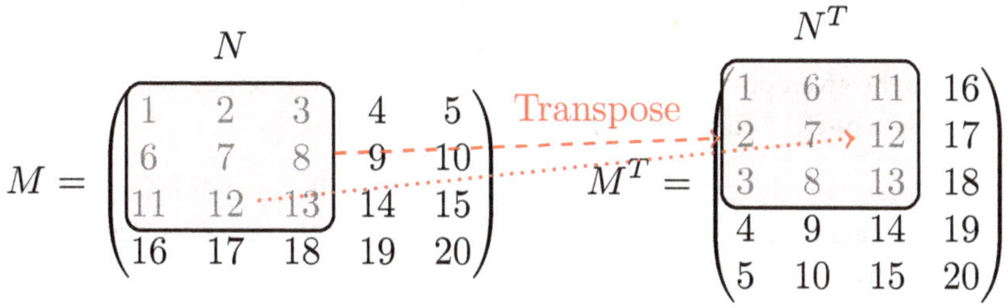

Figure 10.9 – Highlighting parts of a matrix

How it works...

The key is the small \overlay macro, which is used in the following manner:

```
\overlay[options]{drawing commands}
```

This creates a TikZ picture with three significant properties:

- The overlay option ensures that the bounding box of the current image remains unchanged. It's essentially drawing but without requiring space.

- The remember picture option lets TikZ remember the position of the current picture. It writes this value into the .aux file. Using the value from the .aux file is the reason, while a subsequent run may be required for correct positioning.

- The third property is determined by the optional argument of \overlay, denoted by #1, and defaults to being empty. This allows for the addition of options as needed.

Our next key command is the \flag macro:

```
\flag{name}{content}
```

This macro prints the content while labeling it with a specific name, internally utilizing the \overlay macro. It adds the baseline=(#1.base) option, which makes the baseline of the generated node correspond to the content's baseline, not the center.

Regarding highlighting, initially, we utilized the \tikzset command to establish a global style named highlighted. We chose the shape of a rounded rectangle and added color and transparency. You can freely customize this style using colors, shapes, shadings, and more, whatever TikZ provides.

Now consider this macro:

```
\highlight{name}
```

Also, this macro uses \overlay to apply our style to an area. This necessitates flagging two positions beforehand with the names left and right. It utilizes TikZ's fit feature to calculate a rectangular area that exactly fits the given positions. In our case, these are the top-left corner (northwest of the left node) and the bottom-right corner (southeast of the right node).

Once the desired flags were added, we created another overlay with some drawing commands. We can use any TikZ drawing command and the names we defined with the \flag command. So, we added arrows and labels to the drawing.

We did many tasks in this recipe, such as coloring areas and adding labels and arrows relatively positioned to the content. Having these compact yet sophisticated macros in our document, we can add such flags in text, math, lists, tables, drawings, or any desired location. This allows us to draw over the document independently of the underlying layout.

There's more...

The tikzmark package follows the same approach and can be employed similarly. Our direct method grants maximum control, yet exploring the tikzmark package might align better with your needs. In the book *LaTeX Graphics with TikZ*, in *Chapter 9, Using Layers, Overlays, and Transparency*, I showed you how to use the tikzmark package for this purpose.

Basic commands such as \textcolor for coloring and \boxed from the amsmath package suffice for less complex requirements. The empheq package is another option for emphasizing equations or parts of them. You can check out their documentation using texdoc or visit https://texdoc.org.

The same applies to TikZ: call texdoc tikz at the command prompt or visit https://texdoc.org/pkg/tikz. The website https://texample.net, which I maintain, contains examples similar to this recipe and hundreds of more graphical illustrations.

Stating definitions and theorems

In rigorously structured mathematical documents, specific textual components, such as definitions, theorems, lemmas, examples, and remarks are often numbered for effective cross-referencing. This structured approach is prevalent in self-contained scientific works such as theses.

For example, let's create a definition, a theorem along with its proof, a lemma, and an additional note. All of these elements will be automatically numbered to facilitate cross-referencing. Let's apply this to the Pythagorean theorem we know from school geometry.

How to do it...

We'll continue utilizing the `amsmath` package, specifically a part of it, the `amsthm` package. Here are the steps to follow:

1. As usual, start with a document class. For our recipe, the `article` class is sufficient:

    ```
    \documentclass{article}
    ```

2. Load the `amsmath` and `amsthm` packages:

    ```
    \usepackage{amsmath}
    \usepackage{amsthm}
    ```

3. Define a theorem environment with the internal name `thm`, printing "Theorem" in the document:

    ```
    \newtheorem{thm}{Theorem}
    ```

4. Do the same for `lem` as a lemma environment:

    ```
    \newtheorem{lem}{Lemma}
    ```

5. Switch the theorem style to `definition`:

    ```
    \theoremstyle{definition}
    ```

6. Define a definition environment with the internal name `dfn`, printing "Definition" in the document:

    ```
    \newtheorem{dfn}{Definition}
    ```

7. Switch the theorem style to `remark`:

    ```
    \theoremstyle{remark}
    ```

8. Define an unnumbered environment for notes, so insert a star:

    ```
    \newtheorem*{note}{Note}
    ```

9. Begin the document:

```
\begin{document}
```

10. Write up a definition:

```
\begin{dfn}
  The longest side of a triangle with a right angle
  is called the \emph{hypotenuse}.
\end{dfn}
```

11. Add a note:

```
\begin{note}
  The other sides are called \emph{catheti},
  or \emph{legs}.
\end{note}
```

12. Write a theorem. Give it the optional name `Pythagoras`. Insert a label for cross-referencing:

```
\begin{thm}[Pythagoras]
  \label{pythagoras}
  In any right triangle, the square of the hypotenuse
  equals the sum of the squares of the other sides.
\end{thm}
```

13. Continue with the proof. We keep it short here. Let's have a cross-reference to a later written lemma:

```
\begin{proof}
  The proof has been given in Euclid's Elements,
  Book 1, Proposition 47. Refer to it for details.
  The converse is also true, see lemma \ref{converse}.
\end{proof}
```

14. Add a lemma with an internal label:

```
\begin{lem}
  \label{converse}
  For any three positive numbers \(x\), \(y\),
  and \(z\) with \(x^2 + y^2 = z^2\), there is a
  triangle with side lengths \(x\), \(y\) and \(z\).
  Such triangle has a right angle, and the hypotenuse
  has the length \(z\).
\end{lem}
```

15. Add another note. Refer to the theorem of Pythagoras:

```
\begin{note}
    This is the converse of theorem \ref{pythagoras}.
\end{note}
```

16. End the document:

```
\end{document}
```

17. Compile twice to get the cross-references right. Examine how our environments are printed:

Definition 1. The longest side of a triangle with a right angle is called the *hypotenuse*.

Note. The other sides are called *catheti*, or *legs*.

Theorem 1 (Pythagoras). *In any right triangle, the square of the hypotenuse equals the sum of the squares of the other sides.*

Proof. The proof has been given in Euclid's Elements, Book 1, Proposition 47. Refer to it for details. The converse is also true, see lemma 1.   □

Lemma 1. *For any three positive numbers x, y, and z with $x^2 + y^2 = z^2$, there is a triangle with side lengths x, y and z. Such triangle has a right angle, and the hypotenuse has the length z.*

Note. This is the converse of theorem 1.

Figure 10.10 – Definitions, theorems, lemmas, proofs, and notes

How it works...

The amsthm package provides the \newtheorem command, which creates an environment for us. This environment has a built-in counter that increments automatically, facilitating easy cross-referencing using labels. Notably, the notation and body come with distinct formatting, as you saw in the output:

- The default style is plain. It prints the label in bold, the optional name in parentheses in regular upright font, and the body text in italics.

- The definition style generates a bold label and standard upright body text.

- The note style features an italic label and standard upright body text.

Switching the style using the \theoremstyle command is valid for the subsequent \newtheorem definitions.

Choosing environment names that aren't already used by TeX or LaTeX commands is essential, ensuring they're unique. So, `\newtheorem{def}{Definition}` would not work, as `\def` is already a TeX command.

We can utilize cross-references as usual: insert a `\label` with a name. Then, you can use `\ref` anywhere to point to the number of the environment where we placed the label. Usually, not-referenced environments, such as notes or corollaries, can be defined without numbers if you use the starred form `\newtheorem*` as we did previously for notes.

The `proof` environment is an exceptional predefined environment that starts with "Proof" and automatically includes the *quod erat demonstrandum* symbol as an endmark.

The `amsthm` package provides an additional `\newtheoremstyle` command that takes nine arguments so that you can customize the fonts and spacing of the environment for both the head and body. You can find the parameters in the manual, accessible by `texdoc amsthm` at the command line or online at `https://texdoc.org/pkg/amsthm`, enabling you to create customized designs.

There's more...

While styling and customizing the design aspects are crucial, ensuring accurate and systematic numbering within these environments is equally fundamental. Let's look at this and more.

Adjusting the numbering

When dealing with various definitions, theorems, lemmas, and similar elements, it can be beneficial to avoid separate numbering sequences. It can feel disjointed if, for instance, theorem 5 is immediately followed by lemma 2. To unify these numbering sequences, you can utilize an existing counter by specifying it in square brackets after the element's name. Here's an example setup for your recipe:

```
\newtheorem{thm}{Theorem}
\newtheorem{lem}[thm]{Lemma}
\newtheorem{dfn}[thm]{Definition}
```

This configuration will utilize the `thm` counter for numbering theorems, lemmas, and definitions, ensuring a consistent numbering pattern.

Furthermore, you can assign numbering based on sectional units such as chapters or sections if you like. For instance, to number theorems per chapter, use the following:

```
\newtheorem{thm}{Theorem}[chapter]
```

Or, you can number the theorems per section:

```
\newtheorem{thm}{Theorem}[section]
```

Additionally, if you prefer the numbering to appear before the title, such as **1.5 Theorem** instead of **Theorem 1.5**, you can use the \swapnumbers command in the preamble before defining the theorems.

An alternative theorem package

The ntheorem package is a viable alternative to the amsthm package. It provides compatible styles with similar appearances, so the result will be pretty much the same if you load it instead of amsthm in this way:

```
\usepackage[amsmath,amsthm,thmmarks]{ntheorem}
```

One notable advantage of ntheorem is its improved placement of **endmarks**. When concluding a proof with a displayed equation, amsthm might shift the endmark slightly below it. The ntheorem package, however, doesn't exhibit this behavior. Nevertheless, I usually avoid ending a proof abruptly with a formula or diagram, just as I would only conclude a seminar presentation with a final statement. Including a closing note is generally good practice.

Additionally, ntheorem introduces its own styles and offers different customization options. To explore its functionalities further, refer to the package documentation by running the texdoc ntheorem command at the command line or visiting https://texdoc.org/pkg/ntheorem.

Additional theorem tools

The thmtools package is another valuable addition, regardless of whether you use amsthm or ntheorem. Here's what it brings to the table:

- Automatic generation of a list of theorems, similar to lists of tables and figures
- Capability to entirely restate an existing theorem statement at another place
- A key = value interface for managing numbering style and other properties
- Support for intelligent referencing, such as automatically adding the theorem name to a reference
- Shaded and boxed designs, implicitly using the shadethm and thmbox packages
- Additional options for tweaking the design

To generate a list of theorems, add the following line to your preamble:

```
\usepackage{thmtools}
```

Later in your document, use this command:

```
\listoftheorems
```

Make sure to compile your document at least twice. Our small recipe document with shared numbering results in this short list:

List of Theorems

Figure 10.11 – A list of theorems

You can imagine that naming definitions and lemmas adds value, just as we've done with the theorems.

Finally, let's look at the mentioned emphasizing options of `thmtools` through shading and boxing. This can be implemented as follows:

1. Load the `thmtools` package:

    ```
    \usepackage{thmtools}
    ```

2. Load the `xcolor` package so you can use color definitions:

    ```
    \usepackage{xcolor}
    ```

3. Instead of using the `\newtheorem` command, use the following command with a color you like:

    ```
    \declaretheorem[shaded={bgcolor=red!15}]{Theorem}
    ```

4. For definitions, take a box design instead of `\newtheorem`, and use this command with a color you like:

    ```
    \declaretheorem[thmbox=L]{Definition}
    ```

5. In the body text, write your definitions as follows:

    ```
    \begin{Definition}[name]
    ...
    \end{Definition}
    ```

6. Write your theorems like this:

    ```
    \begin{Theorem}[name]
    ...
    \end{ Theorem}
    ```

Applied to our recipe, we get the following result:

Definition 1

> *The longest side of a triangle with a right angle is called the* hypotenuse.

Theorem 1 (Pythagoras). *In any right triangle, the square of the hypotenuse equals the sum of the squares of the other sides.*

Figure 10.12 – Highlighting in theorem environments

To further explore the package, take a look at the manual using `texdoc thmtools` at the command line or by visiting `https://texdoc.org/pkg/thmtools`.

Drawing commutative diagrams

Commutative diagrams are common in algebra, particularly in category theory. Here, vertices represent objects such as groups or modules, while arrows signify morphisms, acting as maps between these objects. The defining feature of these diagrams is their commutativity, ensuring that regardless of the directed path within the diagram, the outcome remains consistent as long as the starting and ending points match.

Such diagrams are vital in visualizing algebraic properties and are pivotal in navigating through entire proofs. That's why our next focus will be on them. To kick things off, we'll explore a diagram representing the first isomorphism theorem in group theory.

How to do it...

We'll employ the TikZ package, though we'll only tap into a fraction of its capabilities. We'll use it because it offers a rich collection of arrowheads, tails, and utilities for positioning and labeling. Here's a breakdown of the document creation:

1. Start with a document class:

   ```
   \documentclass{article}
   ```

2. Load the TikZ package:

   ```
   \usepackage{tikz}
   ```

3. Load the `matrix` library of TikZ:

   ```
   \usetikzlibrary{matrix}
   ```

4. Load the amsmath package:

```
\usepackage{amsmath}
```

5. Declare any operators you will need that are not defined yet:

```
\DeclareMathOperator{\im}{im}
```

6. Begin the document and open a TikZ picture environment:

```
\begin{document}
\begin{tikzpicture}
```

7. Use the \matrix command and provide a name for the matrix. We choose m:

```
\matrix (m)
```

8. Specify the matrix options. We'll set all nodes to be in math mode. Additionally, we'll define the row and column distance:

```
[
    matrix of math nodes,
    row sep    = 3em,
    column sep = 4em
]
```

9. The matrix content is enclosed in curly braces, followed by a semicolon. It's similar to the regular tabular, array, or matrix environments. However, we must conclude the final line with a line break using \\:

```
{
    G                    & \im \varphi \\
    G/\ker \varphi &                 \\
};
```

10. Now, we will draw the arrows. These will be edges, with nodes acting as labels. Start with a path and include the desired arrowhead as an option:

```
\path[-stealth]
```

11. Draw an edge between matrix nodes, referencing them using the implicitly provided name (m-row-column). After the edge, include a node that acts as a label:

```
(m-1-1) edge node [left] {$\pi$} (m-2-1)
```

12. Draw the next edge using the | - operation to achieve a horizontal edge:

```
(m-1-1.east |- m-1-2)
    edge node [above] {$\varphi$} (m-1-2)
```

13. Draw the final edge and conclude the path with a semicolon:

```
(m-2-1) edge
    node [below] {$\tilde{\varphi}$} (m-1-2);
```

14. End the picture and the document:

```
\end{tikzpicture}
\end{document}
```

15. Compile and take a look at the diagram:

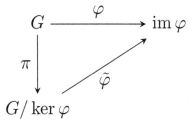

Figure 10.13 – A commutative diagram

How it works...

Besides loading the necessary packages, the basic procedure is as follows:

1. Define macros, operators, or styles.

2. Put all objects in a matrix.

3. Draw labeled arrows as edges with nodes.

For *Step 1*, we just defined the im operator for the "image" of a map. The ker operator is already defined.

In *Step 2*, we chose a matrix of math nodes, ensuring all node content is in math mode. While we just needed the spacing between rows and columns, you could define styles for specific rows or columns. TikZ manual offers further insight into customizing.

In *Step 3*, we made every edge an arrow. This is inherited from the -stealth path option, which rendered an arrow with a stealth tip.

We could apply tip and tail styles for single arrows as well. Let's have a quick demonstration. Load the `arrows.meta` library:

```
\usetikzlibrary{arrows.meta}
```

> **Note**
>
> You can load several libraries simultaneously, such as by \usetikzlibrary{matrix,arrows.meta}.

Now, you have a lot of customizable styles for arrow tips, which you can use at both ends. There are barbs, harpoons, brackets, caps, triangles, and many more than typical arrow styles, and you can customize them via options. The TikZ manual provides a reference section with arrow tips. Here, we have space for a short sample. After you load the `arrows.meta`, change the path to the following:

```
\path
    (m-1-1) edge [->>] node [left] {$\pi$} (m-2-1)
    (m-1-1.east |- m-1-2)
        edge [->] node [above] {$\varphi$} (m-1-2)
    (m-2-1.east) edge [{Hooks[right,length=0.8ex]}->,
        dashed] node [below] {$\tilde{\varphi}$} (m-1-2);
```

The diagram now looks like this:

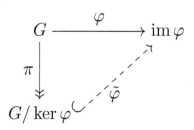

Figure 10.14 – A diagram with customized arrow tips

We gave the arrow specification as an option for each edge. While the dash - means the base edge, tail, and head come before or after. Let's see examples:

- The ->> syntax gives a double head that is commonly used for surjective maps.
- The [{Hooks[right,length=0.8ex]}-> code starts with a hook and ends with a single arrowhead, which stands for an injective map. Furthermore, the edge is dashed, often used to mark the unique structure-preserving map, making the diagram commute.

While it might seem intricate, having this level of control and tuning power is much better than having no flexibility.

There's more...

Diagrams often grow complex, expanding with more columns, rows, an abundance of arrows, and numerous labels. In these instances, employing the \foreach loops with calculation options can offer a solution. Look at this diagram:

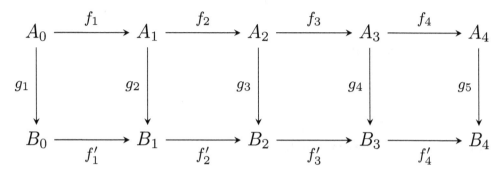

Figure 10.15 – A comprehensive commutative diagram

It's used in proving the so-called **five lemma**. Let's see how to generate it efficiently:

1. Start the document like we did before. In addition, load the calc library:

```
\documentclass{article}
\usepackage{tikz}
\usetikzlibrary{matrix,calc}
\begin{document}
```

2. Begin the TikZ picture. This time, we use the arrow options for the whole picture and define a label style to have labels in smaller sizes:

```
\begin{tikzpicture}[-stealth,
    label/.style = { font=\footnotesize }]
```

3. Write the matrix:

```
\matrix (m) [
    matrix of math nodes,
    row sep    = 4em,
    column sep = 4em ]
{   A_0 & A_1 & A_2 & A_3 & A_4 \\
    B_0 & B_1 & B_2 & B_3 & B_4 \\ };
```

4. Now, let's save work using a for loop:

```
\foreach \i in {1,...,4} {
\path
  let \n1 = { int(\i+1) } in
    (m-1-\i) edge node [above, label] {$f_\i$}
    (m-1-\n1)
    (m-2-\i)
      edge node [below, label] {$f^\prime_\i$}
    (m-2-\n1)
    (m-1-\i)
      edge node [left, label] {$g_\i$} (m-2-\i);

}
```

5. One arrow to go, then we end the picture and the document:

```
\path (m-1-5) edge node [left, label] {$g_5$}
    (m-2-5);
\end{tikzpicture}
\end{document}
```

That's it!

The \foreach command repeats the action for the 1, 2, 3, and 4 values for the \i loop variable here.

We computed \n1 as \i+1 for each path since we're drawing edges to the subsequent node. We used the \let operation provided by the calc library. Roughly said, we can use it for numbers like so:

```
\path let \n1 = { formula } in ... <drawing using
  number n1 somewhere>
```

We can also use it for points like this:

```
\path let \p1 = { formula } in ... <drawing using the
  point p1 somewhere>
```

Multiple expressions can be included within a let operation. The TikZ manual comprehensively describes the let operation; you likely grasp its concept already.

Plotting functions in two dimensions

Function plots are integral in mathematics for visualizing properties such as roots and extreme points. This recipe explores how to create function plots in a coordinate system easily. Let's plot the polynomial function $f(x) = x^3 - 5x$.

How to do it...

We'll use the pgfplots package, built on PGF/TikZ. Now, it's set to plot a function for us. Here's the step-by-step process:

1. Start with a document class. We decided on the standalone class for this recipe, which is great for creating single graphics with just a small margin. However, you can choose the article class or another one as well:

   ```
   \documentclass[border=10pt]{standalone}
   ```

2. Load the pgfplots package:

   ```
   \usepackage{pgfplots}
   ```

3. Begin the document and open a tikzpicture environment:

   ```
   \begin{document}
     \begin{tikzpicture}
   ```

4. Begin an axis environment with centered axis lines:

   ```
   \begin{axis} [axis lines=center]
   ```

5. Call the plot command. As an option, use the range for *x* called the **domain**. Choose a thick line and smooth plotting:

   ```
   \addplot [domain=-3:3, thick, smooth]
       { x^3 - 5*x };
   ```

6. End the axis, tikzpicture, and document environments:

   ```
   \end{axis}
     \end{tikzpicture}
   \end{document}
   ```

7. Compile and take a look at our plot:

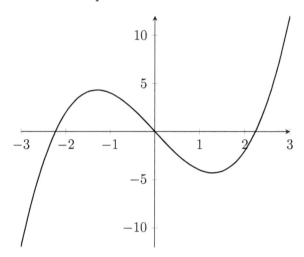

Figure 10.16 – A diagram of a function in the Cartesian coordinate system

How it works...

Within a `tikzpicture` environment, we placed an `axis` environment provided by the `pgfplots` package.

The `axis` environment takes all options for lines, ticks, labels, grids, and styles that apply to the coordinate system and the plot's appearance. We will see some of them later on in the following recipe.

The `\addplot` command receives the function's formula. It understands distinct options dedicated to each individual plot, such as the domain, number of samples, color, thickness, and other styles. You can use multiple `\addplot` commands within a single-axis environment to generate several plots within one drawing.

Our first function plot required a formal setup using environments, but we achieved the plot quite effectively using just a few simple commands.

There's more...

Now that we've covered the fundamental steps for plotting, let's explore various plotting styles.

Adding ticks and grid

At the start of our recipe, we used traditional centered axis lines. However, an axis is often a rectangular box that encapsulates the plot. Let's practice this. In addition, we will add a grid and choose the places for the axis ticks along with their labels.

The settings of our plots are always the same within a `tikzpicture` environment, so we can condense the code shown here to focus solely on the relevant `axis` environment:

```
\begin{axis} [grid, xtick = {-360,-270,...,360}]
  \addplot [domain=-360:360, samples=100, thick]
    { sin(x) };
\end{axis}
```

This gives us the following result:

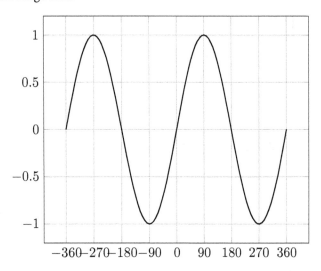

Figure 10.17 – The sine function

Reducing axes

Using a grid and numerous ticks can help examine particular function values. Still, it might be better to have simplified axes, perhaps even slightly offset, for a broader perspective of the function. There's a suitable style that you can use. If you download the file from `https://pgfplots.net/media/tikzlibrarypgfplots.shift.code.tex` and put it into your document folder, you can load this style in your preamble with the following command:

```
\usepgfplotslibrary{shift}
```

Now, change the axis option grid to shift, and you will get this view:

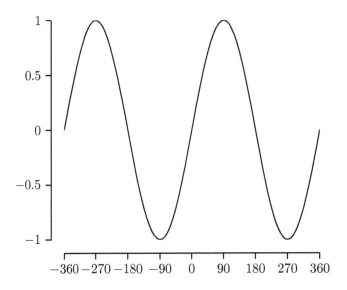

Figure 10.18 – The sine function with reduced axes

You can adjust the default shift value of 10 pt. For instance, alter the code to shift=15pt.

The same library can be used in three dimensions; we return to that in the following recipe.

Plotting in polar coordinates

The standard axis environment uses Cartesian coordinates, but the pgfplots package also offers logarithmic and polar axes.

Functions can also be described within a polar coordinate system. In this setup, each point is defined by its distance from the origin, 0, and the angle to a reference axis. Consequently, the function's argument represents an angle, and its value corresponds to the distance from the origin. Let's attempt a polar plot:

1. In your document preamble, add the following after the \usepackage{pgfplots} command:

   ```
   \usepgfplotslibrary{polar}
   ```

2. Within a tikzpicture environment, like we just saw, write the axis with the plot using the polaraxis package, just hiding the axis lines this time:

   ```
   \begin{polaraxis}[hide axis]
      \addplot[domain=0:180,smooth] {sin(x)};
   \end{polaraxis}
   ```

3.   Compile, and you will get a simple circle:

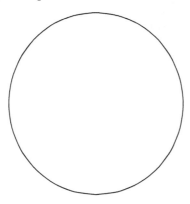

Figure 10.19 – The sine function in a polar coordinate system

So, the sine function, previously represented as a wave in our Cartesian coordinate plot, appears as a circle in polar coordinates. This transition illustrates how altering the axis can provide valuable visual insights.

A comprehensive polar plot shows angles, radius, and a grid featuring circular and radial lines. The earlier sine circle displayed a circle for 180 degrees. If, for example, we adjust the factor in the argument to 6, we'd anticipate a compressed circle every 30 degrees:

```
\documentclass[border=10pt]{standalone}
\usepackage{pgfplots}
\usepgfplotslibrary{polar}
\begin{document}
\begin{tikzpicture}
  \begin{polaraxis}
    \addplot[domain=0:360,samples=300] {sin(6*x)};
  \end{polaraxis}
\end{tikzpicture}
\end{document}
```

Compiling this document results in this output:

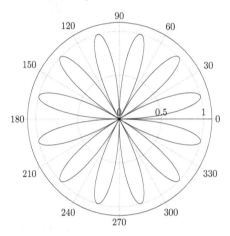

Figure 10.20 – A variant of a sine function in a polar coordinate system

Plotting in three dimensions

Visualizing functions with two arguments can be challenging. We can create three-dimensional plots in documents; however, achieving this in print or as a PDF demands a projection, a viewpoint, or an angle, along with considerations about depth, causing certain portions to be obscured while others remain visible.

Previously, we plotted the function $f(x) = sin(x)$. Now, by adding an additional dimension, we'll visualize the function $f(x,y) = sin(x)sin(y)$.

How to do it...

Like in the previous recipe, we will use the pgfplots package. Follow these steps:

1. Start with a document class. Like in the previous recipe, we use the standalone class. But it's fine if you choose the article class instead:

   ```
   \documentclass[border=10pt]{standalone}
   ```

2. Load the pgfplots package:

   ```
   \usepackage{pgfplots}
   ```

3. Begin the document and open a tikzpicture environment:

   ```
   \begin{document}
     \begin{tikzpicture}
   ```

4. Begin an `axis` environment with options:

```
\begin{axis} [
  title = {$f(x,y) = \sin(x)\sin(y)$},
  xtick = {0,90,...,360},
  ytick = {90,180,...,360},
  xlabel = $x$, ylabel = $y$,
  ticklabel style = {font = \scriptsize},
  grid
]
```

5. Invoke the three-dimensional plot command using the surface style, define the domain (i.e., the range for x and y), and choose a number of samples:

```
\addplot3 [surf, domain=0:360, samples=60]
  { sin(x)*sin(y) };
```

6. End the `axis`, the `tikzpicture`, and document environments:

```
\end{axis}
\end{tikzpicture}
\end{document}
```

7. Compile and take a look at the outcome:

$$f(x,y) = \sin(x)\sin(y)$$

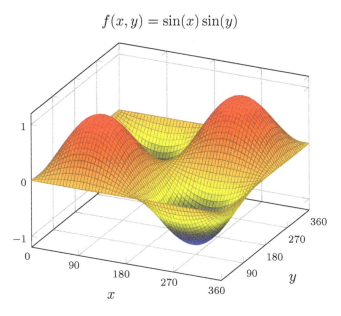

Figure 10.21 – A three-dimensional surface plot

How it works...

The previous recipe already covered the fundamentals of the `pgfplots` package and the `axis` environment.

Now, we employed the `\addplot3` command analogous to the `\addplot` command from the previous recipe, utilizing two variables.

3 in `\addplot3` stands for three-dimensional. As `\addplot` already is the two-dimensional version, there's no `\addplot2` command.

The `\addplot3` command understands similar options. In addition, you can choose a three-dimensional-specific style. We decided on the `surf` option for generating a surface plot.

There's more...

We're going to explore another style for the axis.

Reducing axes

As previously mentioned, we will apply a style for reduced and shifted axes. If you don't have it already, download the file at `https://pgfplots.net/media/tikzlibrarypgfplots.shift.code.tex` and put it into your document folder. Load this style in your preamble with this command:

```
\usepgfplotslibrary{shift}
```

Now, we can use the `shift` style. To see a new function, we will use it with an exponential function. The brief but complete code shall be as follows:

```
\documentclass[border=10pt]{standalone}
\usepackage{pgfplots}
\usepgfplotslibrary{shift}
\begin{document}
\begin{tikzpicture}
  \begin{axis} [shift3d]
    \addplot3 [surf, colormap/hot2, domain = -2:2,
      samples = 50] { x/exp(x^2+y^2) };
  \end{axis}
\end{tikzpicture}
\end{document}
```

Compile and see the distraction-free plot:

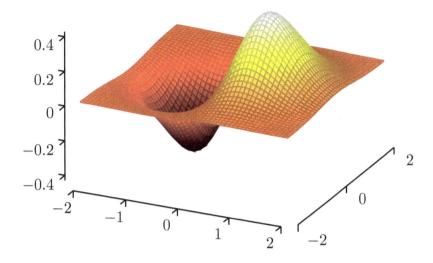

Figure 10.22 – A three-dimensional surface plot with reduced axes

The default shift value is set at 10 pt, but you can customize it, for instance, by employing shift3d=15pt.

While in the previous recipe, the shifted axis style was utilized in two dimensions, in this case, it's applied to a three-dimensional plot.

Drawing geometry pictures

Geometry is a traditional field in mathematics that's familiar from school days, involving compass and ruler constructions. Using LaTeX for drawing geometric constructions and explanations can particularly interest math teachers. These underlying constructions can also aid in general drawings requiring line intersections and circle tangents, even if they don't seem strictly geometric. Therefore, in this recipe, we'll revisit the drawings from school geometry.

How to do it...

We're going to utilize the tkz-euclide package, an extension of TikZ. Our initial objective is to create an equilateral triangle. Afterward, we'll include additional details. Follow these instructions:

1. Start with a document class. It could be any one; here, we can use the standalone class to focus on a single image:

    ```
    \documentclass[border=10pt]{standalone}
    ```

2. Load the `tkz-euclide` package:

```
\usepackage{tkz-euclide}
```

3. Begin the document and open a TikZ picture environment:

```
\begin{document}
\begin{tikzpicture}
```

4. Define some starting points:

```
\tkzDefPoint(0,0){A}
\tkzDefPoint(4,1){B}
```

5. Calculate further points. Here, we will to an intersection of the circle around A through B with the circle around B through A:

```
\tkzInterCC(A,B)(B,A)
```

6. Get the calculated points and give them the names C and D:

```
\tkzGetPoints{C}{D}
```

7. Now, we start drawing. Draw the triangle with the corners A, B, and C:

```
\tkzDrawPolygon(A,B,C)
```

8. Draw all points A, B, C, and D:

```
\tkzDrawPoints(A,B,C,D)
```

9. Print labels to the points and use options for positioning:

```
\tkzLabelPoints[below left](A)
\tkzLabelPoints(B,D)
\tkzLabelPoint[above](C){$C$}
```

10. Add the auxiliary circles of our intersection to the drawing with decent dots:

```
\tkzDrawCircle[dotted](A,B)
\tkzDrawCircle[dotted](B,A)
```

11. Add markers at C and D, like it is done with a compass, for illustration:

```
\tkzCompass[color=red, very thick](A,C)
\tkzCompass[color=red, very thick](B,C)
\tkzCompass[color=red, very thick](A,D)
\tkzCompass[color=red, very thick](B,D)
```

12. End the picture and the document:

```
\end{tikzpicture}
\end{document}
```

13. Compile and have a look at our first result:

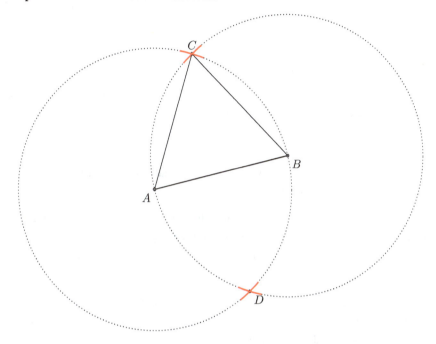

Figure 10.23 – A triangle construction

How it works...

The initial reaction might be, OMG, another syntax! However, this approach ensures unambiguous identification of commands associated with the `tkz-euclide` package by prefixing them with `\tkz`. So, it prevents potential clashes with commands from other packages that might have the same name.

Optional arguments are enclosed in square brackets, allowing the use of general TikZ key-value pairs, such as specifying red color or very thick lines. Mandatory arguments are enclosed in curly brackets as per usual. Coordinates, named points, line segments, and circles are represented using parentheses.

The package documentation is available by typing `texdoc tkz-euclide` at the command line or visiting `https://texdoc.org/pkg/tkz-euclide`.

A practical approach involves the following:

- Define points with coordinates

- Calculate further points, such as by using intersections or projections

- Draw circles and lines in points in the order you like; for instance, you could draw the points later than lines and circles to see them on top

- Add labels

- Optionally, use TikZ commands to include additional elements

Now, let's explore the fundamental commands with sample values for easier syntax comprehension, diverging from the detailed reference manual format.

Defining points

You can assign names to points by specifying coordinates or mathematical formulas. Here are some commands, along with their explanations:

- The `\tkzDefPoint(1,2){P}` command defines a point with the name P at x coordinate 1 and y coordinate 2. `tkz-euclide` employs centimeters as the default length unit.

- The `\tkzDefPoints{1/2/A, 4/5/B}` command defines the points A at (1,2) and B at (4,5). As you see, you can define multiple points simultaneously.

- You can use calculations, such as in the expression `\tkzDefPoint({2*ln(3) }, {sin(FPpi/2}){P}` utilizing the syntax of the `fp` package. Refer to `texdoc fp` or `https://texdoc.org/pkg/fp` for details.

- You can optionally label it directly, such as here:

- `\tkzDefPoint[label=left:$P$]( (1,2){P}`.

Calculating points

For later use, you can let the `tkz-euclide` package calculate points at intersections. Have a look at the following commands and their effect:

- `\tkzInterLL(A,B)(C,D)` intersects the line through the points A and B with the line through C and D

- `\tkzGetPoint{X}` defines a point with the name X as a result of the last operation, like the line intersection above

- `\tkzInterLC(A,B)(C,D)` intersects the line through A and B with the circle around C through D

- `\tkzInterCC(A,B)(C,D)` intersects the circle around A and through B with the circle around C through D

- `\tkzGetPoints{X}{Y}` defines points with the names X and Y as a result of the last operation, like for the intersection above

There are further possible calculations:

- `\tkzDefPointBy[translation = from A to B](X)` defines a point as the translation of X by the line through A and B.

- `\tkzDefPointBy[rotation = center M angle 90](X)` rotates the point X around the center point M by 90 degrees.

- `\tkzDefPointBy[rotation in rad = center M angle pi/2](X)` rotates the point X around the center point M by pi/2, which is in Radian and means 90 degrees like the preceding.

- `\tkzDefPointBy[symmetry = center M](X)` reflects the point X at the point M.

- `\tkzDefPointBy[reflection = over A--B](X)` reflects the point X at the line through A and B.

- `\tkzDefPointBy[projection = onto A--B](X)` defines a point as the orthogonal projection from X to the line through A and B.

- `\tkzDefPointBy[homothety = center M ratio 0.3](X)` calculates a homothety of the point X with center point M and ratio 0.3.

- `\tkzDefPointBy[inversion = center M through P](X)` calculates an inversion of the point X with center point M and through the point P.

  Again, you can get the result of the calculation by `\tkzGetPoint`.

- `\tkzDefPointsBy[operation](A,B,C)` defines point using operations like the preceding operations; the results will be called "A," "B," and "C."

Drawing objects

You can draw objects such as points, lines, and circles using one of these commands:

- `\tkzDrawPoint(A)` draws point A as a filled circle.

- `\tkzDrawPoints(A,B,C)` draws a list of points; here A, B, and C.

- `\tkzDrawLine(A,B)` draws the line through the points A and B with an offset before A and after B. You can modify that offset by an option: `\tkzDrawLine[add=0 and 1](A,B)` starts exactly at A but adds 1 cm after B.

- `\tkzDrawLines(A,B C,D E,F)` draws lines through the points A and B, C and D, E and F, respectively. It understands the same offset as the preceding.

- `\tkzDrawSegment(A,B)` draws the line segment from point A to B.

- `\tkzDrawSegments(A,B C,D)` draws the line segments from point A to point B, and the one from C to D.

- `\tkzDrawCircle(A,B)` draws a circle around points A through B.

All drawing commands understand TikZ options, such as in the following snippet:

```
\tkzDrawCircle[color=blue, fill=yellow, opacity=0.5](A,B)
```

Printing labels

You can print labels to objects using one of the following commands:

- `\tkzLabelPoint(P){$P_1$}` draws a label for the point P, with subscript 1.

- `\tkzLabelPoints(A,B,C)` draws labels for the points A, B, and C.

- `\tkzLabelLine[left, pos=0.2](A,B){$L$}` draws a label L left of the line through A and B, at the position 0.2, so near the start.

- `\tkzLabelSegment[above, pos=0.8](A,B){$S$}` draws a label S above the segment from A to B, at the position 0.8, so near the end. 0.5 is the default position, which means the middle between A and B.

- `\tkzLabelSegments[above](A,B C,D)` labels the segments from A to B and C to D.

- `\tkzLabelCircle[draw, fill=yellow](A,B)(90){Circle of Apollonius}` draws a rectangular node, filled with yellow color and the text "Circle of Apollonius" at a position of 90 degrees.

There's more...

Let's use the same commands from the previous section to expand our drawing. Insert these commands just before the `\end{tikzpicture}` statement:

```
\tkzInterLC(A,B)(B,A)
\tkzGetPoints{F}{E}
\tkzDrawPoints(E)
\tkzLabelPoints(E)
\tkzDrawPolygon(A,E,D)
\tkzMarkAngles[fill=yellow,opacity=0.5](D,A,E A,E,D)
\tkzMarkRightAngle[size=0.65,fill=red,opacity=0.5](A,D,E)
\tkzLabelAngle[pos=0.7](D,A,E){$\alpha$}
```

```
\tkzLabelAngle[pos=0.8](A,E,D){$\beta$}
\tkzLabelAngle[pos=0.5,xshift=-1.4mm](A,D,D){$90^\circ$}
\tkzLabelSegment[below=0.6cm,align=center,
  font=\small](A,B){Reuleaux\\triangle}
\tkzLabelSegment[above right,sloped,
  font=\small](A,E){hypotenuse}
\tkzLabelSegment[below,sloped,font=\small](D,E){opposite}
\tkzLabelSegment[below,sloped,font=\small](A,D){adjacent}
\tkzLabelSegment[below right=4cm,
  font=\small](A,E){Thales circle}
```

Compile the extended code, and take a look at the effect of those commands:

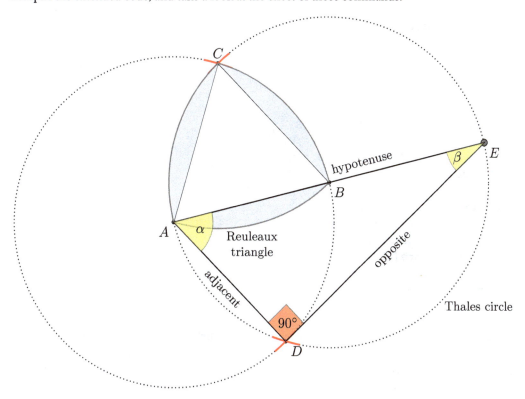

Figure 10.24 – A Reuleaux triangle construction

To witness the simplicity of defining circles tangentially or by their peripheral points, try this short exercise using the commands mentioned previously:

```
\documentclass[border=10pt]{standalone}
\usepackage{tkz-euclide}
\begin{document}
\begin{tikzpicture}
  \tkzDefPoints{0/0/A, 5/0/B, 1/4/C}
  \tkzDefCircle[in](A,B,C)
  \tkzGetPoint{M}
  \tkzDefCircle[circum](A,B,C)
  \tkzGetPoint{N}
  \tkzDefPointBy[projection=onto A--B](M)
  \tkzGetPoint{a}
  \tkzDefPointBy[projection=onto B--C](M)
  \tkzGetPoint{b}
  \tkzDefPointBy[projection=onto A--C](M)
  \tkzGetPoint{c}
  \tkzDrawCircle[very thick](M,a)
  \tkzDrawCircle[very thick](N,B)
  \tkzDrawPolygon[very thick](A,B,C)
  \tkzDrawLines[dotted](N,A N,B N,C)
  \tkzDrawLines[dashed](M,a M,b M,c)
  \tkzMarkRightAngles(M,a,B M,b,C M,c,C)
  \tkzDrawPoints(A,B,C,M,N,a,b,c)
  \tkzLabelPoints[below left](A,M,a,c)
  \tkzLabelPoints[below right](B)
  \tkzLabelPoints[above](C,b)
  \tkzLabelPoints[below](N)
\end{tikzpicture}
\end{document}
```

The command names are self-explanatory. As with most geometric constructions, there's a specific sequence to follow: initially defining objects and then referencing them later. Additionally, drawing commands placed later overlap those drawn earlier, allowing you to control the visibility hierarchy by selecting the drawing order.

When you compile this sample code, you will get this result:

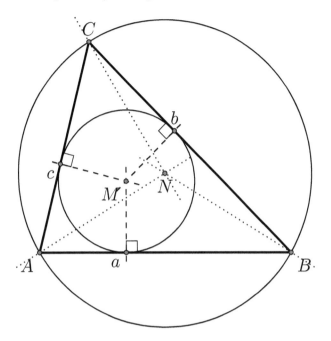

Figure 10.25 – A triangle with inner circle and outer circle

This geometry package built on TikZ significantly simplifies creating geometric constructions.

Doing calculations

Besides writing math, sometimes it's useful to actually calculate something. We have several options:

- The `calc` package offers basic math with LaTeX, with lengths and counters
- The `fp` package provides fixed-point arithmetic with high precision
- `pgfmath` belongs to the PGF/TikZ package, providing many functions and a good parser
- LuaLaTeX is a version of LaTeX that allows programming calculation in **Lua**

Here, let's work with the `pgfmath` functionality, as we already worked with TikZ, and it's better documented than the other options.

How to do it...

Follow these steps:

1. Start a document, load the TikZ package, and begin your document without indentation at the beginning:

   ```
   \documentclass{article}
   \usepackage{tikz}
   \begin{document}
   \noindent
   ```

2. In your text, use the \pgfmathparse command for calculating and the \pgfmathresult command for printing:

   ```
   In a right-angled triangle, the two shortest sides
   got widths of 3 and 7, respectively. The longest
   side has a width of \pgfmathparse{sqrt(3^2 +
   7^2)}\pgfmathresult.
   ```

3. Use the \pgfmathprintnumber command for formatted printing:

   ```
   The smallest angle is about \pgfmathparse{atan(3/7)}
   \pgfmathprintnumber[precision=2]{\pgfmathresult}
   degrees.
   ```

4. End the document:

   ```
   \end{document}
   ```

5. Compile, and look for the values:

In a right-angled triangle the two shortest sides got widths of 3 and 7, respectively. Then, the longest side has a width of 0.0. The smallest angle is about 23.2 degrees.

Figure 10.26 – Calculating within the text

How it works...

There are essentially two steps involved:

1. **Parsing and calculating**: Use the \pgfmathparse command.

2. **Printing or utilizing the result**: Accomplished this using \pgfmathresult. Additionally, \pgfmathprintnumber allows printing the result with the desired precision.

You can construct formulas using typical operation symbols, parentheses, and well-known functions such as sqrt for square root, ln for natural logarithm, min and max, and numerous trigonometric functions such as sin, cos, and tan. For more in-depth information, please refer to the pgfmath section in the PGF/TikZ manual.

If high-precision calculations are necessary, I'd recommend switching to LuaTeX or utilizing the fp package. The reason is that the precision of the pgfmath functions is confined by TeX's internal capabilities. However, for drawing purposes where accuracy in micrometers isn't critical, pgfmath serves well.

Further learning

The previous chapters offered quick-start recipes, but in-depth reference manuals for mathematics with LaTeX exist. The amsmath manual is one such comprehensive resource, detailing the package extensively. Access it by typing texdoc amsmath at the command prompt or online via https:// texdoc.net/pkg/amsmath.

For an even more comprehensive document, visit https://ctan.org/pkg/voss-mathmode.

We used TikZ a lot to visualize mathematics. The manual is available by typing texdoc tikz at the command prompt and at https://texdoc.org/pkg/tikz.

There's a section in the TikZ example gallery with many example math drawings with complete code at https://texample.net/tikz/examples/area/mathematics.

Even more examples are at https://tikz.net/category/mathematics.

There's a gallery for two-dimensional and three-dimensional plots with extensive math at https:// pgfplots.net/tikz/examples/area/mathematics. I maintain the mentioned websites. If you have questions regarding the examples, mathematics with LaTeX, or this book, you can tell them to me in the LaTeX Community forum at https://latex.org.

11

Using LaTeX in Science and Technology

While the prior chapter focused on mathematics, we'll now explore various scientific fields such as chemistry, physics, computer science, technology, and electronics. Given the significant reliance on mathematics in these disciplines, make sure you also explore *Chapter 10, Writing Advanced Mathematics*. This chapter will be an overview, showing specific recipes for how LaTeX can be used across diverse scientific domains.

We'll cover the following main topics:

- Typesetting an algorithm
- Printing a code listing
- Programming with Lua
- Creating graphs
- Writing quantities with units
- Drawing Feynman diagrams
- Writing chemical formulas
- Drawing molecules
- Representing atoms
- Drawing molecular orbital diagrams and atomic orbitals
- Printing a customized periodic table of elements
- Drawing electrical circuits

This chapter aims to showcase various packages through practical examples while providing insights into their utilization. For more intricate details, the manuals of these packages serve as a reference.

Typesetting an algorithm

An **algorithm** constitutes a fundamental concept within computer science. It represents a systematic set of step-by-step operations executed to accomplish specific tasks, such as calculations or data processing, e.g., sorting.

Algorithms can be visualized using a flow chart, which we made in *Chapter 6, Creating Graphics*. In this recipe, we will print an algorithm using **pseudocode** with syntax highlighting. Our example will show the calculations that display the **Mandelbrot** set, a visually stunning classic fractal generated by computations involving complex numbers.

How to do it...

We will utilize the `algorithmicx` package written by Szász János. We will break down the process into several small steps for more transparent comprehension. As usual, the complete code is available for download from `https://latex-cookbook.net`, eliminating the need for manual typing. At the end, you will see an image with the output. Consider switching between the output image and the quite comprehensive instructional steps to observe the incremental construction of the algorithm layout. Here it goes:

1. As usual, start with a document class. Load additional packages you intend to use; in this case, we need the `dsfont` and `mathtools` packages:

   ```
   \documentclass{article}
   \usepackage{dsfont}
   \usepackage{mathtools}
   ```

2. Load these three algorithm packages:

   ```
   \usepackage{algorithm}
   \usepackage{algorithmicx}
   \usepackage{algpseudocode}
   ```

3. You can define your own commands—in our case, a statement for local variables:

   ```
   \algnewcommand{\Local}{\State\textbf{local
     variables: }}
   ```

4. We define any other macros we need. We'll also create a shortcut `\Let` command for recurring variable assignments using the `\State` command. To ensure proper left-hand side alignment, we'll use the `\mathmakebox` command to put an argument in a box with a minimum width of `1em`:

   ```
   \newcommand{\Let}[2]{\State
     $\mathmakebox[1em]{#1} \gets #2$}
   ```

5. Start the document:

    ```
    \begin{document}
    ```

6. Open an `algorithm` environment:

    ```
    \begin{algorithm}
    ```

7. Provide a caption and a label for cross-referencing:

    ```
    \caption{Mandelbrot set}
    \label{alg:mandelbrot}
    ```

8. Start an `algorithmic` environment with an *n* option for numbering every *n*th line. We choose 1 as this option, numbering each single line:

    ```
    \begin{algorithmic}[1]
    ```

9. You can state requirements if any exist:

    ```
    \Require{$c_x, c_y, \Sigma_{\max} \in \mathds{R},
        \quad i \in \mathds{N}, \quad i_{\max} > 0,
        \quad \Sigma_{\max} > 0$}
    ```

10. We write down the function name with arguments:

    ```
    \Function{mandelbrot}{$c_x, c_y, i_{\max},
                \Sigma_{\max}$}
    ```

11. Now we use our own `\Local` macro for declaring local variables:

    ```
    \Local{$x, y, x_1, y_1, i, \Sigma$}
    ```

12. We use a statement to initialize local variables:

    ```
    \State $x, y, i, \Sigma \gets 0$}
    ```

13. We can add a comment to the line:

    ```
    \Comment{initial zero value for variables}
    ```

14. Now, write down a `while` loop that contains assignments:

    ```
    \While{$\Sigma \leq \Sigma_{\max}$
            and $i < i_{\max}$}
        \Let{x_1}{x^2 - y^2 + c_x}
        \Let{y_1}{2xy + c_y}
        \Let{x}{x_1}
        \Let{y}{y_1}
    ```

```
        \Let{\Sigma}{x^2 + y^2}
      \EndWhile
```

15. Add an `if` … `then` conditional statement:

```
        \If{$i < i_{\max}$}
          \State \Return{$i$}
        \EndIf
```

16. We specify a return value and end the function:

```
        \State \Return{0}
      \EndFunction
```

17. End all open environments and the document:

```
    \end{algorithmic}
  \end{algorithm}
  \end{document}
```

18. Compile and take a look at the outcome:

Algorithm 1 Mandelbrot set

Require: $c_x, c_y, \Sigma_{\max} \in \mathbb{R}, \quad i \in \mathbb{N}, \quad i_{\max} > 0, \quad \Sigma_{\max} > 0$

  1: **function** MANDELBROT($c_x, c_y, i_{\max}, \Sigma_{\max}$)
  2:      **local variables:** $x, y, x_1, y_1, i, \Sigma$
  3:      $x, y, i, \Sigma \leftarrow 0$ ▷ initial zero value for variables
  4:      **while** $\Sigma \leq \Sigma_{\max}$ and $i < i_{\max}$ **do**
  5:         $x_1 \leftarrow x^2 - y^2 + c_x$
  6:         $y_1 \leftarrow 2xy + c_y$
  7:         $x \leftarrow x_1$
  8:         $y \leftarrow y_1$
  9:         $\Sigma \leftarrow x^2 + y^2$
10:      **end while**
11:      **if** $i < i_{\max}$ **then**
12:         **return** i
13:      **end if**
14:      **return** 0
15: **end function**

Figure 11.1 – An algorithm with pseudocode

How it works...

The `algorithm` environment is a wrapper that allows the algorithm to float to a good position, just like figures and tables. So, page breaks within algorithms are avoided and pages can be well filled. Furthermore, it supports captions and labels for cross-referencing and adds the `\listofalgorithms` command, which generates a list of algorithms similar to a list of figures.

The inner `algorithmic` environment does the specific typesetting. It supports commands that are commonly used in algorithm descriptions. These are the commands we used:

- The `\Require` command is for a short list of requirements for the algorithm. The output starts with the **Require:** keyword in bold.

- The `\Function` command prints the **function** keyword in bold, followed by the function name in small caps and parameters in parentheses. The `\EndFunction` command prints **end function** in bold.

- The `\While` and `\EndWhile` commands generate a loop in the manner **while** ... **do** ... **end while**.

- The `\If` and `\EndIf` commands generate a conditional statement in the manner **if** ... **then** ... **end if**.

- The `\State` command starts a new algorithm line with a suitable indentation.

The complete set of commands is described in the package manual, accessed by inputting `texdoc algorithmicx` or going to `https://texdoc.org/pkg/algorithmicx`.

There's more...

There's more than the pseudocode style. You can use the `algpascal` layout, which supports **Pascal** language syntax and performs the block indentation automatically. To achieve this, replace the command `\usepackage{algpseudocode}` with the command `\usepackage{algpascal}`. In the same way, you can use the `algc` layout instead, which is the equivalent of the **C** language.

Experienced users may define their own command sets. This and existing layout features are described in the package manual.

Printing a code listing

Documentation often includes code snippets, as well as computer science theses. While the first recipe of this chapter handed pseudocode for algorithms and the subsequent recipe did actual programming, our focus now shifts to typesetting the code. To keep it concise, we'll use a simple "hello world" program as an example.

How to do it...

We'll utilize the `listings` package initially written by Carsten Heinz and designed explicitly for this task. Follow these steps:

1. Start with any document class:

    ```
    \documentclass{article}
    ```

2. Load the `listings` package:

```
\usepackage{listings}
```

3. Begin the document:

```
\begin{document}
```

4. Begin a `lstlisting` environment with an option for the language:

```
\begin{lstlisting}[language = C++]
```

5. Continue with the code you would like to print:

```
// include standard input/output stream objects:
#include <iostream>
// the main method:
int main()
{
    std::cout << "Hello TeX world!" << std::endl;
}
```

6. End the `lstlisting` environment and the document:

```
\end{lstlisting}
\end{document}
```

7. Compile and have a look at the output:

```
// include standard input/output stream objects:
#include <iostream>
// the main method:
int main()
{
    std::cout << "Hello_TeX_world!" << std::endl;
}
```

Figure 11.2 – A C++ listing

How it works...

The fundamental steps are straightforward:

1. Load the `listings` package.

2. Enclose each code listing within a `lstlisting` environment, optionally specifying the language as seen previously.

The manual provides a comprehensive list of supported languages, continually expanding for over 25 years. You can define your own language style or find one for your favorite language online.

Commands and environments within the listings package use the \lst prefix to avoid naming conflicts with other packages.

You can tailor the appearance of all your listings with a single command:

```
\lstset{key1 = value1, key2 = value2}
```

This command offers an extensive key=value interface with numerous keys. Let's look at how to use it, focusing on particularly useful keys.

Modify the preceding example in this way:

1. Add the xcolor package to your document preamble:

   ```
   \usepackage{xcolor}
   ```

2. Load the inconsolata package to utilize an excellent typewriter font:

   ```
   \usepackage{inconsolata}
   ```

3. Define macros, such as the programming language logo, to maintain a consistent appearance:

   ```
   \newcommand{\Cpp}{C\texttt{++}}
   ```

4. After \usepackage{listings}, insert settings via key=value:

   ```
   \lstset{
       language         = C++,
       basicstyle       = \ttfamily,
       keywordstyle     = \color{blue}\textbf,
       commentstyle     = \color{gray},
       stringstyle      = \color{green!70!black},
       stringstyle      = \color{red},
       columns          = fullflexible,
       numbers          = left,
       numberstyle      = \scriptsize\sffamily\color{gray},
       caption          = A hello world program in \Cpp,
       xleftmargin      = 0.16\textwidth,
       xrightmargin     = 0.16\textwidth,
       showstringspaces = false,
       float,
   }
   ```

5. With these settings, you can now utilize the \begin{lstlisting} command without additional arguments. Compile your adjusted example and observe the changes:

Listing 1: A hello world program in C++

```cpp
// include standard input/output stream objects:
#include <iostream>
// the main method:
int main()
{
    std::cout << "Hello TeX world!" << std::endl;
}
```

Figure 11.3 – A customized listing

There's more...

Like the standard LaTeX verbatim environment and the \verb command, lstlisting provides a companion for embedding small code snippets inline—the command \lstinline does it. Write it as follows:

```
Use \lstinline!#include <iostream>! for
including i/o streams.
```

You can use any character as a delimiter instead of the exclamation mark as long as it doesn't appear in the code snippet.

For longer listings, you can save them in external files. Instead of the standard \input command, use the following command:

```
\lstinputlisting[options]{filename}
```

The same options available for the lstlisting environment can be applied here. For instance, the following command includes only lines 4 to 10:

```
\lstinputlisting[firstline=4, lastline=10]{filename}
```

This allows the breakdown of lengthier listings along with explanatory text.

Similar to the regular LaTeX \listoffigures command, you can generate a list of listings with their captions using the \lstlistoflistings command.

Programming with Lua

While LuaTeX comes with numerous more advancements regarding, for example, font support and **MetaPost** graphics support, we will focus on pure Lua programming in this section to carve out benefits to program and use algorithms.

TeX, primarily a text-processing language, has limited programming capabilities and needs advanced data-handling functionalities. That makes general-purpose programming a challenge. To address this, TeX developers sought a scripting language to add modern programming capabilities. Their strategic choice was **Lua**, a versatile, lightweight, and highly portable scripting language designed to be embedded in other applications. This decision led to the development of **LuaTeX**, a new TeX engine that, combined with the LaTeX format, is called **LuaLaTeX**.

While LuaTeX offers various advancements, including enhanced font and MetaPost support, this recipe uses pure Lua programming to run algorithms directly within our LaTeX document.

> **Note**
>
> Use the LuaLaTeX compiler option in your LaTeX editor for the examples in this chapter.

How to do it...

Let's implement an iterative algorithm, **Heron's method** (also called the **Babylonian method**), to calculate the square root of a number. This method is detailed at https://en.wikipedia. org/wiki/Methods_of_computing_square_roots#Heron's_method. In essence, it works as follows:

1. Start with an estimate, x, which could approximate the square root of n.

2. If x is smaller than the actual square root, then n/x is larger than the root since $x*x = $ n is our objective. Conversely, if x is greater than the root, n/x would be smaller. To refine our approximation, we select the average of x and n/x as the new value for x.

3. Go back to *step 2* and repeat this process multiple times.

Let's see how to do this calculation in LaTeX! Follow these steps to get the square root of 2:

1. Start with any document class:

    ```
    \documentclass{article}
    ```

2. Load the `luacode` package for extended Lua support:

    ```
    \usepackage{luacode}
    ```

3. Begin the document with some text:

```
\begin{document}
The value of $\sqrt{2}$ is \approx
```

4. Open a `luacode` environment:

```
\begin{luacode}
```

5. Now use Lua—declare your variable x with an initial value of 1:

```
local x = 1
for i=1,10 do
  x = (x + 2/x)/2
end
```

6. Print the result to the LaTeX document:

```
tex.print(x)
```

7. End the `luacode` environment and the document:

```
\end{luacode}
\end{document}
```

8. Compile using LuaLaTeX and have a look at the output:

The value of $\sqrt{2}$ is ≈ 1.4142135623731

Figure 11.4 – Output of text and calculated result

How it works...

We utilized a `luacode` environment from the package by Manuel Pégourié-Gonnard to embed a Lua program in our LaTeX document. We defined a variable and employed a for loop to compute the final value through ten iterative repetitions. Using the `tex.print` command, we displayed the value of the Lua variable within our document.

The Lua language is comprehensively documented at https://www.lua.org/docs.html.

While we went through this example to understand how to embed Lua code, there's an alternate calculation method. Lua features a mathematical library that provides various mathematical functions. For instance, to print the value of the square root of 2, you could execute this command:

```
tex.print(math.sqrt(2))
```

You don't need the `luacode` environment and package for small Lua code snippets such as this. You can execute any single-line Lua code using the `\directlua` command. You can modify the previous code to have this as the LaTeX document body:

```
The value of $\sqrt{2}$ is
\approx\directlua{tex.print(math.sqrt(2))}.
```

The output will be the same as in the previous figure. The mathematical library is documented in *Section 6.7* of the current Lua reference manual, with version 5.4 available at https://www.lua.org/manual/5.4/manual.html#6.7, and you can find examples for all functions at http://lua-users.org/wiki/MathLibraryTutorial.

There's more...

Let's explore a more comprehensive example that shows the excellent integration of Lua with LaTeX. Utilizing the `pgfplots` package developed by Christian Feuersänger alongside Lua, we'll generate an image illustrating the Mandelbrot set through the algorithm outlined at the beginning of this chapter. Follow these steps:

1. Start with any document class. I opted again for the `standalone` class with some white margin:

   ```
   \documentclass[border=10pt]{standalone}
   ```

2. Load the `pgfplots` package and initialize it with options for the plot width and the version for compatibility:

   ```
   \usepackage{pgfplots}
   \pgfplotsset{width=7cm, compat=1.18}
   ```

3. Load the `luacode` package and open a `luacode` environment:

   ```
   \usepackage{luacode}
   \begin{luacode}
   ```

4. Enter the following Lua code for a function declaration following the algorithm detailed at the beginning of this chapter. Define and initialize local variables with an initial value of zero, perform calculations within a while loop, and transfer the result to TeX:

   ```
   function mandelbrot(cx, cy, imax, smax)
     local x, y, x1, y1, i, s
     x, y, i, s = 0, 0, 0, 0
     while (s <= smax) and (i < imax)   do
       x1 = x * x - y * y + cx
       y1 = 2 * x * y + cy
       x = x1
       y = y1
   ```

```
        i = i + 1
        s = x * x + y * y
    end
    if (i < imax) then
        tex.print(i)
    else
        tex.print(0)
    end
end
```

5. End the luacode environment, begin the document body, and open a tikzpicture environment:

```
\end{luacode}
\begin{document}
\begin{tikzpicture}
```

6. Like in the previous chapter, open a pgfplots axis environment with the following options in square brackets:

```
\begin{axis}[
  colorbar,
  point meta max = 30,
  tick label style = {font=\tiny},
  view={0}{90}]
```

7. Use the \addplot3 command to generate a 3D plot. The Z-values of the plot command are calculated using the \directlua command with the mandelbrot function:

```
\addplot3 [surf, domain = -1.5:0.5, shader = interp,
          domain y = -1:1, samples = 200]
    { \directlua{mandelbrot(\pgfmathfloatvalueof\x,
        \pgfmathfloatvalueof\y,10000,4)} };
```

8. Close the axis and tikzpicture environment and finish the document:

```
\end{axis}
\end{tikzpicture}
\end{document}
```

9. Compile the document using LuaLaTeX. The complex calculation may take some time. This is the generated plot:

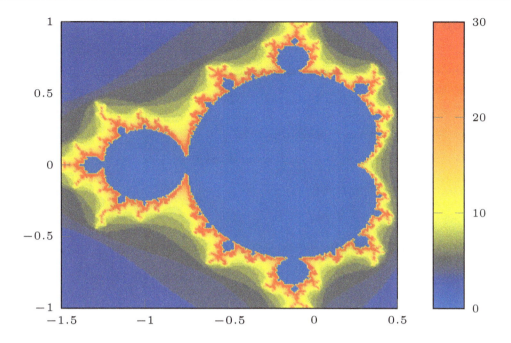

Figure 11.5 – The Mandelbrot set

How it works...

We combined a `luacode` environment, where we defined a Lua function, with the `\directlua` command in the document.

We utilized the `pgfplots` package to iterate through (x,y) values. The result of the Lua `mandelbrot` function is a color. While we aimed to generate a two-dimensional image, the result is used as the Z-value in a 3D plot. That Z-value is colored in proportion to its value. The picture looks two-dimensional because we chose a viewing angle directly above the xy-plane.

Creating graphs

Graph theory, commonly employed in fields such as operations research and computer science, typically involves models and drawings primarily composed of repeated vertices, edges, and labels. There are LaTeX packages that help efficiently generate consistent graphs.

How to do it...

The `tkz-graph` package developed by Alain Matthes provides a user-friendly interface, various preconfigured styles, and extensive customization options. Let's start with a minimal example:

1. Begin with any document class. In this case, I've opted for the standalone class to generate a compact PDF containing the desired image. Additionally, I've included an option for a border value to create a slight margin around the graph.

   ```
   \documentclass[border=10pt]{standalone}
   ```

2. Load the `tkz-graph` package:

   ```
   \usepackage{tkz-graph}
   ```

3. Define the distance between two vertices in cm:

   ```
   \SetGraphUnit{3}
   ```

4. Begin the document body:

   ```
   \begin{document}
   ```

5. Open a `tikzpicture` environment. Here, you may optionally rotate the graph, giving a value in degrees:

   ```
   \begin{tikzpicture}[rotate=18]
   ```

6. Define a set of vertices. Optionally, choose a shape for their positioning:

   ```
   \Vertices{circle}{A,B,C,D,E}
   ```

7. Decide which vertices shall be connected by edges in which order:

   ```
   \Edges(A,B,C,D,E,A,D,B,E,C,A)
   ```

8. Close the `tikzpicture` environment and end the document:

   ```
   \end{tikzpicture}
   \end{document}
   ```

9. Compile and have a look at the picture:

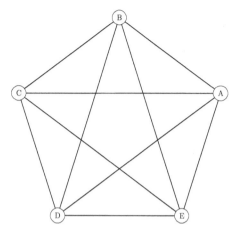

Figure 11.6 – A basic graph

How it works...

After loading the `tkz-graph` package, we used the `\SetGraphUnit` command to choose a value in centimeters for the distance between the vertices because the default value of 1 cm is pretty small. We did this in the preamble, so it's applied to all graphs consistently. We can also use the `\SetGraphUnit` command in the document within the `tikzpicture` environment. In that case, it applies only to the current TikZ picture.

We used the `\Vertices` command to define a set of vertices. We can name them using capital letters, small letters, numbers, or even mathematical expressions such as `$x_1$`. The initial argument defines the geometric structure of the graph, providing various options:

- `line`: This option places the vertices along a line.
- `circle`: This option places all vertices on a circle.
- `square`: With this option, the vertices are positioned as corners of a square. This should be used only with exactly four vertices.
- `tr1, tr2, tr3, tr4`: The vertices are placed in four different types of rectangular triangle formations. Use it with precisely three vertices.

While that doesn't look like many choices, you can use several `\Vertices` commands to build a complex graph. There's a node option to help with positioning. First, define a node or, better, a coordinate as follows:

```
\coordinate (a) at (4,2);
```

Then, you can use the Node option to place the vertices starting at that node or coordinate position like so:

```
\Vertices[Node]{square}{a,b,c,d}
```

That helps in assembling larger graphs by combining multiple smaller graphs.

Finally, we used the \Edges command that generates a sequence of edges by connecting a list of vertices in their given order.

We can easily modify the appearance of the graph using a single command. Insert the following command into your document preamble after you loaded the tkz-graph package:

```
\GraphInit[vstyle=Shade]
```

Compile and see how the graph has changed:

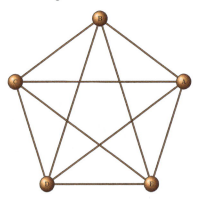

Figure 11.7 – A graph with a shading style

The vstyle option provides various graph styles, defining how vertices are displayed, and some styles produce non-regular edges:

- Empty: This option gives simple vertices without a circle or any border.

- Classic: Using this option, vertices are displayed as filled circles, and the vertex name is positioned outside of the circle.

- Normal: This option gives circular vertices with the vertex name inside.

- Simple: This option generates black-filled circular vertices without printing the vertex names.

- Art: This option turns vertices to shaded balls without printing the vertex name in orange by default. The edges are regular lines but colored orange, too.

- Shade Art: This works like the Art option but with thicker orange lines and black borders for edges.

- `Shade`: This option looks like `Shade Art` but has vertex names inside the balls, just as you saw in *Figure 11.7*.

- `Hasse`: This style produces circular, non-filled vertices without printing names.

- `Dijkstra`: This style prints circular vertices with the name inside

- `Welsh`: This style produces circular vertices with the name outside the vertex node.

The edges are regular black lines except with the `Art`, `Shade`, and `Shade Art` options.

There's more...

You can create your own graph style or customize the existing styles. Let's explore the additional features with a more complex example. Follow these steps:

1. Like in the previous example, start with the document class, load the `tkz-graph` package, choose a basic style, and set a distance between the nodes in centimeters:

```
\documentclass{standalone}
\usepackage{tkz-graph}
\GraphInit[vstyle = Shade]
\SetGraphUnit{5}
```

2. Modify the styles called `VertexStyle`, `EdgeStyle`, and `LabelStyle`. Use the `.append style` syntax to add new settings to the pre-defined style without replacing them. You can use regular TikZ options as follows:

```
\tikzset{
   VertexStyle/.append style =
     { inner sep = 5pt, font = \Large\bfseries},
   EdgeStyle/.append style   = {->, bend left},
   LabelStyle/.append style  =
     { rectangle, rounded corners, draw,
       minimum width = 2em, fill = yellow!50,
       text = red, font = \bfseries}
}
```

3. You can also use the `\renewcommand` macro to modify style elements like this for a different vertex ball color:

```
\renewcommand{\VertexBallColor}{blue!30}
```

4. Begin the document and open a `tikzpicture` environment:

```
\begin{document}
\begin{tikzpicture}
```

5. Declare a first vertex B:

```
\Vertex{B}
```

6. Set a vertex A to the west (WE) and C to the east (EA):

```
\WE(B){A}
\EA(B){C}
```

7. Draw edges between the vertices:

```
\Edge[label = 1](A)(B)
\Edge[label = 2](B)(C)
\Edge[label = 3](C)(B)
\Edge[label = 4](B)(A)
```

8. Add loops, which are edges from a vertex to itself:

```
\Loop[dist = 4cm, dir = NO, label = 5](A.west)
\Loop[dist = 4cm, dir = SO, label = 6](C.east)
```

9. Adjust the bend angle of the edges for the final two wider edges:

```
\tikzset{EdgeStyle/.append style = {bend left = 50}}
\Edge[label = 7](A)(C)
\Edge[label = 8](C)(A)
```

10. End the picture and the document:

```
\end{tikzpicture}
\end{document}
```

11. Compile and have a look at the result:

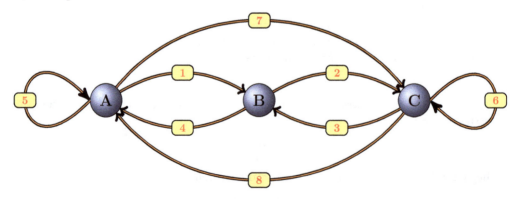

Figure 11.8 – A customized graph

How it works...

Similar to other recipes in this book, the basic procedure is as follows:

1. Define styles.
2. Position vertices.
3. Add edges.
4. Repeat if needed.

For positioning vertices, there's a simple syntax:

```
<direction>(B){A}
```

`<direction>` can be as follows:

*   `\EA` for placing B to the east of A
*   `\WE` for positioning it to the west
*   `\NO` for positioning it to the north
*   `\SO` for positioning it to the south
*   `\NOEA`, `\NOWE`, `\SOEA`, and `\SOWE` work as combinations of the preceding directional commands

The entire `\Edge` syntax is as follows:

```
\Edge[options](vertex1)(vertex2)
```

Options can be line width, labels, styles, and colors. For such detailed options, please refer to the package manual available by running `texdoc tkz-graph` via the command line or online at `https://texdoc.org/serve/tkz-graph/0`.

Writing quantities with units

Unlike pure mathematics, we often encounter units alongside quantities in natural sciences such as chemistry, physics, and engineering. It's essential to distinguish units from variables. Consider this example: let's create a formula that multiplies the speed s of one meter per second by the factor m. At first glance, it might seem straightforward like this:

```
\( m \cdot s = m \cdot 1 m s^{-1} \)
```

The LaTeX standard output would be as follows:

$$m \cdot s = m \cdot 1ms^{-1}$$

Figure 11.9 – A bad example of printing variables and units

What do you think about this? Units and variables seem identical. Imagine multiplying both sides of the equation by s or dividing by m... it becomes pretty perplexing. Furthermore, our space between 1 and m has been lost.

To adhere to common standards in writing, we often require the following:

- Upright presentation of units to differentiate them from italicized math variables
- A small space between a quantity and its accompanying unit
- Customizable appearance without changing the formula code, especially when a journal requests a different style
- Semantic writing—replacing abbreviations such as "m" and "s" with complete terms such as "meters" and "seconds"—enhances clarity
- Intelligent parsing of numbers within quantities
- Incorporating features such as striking out or highlighting to explain a calculation effectively

Is it possible to achieve all of these requirements? Definitely!

How to do it...

The siunitx package by Joseph Wright offers methods to align with international standards for unit systems while allowing customization to suit various typographic styles.

Now, let's rectify the formula mentioned earlier by following these steps:

1. Start with any document class:

   ```
   \documentclass{article}
   ```

2. Load the siunitx package:

   ```
   \usepackage{siunitx}
   ```

3. Begin the document:

   ```
   \begin{document}
   ```

4. Write the preceding formula but this time use the command `\SI{quantity}{units}`:

```
\( m \cdot s = m \cdot \qty{1}{\m\per\s} \)
```

5. End the document for now:

```
\end{document}
```

6. Compile and take a look:

$$m \cdot s = m \cdot 1\,\mathrm{m\,s}^{-1}$$

Figure 11.10 – Improved display of variables, values, and units

7. You can also opt for longer, more natural unit names to achieve the same result as mentioned earlier:

```
\( m \cdot s = m \cdot \qty{1}{\meter\per\second} \)
```

8. Let's adjust the reciprocal units. After loading the `siunitx` package, add the following line to your preamble:

```
\sisetup{per-mode = symbol}
```

9. Compile to see the difference:

$$m \cdot s = m \cdot 1\,\mathrm{m/s}$$

Figure 11.11 – Alternative display of units

10. If you want to emphasize changes, you can use the `cancel` and `color` packages. Add them to your preamble:

```
\usepackage{cancel}
\usepackage{color}
```

11. Let's test this together with scientific, exponential notation. So, modify your formula line as follows:

```
\( m \cdot s = m \cdot
\qty{1e-3}{\cancel\m\highlight{red}\km\per\s} \)
```

12. Compile to see the latest result:

$$m \cdot s = m \cdot 1 \times 10^{-3}\,\cancel{\mathrm{m}}\mathrm{km/s}$$

Figure 11.12 – Emphasizing in a formula

How it works...

The command `\qty{quantity}{units}` accomplishes two tasks:

- It interprets the quantity in its initial argument, effectively formatting numbers and comprehending complex numbers and exponential notations. The output formatting eliminates unnecessary spaces and groups large numbers into blocks of three with a thin space.

- It processes the units provided, ensuring proper typesetting with a thin space between the quantity and unit.

In essence, `\qty` combines two commands, which you also can use directly:

- `\num{numbers}` parses numbers in the argument and formats them properly.

- `\unit{units}` typesets the units. For example, `\unit{\kilo\gram\meter\per\square\second}`, or the shorter `\unit{\kg\m\per\square\s}`, gives the following:

$$\mathrm{kg\,m/s^2}$$

Figure 11.13 – Combined units

The package implements a basic set of SI standardized units via macros, including derived units. You can utilize `\meter`, `\metre`, `\gram`, and so on, as well as derived units such as `\newton`, `\watt`, `\hertz`, among many others. Even non-SI units are supported, such as `\hour` or `\hectare`. The package also supports common prefixes such as `\kilo`, `\mega`, and `\micro`. For a comprehensive list of features, refer to the detailed manual accessible via the `texdoc siunitx` command from the command line or by visiting `https://texdoc.org/pkg/siunitx`.

Drawing Feynman diagrams

A Feynman diagram is a mathematical visualization of the behavior of subatomic particles. There are several ways to generate them using LaTeX.

How to do it...

We will use the `tikz-feynman` package. The author documented it in *J. Ellis, 'TikZ-Feynman: Feynman diagrams with TikZ', (2016), arXiv:1601.05437 [hep-ph]*, and you can access the documentation executing `texdoc tikz-feynman` via the command line or at `https://texdoc.org/pkg/tikz-feynman`.

The positions of the vertices are calculated using Lua, so we must compile with **LuaLaTeX**. Follow these steps:

1. Start with any document class:

   ```
   \documentclass[border=10pt]{standalone}
   ```

2. Load the `tikz-feynman` package:

   ```
   \usepackage{tikz-feynman}
   ```

3. Load additional useful TikZ libraries and begin the document:

   ```
   \usetikzlibrary{positioning,quotes}
   \begin{document}
   ```

4. Utilize the `\feynmandiagram` command as follows:

   ```
   \feynmandiagram [horizontal=a to b] {
     i1 [particle=$e^-$] -- [fermion] a
       -- [fermion] f1 [particle=$e^-$],
     a -- [photon, "$\gamma$", red, thick,
         momentum' = {[arrow style=red]$k$}] b,
     i2 [particle=$\mu^-$] -- [anti fermion] b
       -- [anti fermion] f2 [particle=$\mu^-$],
   };
   ```

5. End the document:

   ```
   \end{document}
   ```

6. Compile and look at the result:

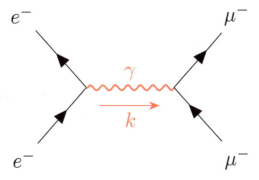

Figure 11.14 – A Feynman diagram

How it works...

We used i1 and f1 as initial and final nodes for one part and i2 and f2 for the other part. a and b are the nodes in the middle.

fermion, anti fermion, and photon are predefined line styles. You can also add TikZ styles.

The particle option is used to set labels. The momentum option adds further annotations.

There's more...

You can consider the alternative packages feynmf and feynmp. Visit https://feynm.net to explore a gallery of Feynman diagrams generated by various packages. Visit https://wiki.physik.uzh.ch/cms/latex:feynman to see a vast amount of examples.

Writing chemical formulas

The presentation of chemical formulas and equations differs from mathematical ones in several ways:

- Atomic symbols are represented by upright letters, distinct from italicized mathematical variables
- Numbers are often employed as subscripts, signifying the count of atoms.
- The alignment of numerous subscripts and superscripts is essential for a good formula layout
- Left subscripts and superscripts are also required in some cases
- Special symbols for bonds and arrows are necessary for chemical equations

However, accomplishing such requirements is challenging with basic LaTeX. Let's find a more effective solution.

How to do it...

We'll utilize the chemformula package that Clemens Niederberger wrote to practice chemical notation in LaTeX. Let's start:

1. Choose a document class, such as scrartcl of the **KOMA-Script** bundle, and the chemformula package and begin with the document:

    ```
    \documentclass{scrartcl}
    \usepackage{chemformula}
    \begin{document}
    ```

2. Start with an unnumbered section to verify that formulas work in headings. Use the \ch command for writing formulas. Give atoms and numbers as arguments straight away, without the _ and ^ syntax used when writing mathematics:

```
\section*{About \ch{Na2SO4}}
\ch{Na2SO4} is sodium sulfate.
```

3. Electric charges of ions are written directly without using _ and ^:

```
It contains \ch{Na+} and \ch{SO4^2-}.
```

4. Adducts can be denoted with a star or a dot, with numbers automatically identified as stoichiometric factors. Leave a blank space as a separator as here:

```
\ch{Na2SO4 * 10 H2O} is a decahydrate.
```

5. Chemical formulas can also be used in math mode. For instance, create a centered equation with a forward arrow, also called a reaction arrow, indicated by - >:

```
\[
   \ch{Na2SO4 + 2 C -> Na2S + 2 CO2}
\]
```

6. We can have it numbered, too, like math equations. This time, we use an equilibrium arrow, <=>:

```
\begin{equation}
   \ch{Na2SO4 + H2SO4 <=> 2 NaHSO4}
\end{equation}
```

7. If a number is left of an atom, it acts as a left subscript. But we can clearly indicate the meaning using _ and ^ before an atom, such as for isotopes:

```
\section*{Isotopes}
\ch{^{232}_{92}U140} is uranium-232.
```

8. Different bond types (single, double, triple) are represented by -, =, or +, respectively. We can see this in a list of hydrocarbons:

```
\begin{itemize}
   \item \ch{H3C-CH3} is ethane,
   \item \ch{H2C=CH2} is ethylene,
   \item \ch{H2C+CH2} is ethyne.
\end{itemize}
```

9. That's enough for now, let's finish the document:

```
\end{document}
```

10. Compile and see what you have done:

About Na_2SO_4

Na_2SO_4 is sodium sulfate. It contains Na^+ and SO_4^{2-}. $Na_2SO_4 \cdot 10\,H_2O$ is a decahydrate.

$$Na_2SO_4 + 2\,C \longrightarrow Na_2S + 2\,CO_2$$

$$Na_2SO_4 + H_2SO_4 \rightleftharpoons 2\,NaHSO_4 \tag{1}$$

Isotopes

$^{232}_{92}U_{140}$ is uranium-232.

Hydrocarbons

- H_3C-CH_3 is ethane,
- $H_2C{=}CH_2$ is ethylene,
- $H_2C{\equiv}CH_2$ is ethyne.

Figure 11.15 – Chemical formulas

How it works...

The input syntax is designed to be natural and straightforward:

- Atoms are represented by letters
- Numbers are automatically formatted as subscripts, signifying the number of atoms in the formula
- Stoichiometric numbers, representing molecule quantities, precede the molecule with a space in between

This simplicity not only aids in typing but also allows effortless copy-pasting from PDFs, Word documents, or the internet.

The most common bonds are written as follows:

- - represents a single bond
- = indicates a double bond
- + signifies a triple bond

The following syntax defines reaction arrows:

- - >, < -: These draw regular arrows pointing to the right or the left
- - / >, < / -: These draw broken arrows pointing to the right or the left (do not react)
- < - >: This draws a resonance arrow (arrows with tips at the left and the right)

- `<>`: This draws a right-facing arrow at the top and a left-facing arrow under it

- `<=>`: This draws an equilibrium arrow (half of an arrow tip at each side)

- `<=>>`: This draws an equilibrium arrow with a tendency to the right, so the top arrow to the right is larger

- `<<=>`: This draws an equilibrium arrow with a tendency to the left, so the lower arrow to the left is larger

You can incorporate mathematical equations, chemical expressions, or text above or below arrows by using this syntax:

```
<=>[\text{above}] [\text{below}]
```

The package manual elaborates on more arrow types and additional features. Access it using the command `texdoc chemformula` using the command line or open it at `https://texdoc.org/pkg/chemformula`.

There's more...

The mhchem package operates similarly but varies in certain aspects, as outlined in the `chemformula` manual. The newer `chemformula` package was designed for enhancements and is part of the `chemmacros` bundle, which brings even more features for chemical notation.

A comprehensive collection of TeX chemistry packages, along with descriptions, is accessible at `https://www.cnltx.de/known-packages`.

There's another package list on CTAN: `https://ctan.org/topic/chemistry`.

We'll explore another exceptional package for drawing molecules in our upcoming recipe.

Drawing molecules

In the previous example, we practiced writing molecular formulas. Now, let's delve into visualizing them. We'll create a visual representation of a cluster of atoms interconnected by various types of lines.

How to do it...

This seemingly complex task becomes much simpler with the `chemfig` package developed by Christian Tellechea. It offers a concise syntax for rendering molecular structures. Let's create a few:

1. Start with any document class and load the `chemfig` package:

    ```
    \documentclass{article}
    \usepackage{chemfig}
    ```

2. Let's organize molecules in a table. To do this, widen the rows slightly and initiate a `tabular` environment with a column aligned to the right and another to the left:

    ```
    \renewcommand{\arraystretch}{1.5}
    \begin{tabular}{rl}
    ```

3. For molecules, use the `\chemfig` command. Represent atoms as letters and depict a single bond using a dash:

    ```
    Hydrogen: & \chemfig{H-H} \\
    ```

4. Depict a double bond using an equal sign:

    ```
    Oxygen:    & \chemfig{O=O} \\
    ```

5. Use a tilde for a triple bond:

    ```
    Ethyne:    & \chemfig{H-C~C-H}
    ```

6. End the table and add some space:

    ```
    \end{tabular}
    \qquad
    ```

7. Enclose branches within parentheses. Incorporate options using square brackets separated by commas. The first option indicates an angle. As we'll see later, you can specify multiples of 45 degrees or arbitrary angles. The second option signifies a factor for interatomic distance. We'll set it to 0.8 for a more compact drawing. Use this for the methane structure:

    ```
    Methane: \chemfig{[,0.8]C(-[2]H)(-[4]H)(-[6]H)-H}
    ```

8. Finish the document:

    ```
    \end{document}
    ```

9. Compile and take a look at the drawings:

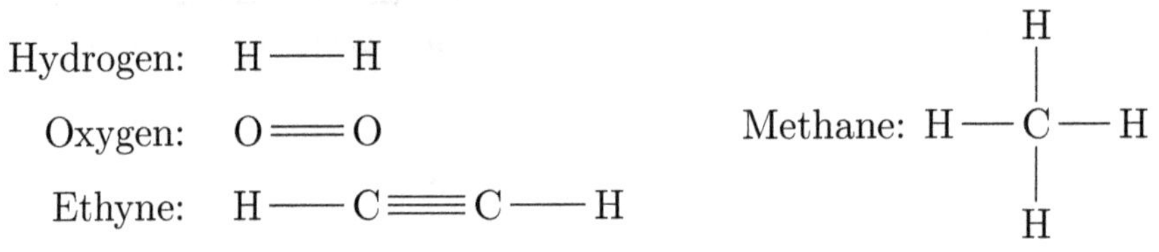

Figure 11.16 – Visual representations of molecules

How it works...

The chemfig employs TikZ for its drawing functions, handling the bounding box automatically to prevent overlap with other text. Experienced users have the flexibility to embed TikZ code if needed.

The primary command is \chemfig, which requires an argument consisting of the following arguments:

- Letters for atoms

- Symbols for bonds, such as -, =, and ~ for simple, double and triple bonds, respectively

- Options for bonds in square brackets, separated by commas

- Branches of atoms and bonds within parentheses

The most crucial option for bonds is the angle. It can be specified as follows:

- An integer number representing a multiple of 45 degrees, such as [2] for 90 degrees

- An absolute angle in degrees, indicated by a double colon, such as [:60] for 60 degrees

- A relative angle in degrees, marked by two double colons, such as [::30] for 30 degrees in relation to the previous bond

Positive and negative numbers are allowed.

A branch enclosed in parentheses allows you to open a path using an opening parenthesis, structure it as shown previously, and conclude it using a closing parenthesis. This returns you to the same position from where the branch started.

> **Tip**
> In complex molecules, find the longest chain and draw it first. Then, add the branches. Use relative angles for easy rotation of the entire molecule.

There's more...

There are further features we should take a look at.

Drawing rings

Molecular rings are commonly represented as regular polygons. They can be drawn using this syntax:

```
atom*n*(code)
```

Here, n indicates the number of sides of the polygon, and the chemfig code within parentheses depicts the structural arrangement within the ring.

For instance, the famous Benzene ring with all its atoms can be drawn this way:

```
\chemfig{C*6((-H)-C(-H)=C(-H)-C(-H)=C(-H)-C(-H)=)}
```

This line gives us the following picture:

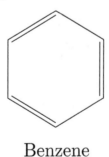

Figure 11.17 – The Benzene ring with all atoms

Naming molecules

Underneath a molecule, its name can be written using this syntax:

```
\chemname[distance]{\chemfig code}{name}
```

The optional distance value defines the distance to the baseline of the molecule, defaulting to 1.5 ex. For instance, to place the name Benzene below the carbon skeleton of a Benzene ring, use the following:

```
\chemname{\chemfig{*6(=-=-=-)}}{Benzene}
```

This will result in the following drawing:

Benzene

Figure 11.18 – The simplified Benzene ring with a label

Using building blocks

In LaTeX, you can create new macros using the \newcommand syntax. The chemfig package provides a similar feature—you can create your own macros for recurring use as follows:

```
\definesubmol{name}{code}
```

Now, we can use this macro in formulas by writing !name as a shortcut. For instance, this defines a molecular section with a carbon atom and two hydrogen atoms:

```
\definesubmol{C}{-C(-[2]H)(-[6]H)}
```

We can use the !C shortcut to draw the Pentane molecule:

```
\chemfig{H!C!C!C!C!C-H}
```

Remarkably, this concise code generates a considerably large molecule representation:

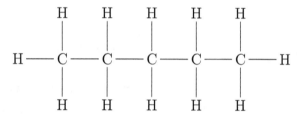

Figure 11.19 – The Pentane molecule

Applying style options

We can apply various style options to molecule drawings. The \chemfig command takes one optional argument in square brackets, which is a list of key=value options, and a mandatory argument for the molecule code in curly braces. It looks like this:

```
\chemfig[key1=value1, key2=value2, ...]{code}
```

Here are two commonly used styles:

- chemfig style: This is a list of options that apply to the entire tikzpicture environment of the molecule, grouped in braces
- atom style: This is a list of options for the atom nodes, again grouped in braces

For instance, applying these options would scale the entire picture and set the nodes to appear blue:

```
\chemfig[chemfig style = {scale=1.5, transform shape},
    atom style = {color=blue}]{H-C~C-H}
```

These options would result in thicker lines and a 15-degree rotation of the nodes:

```
\chemfig[chemfig style = {thick},
    atom style = {rotate=15}]{C(-[2]H)(-[4]H)(-[6]H)-H}
```

Here is the combined output from both lines:

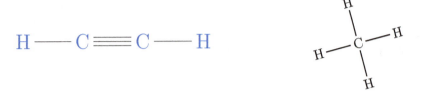

Figure 11.20 – Customized molecule drawings

> **Note**
>
> You may come across an outdated syntax on the internet: in a previous version of the package, the `\chemfig` command had two optional arguments, each enclosed in square brackets, as follows:
>
> `\chemfig[options for tikzpicture][options for nodes]{code}`
>
> The first argument's options modified the entire `tikzpicture` environment of the molecule, and the second argument's options adjusted the style of each node. Rewrite it using `chemfig` and `atom` styles.

For more options and features, please read the package manual by inputting `texdoc chemfig` using the command line or online at `https://texdoc.org/pkg/chemfig`.

Using ready-drawn carbohydrates

Though `chemfig` simplifies drawing, creating complex molecules can still be time-consuming, especially when dealing with numerous structures when you write lecture notes or a thesis covering carbohydrates. Fortunately, we don't have to start from scratch every time.

The `carbohydrates` package provides a lot of `chemfig`-drawn carbohydrates for you to use. It includes trioses, tetroses, pentoses, and hexoses in various models: the **Fischer** (full and skeleton), **Haworth**, and **chain** models. You can draw them as ring isomers and as chain isomers.

Let's have a look at how easy it becomes, for example, with glucose:

```
\glucose[model=fischer, chain]\quad
\glucose[model={fischer=skeleton}, chain]
```

This draws the Fischer models; the skeleton version doesn't show the H and C atoms:

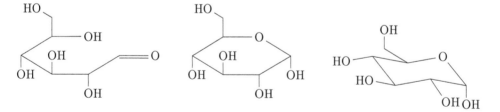

Figure 11.21 – Glucose molecules displayed using the Fischer models

Now let's draw glucose but with other models:

```
\glucose[model=haworth, chain]\hfill
\glucose[model=haworth, ring]\hfill
\glucose[model=chain, ring]
```

We get the following drawings:

Figure 11.22 – Glucose molecules displayed using the Haworth and chain models

Already implemented are the following molecules:

- \glycerinaldehyde (triose)

- \erythrose, \threose (tetroses)

- \ribose, \arabinose, \xylose, \lyxose (pentoses)

- \allose, \altrose, \glucose, \mannose, \gulose, \idose, \galactose, \talose (hexoses)

The package manual tells you all the details about options and usage. You can open it using the command line by running the command `texdoc chemformula` or online at `https://texdoc.org/pkg/carbohydrates`.

Representing atoms

Now that we've mastered drawing molecules, shall we explore further? Can we draw atoms? Absolutely!

How to do it...

We'll utilize a package named after the renowned physicist Niels Bohr and written by Clemens Niederberger—the `bohr` package. Follow these steps:

1. Start with a document class, load the `bohr` package, and begin with the document:

   ```
   \documentclass{article}
   \usepackage{bohr}
   \begin{document}
   ```

2. Use the command `\bohr{number of electrons}{element name}`, to draw the Fluorine atom:

   ```
   \bohr{10}{F}
   ```

3. For the next drawing, adjust the nucleus radius as follows:

   ```
   \setbohr{nucleus-radius=1.5em}
   ```

4. With this adjustment, there's more space at the center for an ion symbol. In this instance, employ the `\bohr` command with an optional argument specifying the number of electron shells within square brackets. This will illustrate a sodium ion:

   ```
   \bohr[3]{10}{$\mathrm{Na^+}$}
   ```

5. That's all for now! Conclude the document:

   ```
   \end{document}
   ```

6. Compile to see the result:

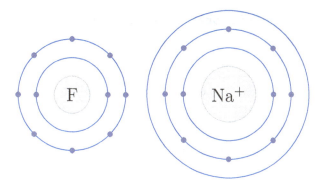

Figure 11.23 – Atoms and electrons

How it works...

It was pretty straightforward. However, I wanted to demonstrate how one can write about science effortlessly today.

After loading the package, all we required was this single command:

```
\bohr[number of shells]{number of electrons}{element name}
```

The \setbohr command provides a key=value interface for further fine-tuning. We'll skip over the extensive list of optional parameters to avoid overwhelming those who aren't working with physics or chemistry. You can read all customization details in the manual, which you can open by running texdoc bohr via the command line or online at https://texdoc.org/pkg/bohr.

Drawing molecular orbital diagrams and atomic orbitals

A **molecular orbital** (**MO**) diagram describes chemical bonding in molecules and displays energy levels. First, we will create such an MO diagram, and then we will draw atomic orbitals with a more visual approach.

How to do it...

We will use the tikzorbital package written by Germain Salvato-Vallverdu. These are the steps:

1. Start with any document class; we choose the standalone class here. Then load the tikzorbital package that implicitly loads TikZ:

    ```
    \documentclass[border=10pt]{standalone}
    \usepackage{tikzorbital}
    ```

2. Load the `positioning` and `quotes` TikZ libraries and begin the document:

```
\usetikzlibrary{positioning,quotes}
\begin{document}
```

3. Open a `tikzpicture` environment, and define a custom ∧ style to get small, center-aligned sans-serif text where we want it:

```
\begin{tikzpicture}[note/.style =
  {align = center, font = \sffamily\scriptsize}]
```

4. Use the `\drawLevel` command to draw an energy level line, that we call `1s1`, with an electron visualized in the upward direction:

```
\drawLevel[elec = up]{1s1}
```

5. Continue using `drawLevel` commands, now with a positioning coordinate and a width option:

```
\drawLevel[elec = up, pos = {(5,0)}]{1s2}
\drawLevel[elec = pair, pos = {(2,-2)},
  width = 2]{sigma}
\drawLevel[pos = {(2,2)}, width = 2]{sigmastar}
```

6. Draw a dashed line between the various right and left anchors of the energy level lines:

```
\draw[dashed]
  (right 1s1) -- (left sigma)
  (right 1s1) -- (left  sigmastar)
  (left  1s2) -- (right sigmastar)
  (left  1s2) -- (right sigma);
```

7. Draw labels for the energy levels:

```
\node[left]  at (left 1s1) {{$1s_1$}};
\node[right] at (right 1s2) {{$1s_2$}};
\node[right] at (right sigma) {$\sigma$};
\node[right] at (right sigmastar) {$\sigma^*$};
```

8. Print some text nodes for explanation using our `note` style:

```
\node[below = 0.4cm of middle 1s1, note]
  {Atomic\\Orbital};
\node[below = 0.4cm of middle 1s2, note]
  {Atomic\\Orbital};
\node[below = 0.4cm of middle sigma, note]
  {Molecular Orbital};
```

9. Finish the drawing with an arrow indicating the energy level:

```
\draw[very thick, -stealth] (-1.5,-2.5)
   to["Energy", note, sloped] (-1.5,2.5);
```

10. End the `tikzpicture` environment and the document:

```
\end{tikzpicture}
\end{document}
```

11. Compile and look at the outcome:

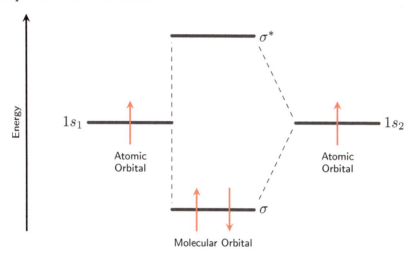

Figure 11.24 – A molecular orbital diagram

How it works...

The `\drawLevel` command is the most relevant here, as it draws a thick line with arrows representing the spin of the electrons at that level. It understands the following options:

- `elec`: This defines the number of electrons with their direction. The value can be up, down, updown, or pair, with the last two both having the same effect of displaying two electrons in the up and down directions, as seen in *Figure 11.24*.

- `pos`: This is the position of the left side of the energy level as (x,y) coordinate, enclosed in curly braces to ensure the correct parsing. If you omit it, $(0,0)$ will be used.

- `width`: This is the width of the energy level, which is 1 by default.

Some style options allow customizing color, thickness, arrows, and line style, as listed in the manual. You can open the manual by running `texdoc tikzorbital` at the command prompt or visiting `https://texdoc.org/pkg/tikzorbital`.

The `\drawLevel` command generates anchors to the `left`, `right`, and `middle` of it that we can use for drawing.

Apart from the `\drawLevel` command, we used TikZ commands for drawing lines and nodes; you can read more about the TikZ commands in my book, *LaTeX Graphics with TikZ*, or start at `https://tikz.org`.

A good starting point to learn more about MO diagrams is `https://en.wikipedia.org/wiki/Molecular_orbital_diagram`. I wrote this example in LaTeX to represent one of the figures at `https://www.ch.ic.ac.uk/vchemlib/course/mo_theory/main.html`, where you can also find more MO diagrams.

There's more...

The `tikzorbital` package provides the `\orbital` command to visualize atomic orbitals. Here's a quick example:

```
\begin{tikzpicture}
  \orbital{dyz}
  \orbital[pos = {(2.4,0)}]{dx2y2}
  \orbital[pos = {(4.5,0)}]{dz2}
\end{tikzpicture}
```

This gives us the following picture:

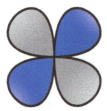 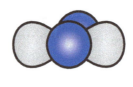 

Figure 11.25 – Atomic orbitals

Furthermore, the package provides an `\atom` command that can even be used to build molecule drawings. Here's an example that displays the diatomic molecule hydrogen fluoride (HF):

```
\begin{tikzpicture}
  \atom[name=F, color=red]{
    blue/270/south/2, blue/180/west/2,
    blue/90/north/2,  blue/0/east/1}
  \atom[name=H, color=gray, pos={(1.5,0)},
      scale=0.7]{gray/180/west/1}
\end{tikzpicture}
```

The output of this code is the following:

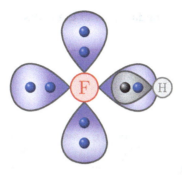

Figure 11.26 – The hydrogen fluoride molecule

This shall quickly demonstrate what we can achieve using a few commands of the `tikzorbital` package. If you are interested, you can take a deep dive into the package manual, which also provides other examples.

Printing a customized periodic table of elements

In the previous recipes, we read a lot about atoms and elements. Do you remember that huge poster of the periodic table of elements in the chemistry room at your school? Let's make it ourselves!

How to do it...

We will use the `pgf-PeriodicTable` package written by Hugo Gomes. Take the following steps:

1. Start with any document class:

   ```
   \documentclass[border=10pt]{standalone}
   ```

2. Load the `pgf-PeriodicTable` package:

   ```
   \usepackage{pgf-PeriodicTable}
   ```

3. Begin the document:

   ```
   \begin{document}
   ```

4. Use the `\pgfPT` command:

   ```
   \pgfPT
   ```

5. End the document:

   ```
   \end{document}
   ```

6.   Compile and look at the result:

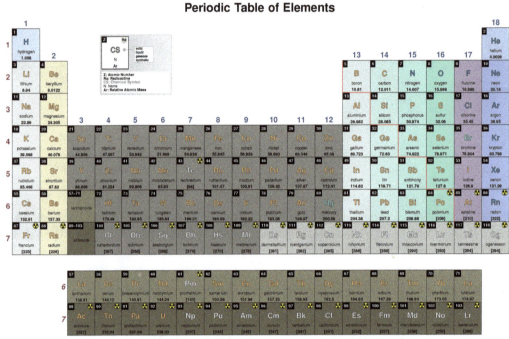

Figure 11.27 – The periodic table of elements

How it works...

That was too easy. The `\pgfPT` command understands many options, and you can customize a lot, including the colors. Let's leave a detailed reference to the package manual that you can find at `https://texdoc.org/pkg/pgf-PeriodicTable`.

Let's use that command to print, for example, the **IUPAC** groups 1 and 2 (also known as the **lithium group** and the **beryllium group**), periods 2 and 3, as follows:

```
\documentclass[border=10pt]{standalone}
\usepackage{pgf-PeriodicTable}
\usepgfPTlibrary{colorschemes}
\pgfPTGroupColors{example}{G1=red!90!black, G2=orange}
\begin{document}
\pgfPT[show title = false, back color scheme = example,
  legend box = {draw=blue!50, fill=blue!20},
  show extra legend,
  Z list = {1,3,4,11,12}]
\end{document}
```

This gives us the following output:

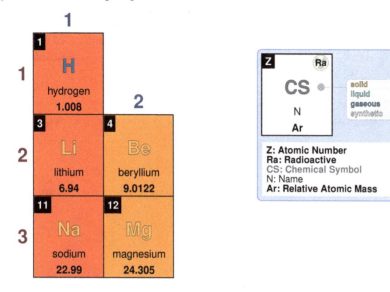

Figure 11.28 – A customized part of the periodic table of elements

Drawing electrical circuits

Technical documents in the domain of electrical engineering often comprise numerous formulas and many drawings. LaTeX excels in math typesetting, making it a top choice for authors. As we explored in a prior section of this chapter, the `siunitx` package makes representing electrical units in compliance with standards easy.

Drawing electrical circuits directly in LaTeX has various benefits. Unlike importing external images, drawings done within LaTeX can have annotations that precisely match the text regarding fonts and styles for perfect consistency.

Therefore, this section focuses on generating circuit diagrams. We aim to design a circuit featuring typical electrical components such as resistors, diodes, capacitors, bulbs, and more.

> **Note**
> The drawing in this recipe serves as a sample, and attempting to replicate it with actual components at home is not advised.

How to do it...

The TikZ graphics package provides several libraries for drawing electrical and logical circuits. We'll select one that adheres to the IEC standard. The code is a bit long, so it's recommended to download it with the code bundle from the publisher's website or from `https://latex-cookbook.net/chapter-11`. Here's a step-by-step guide:

1. Start with a `document` class. For this illustration, choose the `standalone` class, which generates a PDF file matching the size of our drawing. Then, load the `tikz` package:

   ```
   \documentclass[border=10pt]{standalone}
   \usepackage{tikz}
   ```

2. Load the `circuits.ee.IEC` TikZ library, symbols complying with the IEC norm:

   ```
   \usetikzlibrary{circuits.ee.IEC}
   ```

3. Begin the document:

   ```
   \begin{document}
   ```

4. Open a `tikzpicture` environment and define the following options:

   - The desired style

   - The x and y unit dimensions

   - An annotation style for a smaller font size

   - Graphic symbol settings, if desired

   - A switch contact style

   Here's the command with selected sample values:

   ```
   \begin{tikzpicture}[
       circuit ee IEC,
       x = 3cm, y = 2cm,
       every info/.style = {font = \scriptsize},
       set diode graphic = var diode IEC graphic,
       set make contact graphic =
         var make contact IEC graphic,
   ]
   ```

5. Start by drawing six contact points in two rows, three per row. Utilize a `\foreach` loop for convenience:

   ```
   \foreach \i in {1,...,3} {
     \node [contact] (lower contact \i) at (\i,0) {};
   ```

```
    \node [contact] (upper contact \i) at (\i,1) {};
}
```

6. As we defined the contacts' names, given in parentheses, we can refer to them using upper contact 1, lower contact 3, and similar. So, we will connect the upper-left contact and the lower-left contact by a line with a diode in the middle:

```
\draw (upper contact 1) to [diode]
   (lower contact 1);
```

7. We saw that we stated the component name as an option for the path. We can do the same for a capacitor:

```
\draw (lower contact 2) to [capacitor]
   (upper contact 2);
```

8. The component keys can have options. So, we draw a line with a resistor, which has an electrical resistance of 6 ohm, with that value as annotation:

```
\draw (upper contact 1) to [resistor = {ohm = 6}]
   (upper contact 2);
```

9. Annotations can be different. Here, we use a symbol for an adjustable resistor:

```
\draw (lower contact 2) to [resistor = {adjustable}]
   (lower contact 3);
```

10. We can have even more options. Useful options are near start and near end for positioning two components at a line:

```
\draw (lower contact 1) to [
      voltage source = {near start,
      direction info = {volt = 12}},
            inductor = {near end}]
   (lower contact 2);
```

11. Do it similarly for an open contact and a battery with some text as annotation:

```
\draw (upper contact 2) to
      [ make contact = {near start},
             battery = {near end,
                info = {loaded}}]
   (upper contact 3);
```

12. Let's finish with a bulb. We will make it a bit bigger than the default:

```
\draw (lower contact 3) to
    [bulb = {minimum height = 0.6cm}]
  (upper contact 3);
```

13. End the `tikzpicture` environment and the document:

```
\end{tikzpicture}
\end{document}
```

14. Compile and have a look at the circuit:

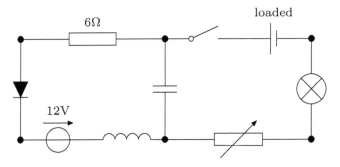

Figure 11.29 – A fictional electronic circuit

How it works...

The TikZ manual references the circuit libraries, showcasing symbols and their associated options. We can only outline some selected details of the breadth of content here. But here's a stepwise summary of our approach:

1. Load the necessary library and defining styles, either as an option to the `tikzpicture` environment or globally through the `\tikzset` command.

2. Position contacts and other nodes, which can be done using pure coordinates combined with a `\foreach` loop or with the aid of the `positioning` TikZ library. Another option would be utilizing a TikZ `matrix of nodes`.

3. Draw lines between the nodes using `to` paths, which take components as options.

Components can have further options, such as for additional information (`info above`), positioning (`near start` or `near end`), or color and size.

In our example, we opted for verbose naming and ample spacing to enhance code readability, a practice particularly beneficial in complex drawings.

Access the TikZ manual by entering `texdoc tikz` via the command line or read it online by visiting `https://texdoc.org/pkg/tikz`. The relevant sections are in a *Circuit Libraries* section in the *Libraries* part. You can also go directly to `https://tikz.dev/library-circuits` to read that section online.

See also

While scientific and technical writing is often based on mathematical writing, there are distinct field-specific notations, conventions, and requisites.

Developers and power users in the LaTeX community created numerous LaTeX packages and classes dedicated to a certain scientific field. The CTAN catalog is a good place to explore what's out there. Visit the CTAN topic categories; here are a few examples:

- `https://ctan.org/topic/physics`

- `https://ctan.org/topic/biology`

- `https://ctan.org/topic/chemistry`

- `https://ctan.org/topic/astronomy`

- `https://ctan.org/topic/electronic`

You can also visit `https://ctan.org/topics/cloud` to find the field of science you are looking for.

LaTeX's capability to generate scientific illustrations is fascinating. There's an abundance of examples available, and I curate a TikZ gallery featuring diverse drawings alongside different scientific disciplines. The gallery is conveniently organized by scientific field, allowing you to explore various graphics created using LaTeX. For example:

- `https://texample.net/tikz/examples/area/physics/` showcases approximately 50 examples, encompassing 3D atom clusters, energy level diagrams, optics, mechanics, astronomy, and more

- `https://texample.net/tikz/examples/area/chemistry/` presents 15 illustrations for chemistry, including a periodic table of elements

- `https://texample.net/tikz/examples/area/computer-science/` contains around 40 drawings covering networks, database topics, protocols, algorithms, and related topics

Even more drawings with their code can be found at `https://tikz.net`. Over 500 TikZ examples are available to explore by topic, spanning physics, engineering, computing, mathematics, and beyond.

These curated resources offer a rich repository of LaTeX-generated graphics across various scientific domains. Take their source code as a basis for your own drawings.

12

Getting Support on the Internet

During the initial stages of LaTeX, user groups were the primary support sources, helping through installation disks and personalized help. However, the advent of the internet has made information incredibly accessible. Although groups such as TeX User Group and DANTE still play crucial roles in significant resources such as **TeX Live** and **Comprehensive TeX Archive Network (CTAN)**, you can independently update and find information today. Additionally, various online TeX communities provide avenues for seeking help. This chapter will guide you through utilizing these resources effectively.

In this chapter, we will talk about the following topics:

- Exploring available LaTeX resources on the web
- Utilizing web forums effectively
- Crafting high-quality questions
- Generating minimal working examples

Exploring available LaTeX resources on the web

There are many LaTeX websites, and I've compiled a concise guide highlighting some excellent starting points.

How to do it...

In this recipe, you'll find a list of internet addresses and brief descriptions. Click on any of them to delve deeper into their content and explore further sites. Over time, website links might change, leading to some links becoming inactive. For the most recent list of addresses, you can visit `https://latex-cookbook.net/chapter-12`.

Software archives and catalogs

Some sites function as archives and catalogs, simplifying the search and navigation of the extensive software available:

- `https://ctan.org` is the most significant software and package archive. CTAN houses over 6,500 packages for TeX, LaTeX, and associated tools. You can peruse packages by name or topic and utilize a site-wide search function. CTAN serves as a distribution network for TeX distributions, TeX Live, and MiKTeX, operating via a central server and mirrored servers worldwide.

- The traditional **TeX Catalogue** is a manually curated catalog of the most significant TeX and LaTeX packages, organized for browsing by topic, alphabetically, or in a logical hierarchy. It is no longer maintained but is still available at `https://ctan.net/obsolete/help/Catalogue`.

- `https://tug.org/FontCatalogue` is the **LaTeX Font Catalogue**. It showcases an indexed list with examples of numerous fonts with direct LaTeX support.

User groups

Longstanding user groups form the backbone of LaTeX support on the internet, contributing to TeX development and CTAN while maintaining their independent home pages. Here are some of their websites:

- The home of the international **TeX Users Group** (**TUG**) is `https://tug.org`. The website is a gateway to the world of TeX with a lot of content.

- The website of the German-speaking TeX user group **DANTE** is `https://www.dante.de`. It has a lot of links to information in German, member journals, and event information.

- The homepage of the French-speaking TeX user group **GUTenberg** is `https://www.gutenberg-asso.fr`. It includes newsletters and periodicals.

- The **UK TeX Users Group** has dissolved recently, but their contributions remain relevant. The website archive is available at `http://uk-tug-archive.tug.org`.

- The LaTeX project website `https://www.latex-project.org` primarily serves as a hub for developers of the next LaTeX version, offering informative updates and insights.

Web forums and discussion groups

The most active sites on the internet are web forums. The following sites are the most relevant today:

- The highly active and mature LaTeX community support forum `https://latex.org` has hosted over 100,000 categorized, tagged, and searchable posts since 2008. Queries here are promptly addressed. It also manages an article archive and a LaTeX news portal at `https://latex.net`.

- The commercial question-and-answer platform `https://tex.stackexchange.com` doesn't provide news or articles, only questions and answers. While that platform has been very successful, this business case is now threatened by upcoming artificial intelligence chatbots such as ChatGPT, which are trained to do programming, including with LaTeX. This costs the website page visits and, thus, advertisement revenue.

- A very active question-and-answer site in German is `https://texwelt.de`.

- Another German web forum that is well-frequented and more discussion-based is `https://golatex.de`.

- You can find a French-speaking question-and-answer site at `https://texnique.fr`.

- In the Usenet, accessible via a Usenet reader or Google Groups, you can find a discussion group for TeX and LaTeX called `comp.text.tex`.

- A German-speaking Usenet discussion group is `de.comp.text.tex`.

Frequently asked questions (FAQs)

Discussion groups, web forums, and mailing lists gather frequently asked questions, making them available online. Checking these resources could provide answers to your questions and save you time. Here is a list of sites with FAQs:

- The English language **TeX FAQ** at `https://texfaq.org` was initially collected by the UK TeX Users Group and is today maintained by various contributors, including me. Most topics are covered with links to recommended packages.

- The **Visual LaTeX FAQ** at `https://ctan.net/info/visualfaq` provides a document with more than a hundred text samples. Click on any interesting detail and it will lead you to the corresponding page of the TeX FAQ.

- The LaTeX pictures how-to at `https://ctan.net/info/l2picfaq` is a question-and-answer collection about working with images and floats.

- The FAQ for MacTeX users is hosted at `https://tug.org/mactex/faq.html`.

- Two different German FAQs can be found at `https://texfragen.de` and `https://wiki.dante.de`.

- The GUTenberg group maintains a French TeX FAQ at `https://faq.gutenberg-asso.fr`.

TeX distributions

Several TeX software distributions are available for straightforward installation. Choose the appropriate collection based on your operating system; the following websites offer guidance on installation and updates:

- **TeX Live**: Visit `https://tug.org/texlive` for download information and installation instructions for the cross-platform TeX distribution, compatible with Windows, Linux, macOS, and other Unix systems. The TeX Users Group supports it.

- **MacTeX**: This distribution is derived from TeX Live and has been significantly customized for macOS; details about this distribution can be found at `https://tug.org/mactex`.

- **MiKTeX**: For this Windows-specific distribution, visit `https://miktex.org` for download and documentation. Recently, it has been ported to Unix-based systems.

There's more...

Besides my blog, `https://texblog.net`, there are numerous TeX and LaTeX blogs, many of which are showcased in the Community aggregator on `https://texample.net`. The front page provides a glimpse of the latest posts from the blogosphere, and both blogs and post extracts are archived there.

For LaTeX support via email, various mailing lists are available for subscription. I have compiled collections of these lists on `https://texblog.net/latex-link-archive/mailinglists`.

LaTeX editors, PDF viewers, and supplementary tools each have their own home pages. I have compiled links to these specific pages on my blog at `https://texblog.net/latex-link-archive/distribution-editor-viewer/`. This resource allows you to access information about the editor or tool you use conveniently.

Moreover, online LaTeX editors run directly in a web browser, making LaTeX accessible on tablets and smartphones. The most prominent is Overleaf at `https://www.overleaf.com`, which offers real-time collaborative editing and a code-less mode. It's a commercial service with free access to the basic features, while premium features require a paid subscription. However, many universities and institutes partner with Overleaf to give their students premium access.

The online compiler at `https://texlive.net` is commonly integrated into web forums.

Utilizing web forums effectively

In the early days, LaTeX support was provided through Usenet and mailing lists. Nowadays, internet forums have become the primary platform for LaTeX assistance.

Forums thrive on user questions and community responses. The vitality of forums is rooted in users' inquiries and the collaborative efforts of readers who provide answers. You are encouraged to ask any LaTeX-related questions on these forums, as they warmly welcome queries. Let's explore how to engage here.

How to do it...

As an example, let's take a look at the `LaTeX.org` forum. Established in January 2008, it has accumulated more than 100,000 posts as of the publication of this book. I manage this forum, and I can assure you that we genuinely appreciate good questions.

So let's have a walk together:

1. With any internet browser, visit the address `https://latex.org`. The top of the browser window will show an overview:

Figure 12.1 – A LaTeX web forum

2. Click the header of any category, such as **Graphics, Figures & Tables**, to see the forum category view:

Figure 12.2 – LaTeX forum topics

3. Explore different topics by clicking on bold titles and utilizing the search field at the top right, as shown in the first screenshot of this recipe.

4. To initiate a discussion on a new topic or post a question, click the **New topic** button in the top-left corner.

How it works...

While reading forum posts doesn't require registration, posting does. This is necessary to prevent the influx of spam posts from advertisers. Therefore, please register with a preferred login alias name to contribute. Registering comes with the advantage of being able to subscribe to topics and receive email notifications for any responses to your posts. Select any pseudonym to maintain anonymity.

The forum's post editor includes standard formatting tools for:

- Applying bold or italic styles and adjusting font size or color
- Quoting sections of previous posts
- Creating numbered or bulleted lists
- Adding images
- Inserting hyperlinks (URLs)
- Attaching files such as PDFs or log files

In addition to these general features, LaTeX-specific functionalities include:

- A **Code** button that transforms code snippets into human-readable code with LaTeX syntax highlighting and facilitates one-click access to an online LaTeX editor that compiles your code

- An inline **LaTeX** code button for embedding LaTeX code within text

- A **CTAN** button that converts a package name into a link leading to the CTAN package homepage, making life easier for advisors

- A documentation button that transforms a keyword into a link directing to the corresponding manual at `https://texdoc.org`, again to make it easier to answer with references

- Topic status options such as **Solved** for filtering unsolved questions

These features, particularly the last mentioned and the various shortcuts, aim to make working with LaTeX, CTAN, and documentation as user-friendly as possible. This sets the LaTeX forum apart from general forums and even TeX Stack Exchange, which functions similarly to other commercial Stack Exchange network sites.

As the forum's maintainer, I am directly reachable through the platform, as I consistently visit and review new topics daily. I have already posted more than 10,000 answers in the forum, and I'm reading every single question. I'm more than happy to provide support, especially regarding examples from this book.

While you can ask ChatGPT and other AI chatbots LaTeX-related questions and likely receive a functional answer, as demonstrated in the next chapter, you can get human feedback from qualified experts in a LaTeX forum. So, visit us at `https://latex.org`!

Crafting high-quality questions

As mentioned, I appreciate good questions, and most forum users share this sentiment. Sometimes, I dedicate an hour to creating a TikZ drawing for a user, while others work hard to troubleshoot error messages or output issues. We usually enjoy the process, especially when the questions are well-constructed.

How to do it...

We welcome challenges, particularly when we can figure out solutions. To make this happen, questions should adhere to the following guidelines:

- Provide as much information as possible

- Include the error message text, if available

- Format code properly using the syntax highlighting feature

- Show your effort if you have made some progress

It's also advisable to perform a forum search before posting, using relevant keywords. A similar question may have already been addressed.

And here's the ultimate advice that comes close to guaranteeing a solution for almost every LaTeX problem: post a minimal working example.

The following recipe will explain this.

Generating minimal working examples

The most effective way to seek help from anyone is to post the problem in a readily understandable manner, sparing readers from the need to ask for additional details. That's like serving the problem on a silver platter with a complete, illustrative, and minimal code example that can be easily compiled, making the resolution process straightforward. This approach is perfect in a forum, allowing readers to test and address the issue promptly. In other words:

- Post the complete code so readers can try to compile it

- The code should show the problem

- Remove non-relevant stuff so it's as small as possible

Then, it's usually easy to solve it. It's handy enough to post in a forum, and the readers can quickly try it out.

How to do it...

A good strategy is the "divide and conquer" method—resolving a problem by breaking it into smaller parts until only simple issues remain. To isolate the cause of a problem, follow these steps:

1. Duplicate your document. If it comprises multiple files, copy them all. Proceed with modifications on the duplicate, not the original.

2. Eliminate a substantial portion of the document copy you suspect does not contain the root cause. This can include the following:

   - Moving \end{document} upwards

   - Deleting lines

   - Commenting out lines using the percent sign (%)

   - Commenting out or removing \include or \input commands

   - For included files, deleting or commenting out lines or inserting \endinput, which can be moved upwards later

3. Recompile the document:

    - If the problem persists and still needs to be narrowed down as much as possible, return to step 2 and remove another part.

    - If the problem disappears, you identified the removed part as the likely cause. Restore that part using the editor's undo feature and proceed to step 2, removing other parts and refining the affected area.

4. Simplify the document further using the following steps:

    - Removing non-relevant packages, such as by commenting out or deleting corresponding `\usepackage` lines

    - Removing macro and environment definitions if irrelevant

    - Replacing images with rectangles such as `\rule{...}{...}` or using the `demo` option in the `graphicx` package:

    ```
    \usepackage[demo]{graphicx}
    ```

    - Substituting long texts with generated dummy text from packages such as `blindtext`, `lipsum`, or `kantlipsum`

    - Reducing complex math formulas

    - Replacing a bibliography file with a `filecontents*` environment

5. Verify if the document is now simple enough or if the previous steps must be repeated. Your efforts in isolating the problem may have already revealed the solution. Otherwise, the minimal example is ready for posting in a forum.

Forum regulars love problems where they can copy and paste, fix, verify the solution, and post the answer.

Don't worry if the procedure looks like it requires a lot of effort. The thorough explanation is just a bit long. Often, just a few removals and tests can lead to the solution.

There's more...

In the previous section, we used a top-down approach to contain the problem methodically. An alternative strategy is the bottom-up approach, wherein we initiate with a small test document and progressively expand it to showcase the problem. While this method can be advantageous, mainly when a rough idea of the problem's origin exists, the challenge lies in accurately reproducing the issue. Without successful reproduction, the reduced example lacks relevance.

When employing the bottom-up approach, the document must adhere to specific criteria:

- It should be complete, spanning from `\documentclass` to `\end{document}`
- It should show the problem when compiled
- It should be as concise as possible
- It should be compatible with any basic LaTeX system, so, for instance, not based on a specific journal document class

So, consider the following approaches:

- Use a standard class such as `article`, `book`, or `report`
- Avoid system-dependent configurations such as input encoding and uncommon fonts
- Try loading only commonly used packages

Forum readers or other remote helpers often dislike installing something just to test your code. A reasonable compromise could be using the mwe package, which automatically loads the `blindtext` and `graphicx` packages and provides several dummy images; this makes a minimal example elegant. Or you can use the `standalone` class, which crops the PDF to the actual content, which is better than an A4 or letter page just for showing an issue with a small drawing.

13

Using Artificial Intelligence with LaTeX

In recent years, there has been remarkable progress in **artificial intelligence** (**AI**), which refers to machine or software-simulated intelligence. AI involves processing extensive data and learning through logic, statistics, and algorithmic training.

Generative AI, in particular, can create text, images, and videos. This is highly useful for us, as LaTeX revolves around text, both regarding content and source code. Text generation involves using a **large language model** (**LLM**) trained on vast datasets. You can give it some input text, a so-called **prompt**, and it predicts the following words based on the statistical relationships it has learned. So, based on the LLM's language expertise and training data, you may get an excellent answer to your question or a response that at least seems to fit somehow, as good as it can be.

An example of such an LLM system is **ChatGPT** (**Chat Generative Pre-trained Transformer**), a **chatbot** developed by **OpenAI** research. It has gained widespread popularity for its impressive conversational abilities. Users can engage in conversations with ChatGPT, obtaining answers and refining the interaction in terms of language, writing tone, formality, and level of detail.

This chapter will explore leveraging ChatGPT to assist us in LaTeX writing tasks. We'll cover the following topics:

- Getting started with ChatGPT
- Getting answers to LaTeX questions
- Enhancing content
- Generating code

> **Note**
>
> To showcase ChatGPT, I'll present some output here and highlight prompt and response texts in italics.

Getting started with ChatGPT

In this book, we will use **ChatGPT version 3.5**. This chatbot is available for free and is trained on data up to January 2022. Newer versions are subscription-based paid services.

This version is sufficient for our purposes here, as LaTeX has a history spanning over 30 years and was well established by 2022, ensuring a substantial amount of available data.

With GPT-3.5, the maximum combined limit for input and output is 4,096 **tokens**. A token means a unit of text usually equivalent to a word, a subword, or a single character, so we may estimate about 3,000 words on average.

How to do it...

To get started, all you need is a web browser. Follow these steps:

1. Open the ChatGPT website at `https://chat.openai.com`.

2. If you don't have an account, click on **Sign up**. Once your account is created, click on **Log in**.

3. You can use a Google or Gmail account, a Microsoft account, or an Apple ID for a quick sign-up. Alternatively, enter your email address and choose a password.

4. To verify your email address, you will receive an email from OpenAI, and you need to click the **Verify email address** button.

5. Now, you are logged in and ready to chat! You can ask any question or provide instructions to ChatGPT.

Here's an example where I'll quote ChatGPT's entire response to give you an idea of what to anticipate. I'll keep subsequent examples more concise:

> **Prompt**: *Tell me why LaTeX is excellent.*
>
> **Response**: *LaTeX is fantastic for a few reasons! Here are some:*

1. **Professional Typesetting:** *It's unbeatable for creating high-quality documents, especially for academic papers, reports, theses, and books. The typesetting quality is top-notch, allowing for precise control over formatting, equations, and bibliographies.*

2. **Mathematical Typesetting:** *It's a go-to tool for mathematicians, scientists, and engineers because it beautifully renders complex mathematical equations and symbols, often a pain point in other word processors.*

3. **Cross-Referencing and Citations:** *LaTeX makes referencing and citation management a breeze. Its automated referencing system ensures accurate and consistent numbering and linking throughout the document.*

4. **Portability and Compatibility:** *LaTeX documents can be easily converted to various formats (PDF, HTML, etc.) without compromising quality, and the files themselves are plain text, making them portable and easily readable across different platforms.*

5. **Community and Packages:** *There's a vast collection of packages and templates available, created and shared by a vibrant community. This means you can find solutions to almost any typesetting problem or document style you might need.*

6. **Separation of Content and Formatting:** *LaTeX encourages the separation of content from design, allowing you to focus on writing without getting distracted by formatting concerns.*

7. **Free and Open Source:** *LaTeX is free to use and has been maintained and improved over the years by a dedicated community. It's available on various operating systems.*

   While it has a learning curve, once you get the hang of it, LaTeX can significantly streamline document creation and produce beautiful, professional-looking output.

That takes quite some space here! I'll keep it because every point is on topic here, and you notice ChatGPT's typical response style: it may begin with an introduction, often organizes information into bullet points, and concludes with a final statement. This can lead to lengthy responses.

How it works...

ChatGPT retains information from previous chat interactions. You can reference earlier responses and instruct ChatGPT to condense, elaborate, seek additional details, or even ask for rephrasing or translation into another language. Let's experiment with rephrasing the previous response:

Prompt: *Shorten it without using bullet points.*

Response: *LaTeX is fantastic for professional-quality documents, especially in academia. It excels in mathematical typesetting, automates referencing, and offers portability to various formats. Its community support and open-source nature make it a top choice for precise, beautifully formatted content despite a learning curve.*

It's worth noting that ChatGPT often exhibits an enthusiastic tone. That's why I usually explicitly request a more neutral, non-promotional tone. We will see that in the recipe *Improving your content* later in this chapter. For now, let's take the opposite approach – we'll test how far we can push ChatGPT to get a funny text. We can request increased excitement and repeat the step. I'll skip some responses and just present the final one:

Prompt: *Tell me the same, but more excited.*

...

Prompt: *Be even more excited.*

...

Prompt: *Now get super crazy excited like mad!*

Response: *LaTeX, oh my stars and galaxies, it's the intergalactic wizardry of document creation! It's like wielding the Infinity Gauntlet of academic prowess, effortlessly crafting documents that make textbooks jealous! Think of it as a quantum leap into a universe where math equations sparkle like cosmic fireworks! References? It's like summoning an army of citation superheroes who zip through your document with lightning speed! And transformation? It's shape-shifting into any format faster than the speed of thought—from PDFs to HTML to whatever dimension you desire! The community? It's a supernova explosion of brilliance, sharing secrets and rocketing you toward document perfection at warp speed! Using LaTeX is like being the cosmic conductor of mind-boggling, exhilarating content creation—an adventure that blasts you beyond the stratosphere of awesomeness!*

On one hand, it's fun to play with the language model this way; on the other hand, it shows how capable it is in building vibrant sentences. Even if you tell ChatGPT to construct an entertaining poem about LaTeX with some particular words you like to see in it, it gets it done and responds with a humorous, rhyming text.

> **Note**
>
> The answers may vary depending on the context and what ChatGPT has seen and learned. In particular, initiate a new chat for a new subject so ChatGPT doesn't use unrelated context from a prior conversation.

Now that we know the system, we can discuss more details in the upcoming recipes.

There's more...

You can also use ChatGPT on your smartphone. The ChatGPT mobile app even includes a voice conversation feature. It's powered by **Whisper**, an excellent open source speech recognition system. It converts spoken words into text; you can choose from five voices for audio output. You can use it to engage in questions and answers, take notes on the go, and even have ChatGPT enhance or translate your notes, which can later be shared on your computer.

If you are willing to subscribe with a monthly payment, you can upgrade your plan to **ChatGPT Plus**. Then, you can use version 4, which offers significant advantages, including a higher token limit of 32,000, improved training on newer data, and access to current internet information. An update to version 5 is already anticipated.

There are alternative AI writing assistants available, such as the following:

- **Gemini**: This is considered a top ChatGPT alternative, maintained by Google, and suitable for both writing and coding tasks. Visit `https://gemini.google.com`.

- **Claude**: This is operated by **Anthropic**, with support from Google and Amazon, and is ideal for analyzing large inputs and document analysis. Find more information at `https://claude.ai`.

- **Grok**: This was launched by **xAI** and is backed by Elon Musk. It's tailored for entertaining chats and can be found at `https://x.ai`.

- **Llama**: Version 2 is an open source chatbot developed by **Meta**. Explore it at `https://www.llama2.ai`.

There will be new tools and integration of such AI bots into applications such as word processors, code editors, and web browsers.

> **Note**
>
> AI assistants, including ChatGPT, process and store your input, potentially using it for training and analysis, so avoid using online AI for confidential data.

Getting answers to LaTeX questions

ChatGPT is a vast knowledge base. Ask any questions to get elaborate answers.

How to do it...

You can ask straightforward questions and explore the answers, such as these randomly chosen prompt examples:

- *What are the benefits of LaTeX?*

- *What is the difference between XeLaTeX and LuaLaTeX?*

- *When using LaTeX, how should I determine whether to utilize the* `\include` *command or the* `\input` *command?*

- *How do I create a presentation in LaTeX similar to PowerPoint?*

- *Where is the error in the following LaTeX code?* Then, add the code.

For an excellent question where you can expect an optimal answer, be specific and provide as much context as possible, as you would in a LaTeX support forum.

Follow up with further questions or instructions, such as the following command prompts:

- *Provide more details*

- *Show particular examples*

- *Explain specific details*

- *Break the answer down into smaller steps*

- *Clarify what's not apparent enough*

- *Add more context and make a reattempt to answer*

As long as the conversation remains within the same chat thread, ChatGPT will retain the context for follow-up inquiries.

How it works...

ChatGPT finds the answers in its huge knowledge database and uses its linguistic capabilities to generate natural responses, like in a normal conversation.

Asking questions to a chatbot and engaging in detailed conversations about responses and your further queries differ significantly from interactions in internet forums where any user can publicly comment on your questions, code, or style. ChatGPT may offer a quick and enjoyable conversational experience with a much lower barrier to asking a question, and it's much easier than typing keywords into a search engine. This might contribute to the declining popularity of web forums. However, competent users can still be found online, and ultimately, these forums serve as a valuable source from which AI learns.

In the following recipe, we'll explore the creation of optimal input and learn how ChatGPT processes it.

Improving your content

You can leverage ChatGPT to enhance the quality of your content.

How to do it...

The most direct approach is to provide ChatGPT with your original text and instruct it to enhance it. Clearly outline ChatGPT's role in this task and specify the desired tone.

For instance, use a prompt like the following:

> **Prompt**: *Act as a technical editor. Maintain an informal yet sober and technical tone, and avoid excessive enthusiasm. Rephrase the following texts, preserving what sounds good but improving overall quality.*

Then, provide your text paragraph by paragraph, look at ChatGPT's responses, and see if there are any corrections or improvements that you would like to keep. This ensures corrections to spelling and grammar, adherence to the desired tone, and, also important, identification of synonyms that could amplify the impact and clarity of your initial writing.

As an example, let's consider a brief text excerpt from `https://en.wikipedia.org/wiki/LaTeX`:

> **Prompt**: *LaTeX uses the TeX typesetting program for formatting its output, and is itself written in the TeX macro language.*

Response: *LaTeX formats its output using the TeX typesetting program and is written in the TeX macro language itself.*

In my view, this slight rephrasing improves the sentence.

Various tools and browser extensions utilize ChatGPT in the background. Let's look at one that aids us in editing. **editGPT** is a ChatGPT-powered editor available at `https://editgpt.app`. You can use it as a standalone editor or, if you use Firefox or a Chrome-compatible web browser, as a browser extension directly integrated with the ChatGPT website. Here, we'll opt for the latter. Follow these steps to install the extension:

1. Download and install the editGPT extension from the Chrome or Firefox extension store. As a Microsoft Edge user, you can also use the Chrome extension.

2. Go to the ChatGPT website at `https://chat.openai.com`.

    Start a chat and type any prompt with the text you want to edit and an instruction to rephrase or proofread it.

3. The **editGPT** button will appear at the top of the browser window. You may need to refresh the web page if it doesn't show up.

4. Click the **editGPT** button to enable the editing mode. In this mode, every ChatGPT response will now display statistics while highlighting deleted phrases in red and added phrases in green. In this way, you can evaluate the changes.

5. Click the **editGPT** button again to turn off the editing mode.

The following screenshot shows the previous ChatGPT response in editing mode:

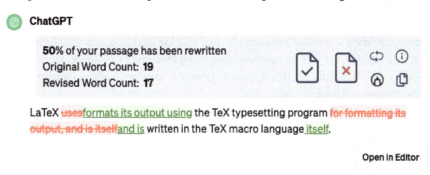

Figure 13.1 – ChatGPT highlighting the changes

When you click the **Open in Editor** button, your text opens in a separate editing window as depicted here:

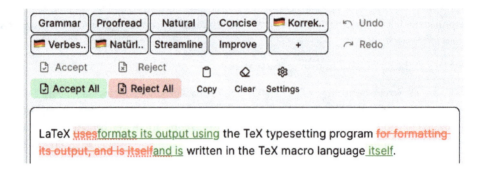

Figure 13.2 – The ChatGPT editor aka editGPT

The buttons allow you to select features such as grammar correction, proofreading, fixing awkward parts, and refining phrases. For more extensive documents or multiple requests, you may need to sign up for a free or paid account at `https://editgpt.app`.

If you are a macOS User, you may also try the **BetterTouchTool** application available at `https://folivora.ai`. It aids with keyboard shortcuts, offers new mouse gestures, and includes ChatGPT support. Briefly said, you can configure the prompt to be used, and then, in any application, such as your LaTeX editor, highlight text, press a key, and the text will be transformed according to the preconfigured prompt. Multiple configurations are possible.

> **Note**
> The ChatGPT website and any ChatGPT-powered tool may change in appearance, features, free availability, or pricing over time.

Our editing demonstration was just a tiny example. In a real-life workflow, you may finish writing an entire chapter, then utilize ChatGPT to rephrase ideas using synonyms for variety, avoiding excessive repetition. Finally, you can apply another excellent grammar checker, such as **Grammarly Pro**, to enhance your grammar and tone further.

How it works...

ChatGPT processes your input text and follows your instructions. Its pre-trained knowledge helps it to contextualize the content. ChatGPT is leveraging its learned language patterns to correct grammar and rephrase your text in the desired tone, as it's trained in many writing styles and linguistic nuances.

In general, you have various options to build your prompt to get the output you desire:

- Define the role of ChatGTP using phrases such as "You are..." and "Act like a..."
- Specify the role of the recipient, such as a child, a student, or a professor

- Tell it what you want, such as "I want..." or "I need..."

- Outline the task, such as "You should..." and "Do the following..."

- Exclude undesired elements using phrases such as "Don't use ..." either at the beginning or later while requesting another try of the response

- Specify the desired tone, such as "Your tone is informal and motivating"

- Request a particular output format, such as a bullet list, a numbered list, a table, or code in any language

- Provide any relevant context imaginable

- Optionally, offer an example of your expectations

As ChatGPT is not human, you may omit friendly words such as "please" to keep your input concise, allowing more words in both your input and output because such a ChatGPT prompt, together with your text, can be comprehensive. You can instruct ChatGPT to apply the prompt to all the subsequent input texts so you don't need to repeat it. Once you have crafted prompts that suit your requirements, copy and store them somewhere, particularly if you work on content over a long period of time.

There's more...

Another helpful use of ChatGPT is to overcome writer's block. You can instruct ChatGPT to generate a few ideas or key points to help you kickstart your writing. Let's say you would like to create some diagrams showing how LaTeX can be used for this purpose. To get to a point where you can start, for example, you could use such a prompt:

Prompt: *Provide the six most commonly used diagram types in a bullet list, explain them, and tell me which field of science or business is most popular for every kind.*

Response:

1. **Flowcharts:**

   - **Explanation:** *A flowchart is a visual representation of a process or workflow, using different shapes to represent different steps or activities and arrows to show the flow of control.*

   - **Popular Applications:**

     - **Business:** *Process optimization, project management, decision-making.*

     - **Science:** *Experimental procedures, data analysis workflows.*

ChatGPT proceeds to explain pie charts, bar charts, Venn diagrams, Gantt diagrams, and mind maps. You can continue like this:

Prompt: *For each diagram type, name a LaTeX package that supports generating such diagrams.*

ChatGPT will list packages for each kind of diagram, even with an entire code example that you may use as a starting point, like the following snippet of the ChatGPT output:

2. **Pie Chart:**
    * **LaTeX Package:** `pgf-pie`
    * **Example Code:**

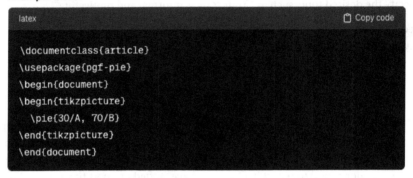

```latex
\documentclass{article}
\usepackage{pgf-pie}
\begin{document}
\begin{tikzpicture}
  \pie{30/A, 70/B}
\end{tikzpicture}
\end{document}
```

Figure 13.3 – ChatGPT output with code

Click the **Copy code** button at the top right corner of the code window to copy the code to the clipboard, and then paste it into your LaTeX editor for further work.

You can quickly get some starting points and continue in your own manner.

The ChatGPT answers may give a kick-off, though I would always be careful to check if an answer is correct and use my thoughts and writing. I would not copy and paste text from ChatGPT to directly use it because it can be considered plagiarism, not just because it's machine output: what ChatGPT says comes from its training data, and that may even contain original phrases of other authors, even though it's machine processed. Creativity and correctness remain the author's responsibility.

Additional ways to integrate ChatGPT into your writing process include the following:

* Brainstorming through curious questions and discussing the answers
* Telling ChatGPT to draft an abstract, introduction, or summary of your original text
* Designing a table of contents
* Structuring your ideas in a bulleted list or using a table
* Drafting content rapidly with less concern for grammar and allowing ChatGPT to suggest corrections
* Writing in your native language and using ChatGPT to translate it into another language
* Generate a LaTeX document based on your text

The last point will be our next topic.

Generating code

ChatGPT was also heavily trained in coding, making it proficient in generating code, including LaTeX. You can use it to create code snippets or even entire document templates, saving time and effort.

How to do it...

Proceed with your AI conversation like you would do with a human programming assistant as follows:

1. Ensure you mention LaTeX as the code language in the input prompt or earlier in the chat. Clearly state your requirement, such as this one:

    Prompt: *Generate the LaTeX code snippet for a matrix with m rows and n columns using a_ij entries and dots.*

2. ChatGPT will respond with an output similar to the following:

     ChatGPT

    Certainly! Here's the LaTeX code snippet for a matrix with m rows and n columns using a_{ij} entries and dots:

    ```latex
    \begin{bmatrix}
        a_{11} & a_{12} & \dots & a_{1n} \\
        a_{21} & a_{22} & \dots & a_{2n} \\
        \vdots & \vdots & \ddots & \vdots \\
        a_{m1} & a_{m2} & \dots & a_{mn} \\
    \end{bmatrix}
    ```

    Figure 13.4 – ChatGPT wrote LaTeX code for a matrix

3. Ask for an explanation of parts you want to know more about, like so:

    Prompt: *What is the* bmatrix *environment doing?*

    ChatGPT will respond by telling you the meaning and explaining the syntax. It will even tell you that the amsmath package is required for this.

4. Request changes if needed using prompts like the ones in these examples:

    Prompt: *Use the variable* x *instead of* a *in the matrix cells.*

Prompt: *Use parentheses instead of square brackets as delimiters.*

ChatGPT will adjust the code as requested, using x_ij in the matrix cells and replacing the `bmatrix` environment with a `pmatrix` environment.

5. Highlight, copy, and paste the code into your LaTeX editor, or use the **Copy code** button.

6. Compile the code to see how it appears in the PDF output:

$$\begin{pmatrix} x_{11} & x_{12} & \cdots & x_{1n} \\ x_{21} & x_{22} & \cdots & x_{2n} \\ \vdots & \vdots & \ddots & \vdots \\ x_{m1} & x_{m2} & \cdots & x_{mn} \end{pmatrix}$$

Figure 13.5 – The ChatGPT code compiled with LaTeX

How it works...

ChatGPT integrates its knowledge of LaTeX with its language processing capabilities, which are also trained in programming languages. It offers more than a mere reproduction of training data: as demonstrated, you can test ChatGPT's comprehension of the code and ask for accurate adjustments. ChatGPT can serve as your coding companion.

There's more...

There are endless possibilities for what you can request. One significant benefit is that you can quickly get usable code snippets, saving you from extensive typing, such as for a large table template, an `axis` plot within a `tikzpicture` environment, or an entire document template to fill in, like with this prompt:

Prompt: *Create a LaTeX beamer presentation with three sections, three slides per section, and a table of contents using the Singapore theme.*

From what I tested, I consistently received usable results. ChatGPT can even draw graphs or plots for you. When it comes to more creativity, ChatGPT gives it a shot, but the results may appear amusing. Try letting it draw a robot; for example, it gets the basics done, but the drawing looks funny.

You are not restricted to LaTeX syntax. For example, you can state some book details, and ChatGPT will understand and generate the corresponding BibTeX entries for you, as demonstrated here:

Prompt: *Create a BibTeX entry of this book: Stefan Kottwitz, LaTeX Graphics with TikZ, Packt Publishing, 2023.*

You will get the following response:

 ChatGPT

Absolutely, here's the BibTeX entry for the book "LaTeX Graphics with TikZ" by Stefan Kottwitz:

```bibtex
@book{kottwitz2023latex,
    author    = "Stefan Kottwitz",
    title     = "LaTeX Graphics with TikZ",
    publisher = "Packt Publishing",
    year      = 2023
}
```

Figure 13.6 – A BibTeX database entry generated by ChatGPT

The AI understood what it meant and autonomously populated the fields in the BibTeX syntax.

> **Note**
>
> You just saw that ChatGPT can translate from LaTeX-generated output, such as single references or an entire bibliography, back to LaTeX code. With ChatGPT version 4 and above, you can upload entire PDF documents and use a prompt such as *Create LaTeX code for the attached document*. You can provide further instructions to adjust the generated code.

If you use the **Overleaf** LaTeX cloud solution, you can try the **Writefull** extension. It's a language tool trained on published papers to support you with language feedback in academic writing. It incorporates the **TeXGPT** feature that allows applying ChatGPT directly in your code editing window and generates code for elements such as tables, figures, and formulas.

Index

Symbols

A

B

Z

www.packtpub.com

Subscribe to our online digital library for full access to over 7,000 books and videos, as well as industry leading tools to help you plan your personal development and advance your career. For more information, please visit our website.

Why subscribe?

- Spend less time learning and more time coding with practical eBooks and Videos from over 4,000 industry professionals

- Improve your learning with Skill Plans built especially for you

- Get a free eBook or video every month

- Fully searchable for easy access to vital information

- Copy and paste, print, and bookmark content

Did you know that Packt offers eBook versions of every book published, with PDF and ePub files available? You can upgrade to the eBook version at packtpub.com and as a print book customer, you are entitled to a discount on the eBook copy. Get in touch with us at customercare@packtpub.com for more details.

At www.packtpub.com, you can also read a collection of free technical articles, sign up for a range of free newsletters, and receive exclusive discounts and offers on Packt books and eBooks.

Other Books You May Enjoy

If you enjoyed this book, you may be interested in these other books by Packt:

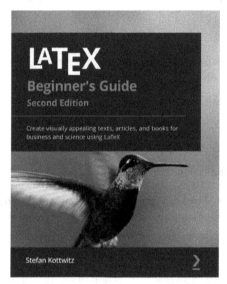

LaTeX Beginner's Guide

Stefan Kottwitz

ISBN: 978-1-80107-865-8

- Make the most of LaTeX s powerful features to produce professionally designed texts
- Download, install, and set up LaTeX and use additional styles, templates, and tools
- Typeset math formulas and scientific expressions to the highest standards
- Understand how to include graphics and work with figures and tables
- Discover professional fonts and modern PDF features
- Work with book elements such as bibliographies, glossaries, and indexes
- Typeset documents containing tables, figures, and formulas